Satan and God's Armor

Satan and God's Armor

WALKING WITH JESUS
VOLUME SEVEN

*An Expository Commentary
based upon Paul's Letter to the Ephesians*

(CHAPTER SIX VERSES 1–12)

ROBERT B. CALLAHAN SR.

RESOURCE *Publications* · Eugene, Oregon

SATAN AND GOD'S ARMOR
An Expository Commentary based upon Paul's Letter to the Ephesians
(Chapter Six Verses 1–12)

Copyright © 2013 Robert B. Callahan Sr. All rights reserved. Except for brief quotations in critical publications or reviews, no part of this book may be reproduced in any manner without prior written permission from the publisher. Write: Permissions, Wipf and Stock Publishers, 199 W. 8th Ave., Suite 3, Eugene, OR 97401.

Resource Publications
An Imprint of Wipf and Stock Publishers
199 W. 8th Ave., Suite 3
Eugene, OR 97401
www.wipfandstock.com

ISBN 13: 978-1-60899-651-3
Manufactured in the U.S.A.

All scripture quotations, unless otherwise indicated, are taken from the Holy Bible, The King James Study Bible, Copyright ©1983, 1988. (Previously published as the Liberty Annotated Study Bible and as The Annotated Study Bible, King James Version) Copyright © 1988 by Liberty University. Thomas Nelson Publishers.

*For my wife, Ginger,
whose encouragement, faith,
love, and objectivity contributed
significantly to Walking with Jesus*

Topical Categories in Walking with Jesus
(An Expository Commentary)

Volume One	Volume Two	Volume Three	Volume Four
The Triune God Speaks to the Saints	*Sin and Redemption*	*Christ's Prisoner*	*Walking As Mature Christians*
To the Faithful in Christ Jesus	Sin and God's Wrath	For This Cause— God's Glory	Living in Harmony With Christ
God's Will— Spiritual Blessings	God, Rich in Mercy and Grace	Revealing God's Hidden Truths	Unity in the Triune God The Holy Spirit
Trusting in Him	A Right Relationship With God	Praying to the Father	The Lord Jesus Christ
Praying for Christians	Reconciliation	Believing God's Power	God, the Father
	Praying Through the Holy Spirit		Grace According to Christ's Gifts
	God's Foundation (Apostles and Prophets)		Maturing in Christ

Topical Categories in Walking with Jesus
(An Expository Commentary)

Volume Five	Volume Six	Volume Seven	Volume Eight
Following Christ	*Walking Wisely*	*Satan and God's Armor*	*Christ's Ambassadors*
Alienated from God	Christ-Like Conduct	Family Relationships	A Call to Discipleship
Ye Have Not So Learned Christ	No Inheritance in the Kingdom of God and Christ	Life's Basic Relationship	Wearing God's Armor
Christ-Like Conduct	Walking in the Light	The Whole Armor of God	Christ's Ambassadors
	Walking Circumspectly	Satan and His Evil Forces	
	The Marriage Relationship		
	Christ and His Church		

Ephesians "brings one into an atmosphere of unbounded spiritual affluence that creates within one's heart deepest peace and assurance. It is impossible to live habitually in Ephesians and be depressed."

Ruth Paxson

Contents

Volume Seven: Topical Categories xi
Foreword xiii
Preface xv
Acknowledgments xvii
The Question of Authorship xix
Introduction xxi

1	Children, Obey Your Parents	1
2	Discipline	10
3	Man's Relationship to God	20
4	Priorities	29
5	Christ's Slaves	38
6	Knowing Your Master in Heaven	46
7	Finally My Brethren, Be Strong . . .	54
8	Separating Ourselves	63
9	Strength, Power, and Might	72
10	To Fall or To Stand	81
11	Prepare to Wrestle	89
12	Satan	99
13	The Combatants	108
14	The Devil and His Forces	118
15	The Devil's Disguises	127

16	Those Damnable Heresies	135
17	Road Blocks and Detours	145
18	Watch and Pray	155
19	False and True Teachings	163
20	Truth and Experience	172
	Outline Questions	181
	Bibliography	222
	Scripture Index	225

Volume Seven: Topical Categories

Category	Scripture	Chapters
Family Relationships	Eph. 6:1–4	1–2
Life's Basic Relationships	Eph. 6:5–9	3–6
The Whole Armor of God	Eph. 6:10–11	7–10
Satan and His Evil Forces	Eph. 6:10–12	11–20

Foreword

Robert Callahan's multi-volume work of Paul's Letter to the Ephesians is both a welcomed and long-overdue guide for Christian living today. The Apostle's sense of the eternity and greatness of God, his emphasis on the living reality and exaltation of Christ, his devotion to God's grace as an unearned gift of enduring love, and his call to an ardent and faithful discipleship all witness to an urgency and renewal critically needed in our time. Callahan's heart and style rise to meet this challenge and to convey God's message of hope and promise, of presence and courage, to Christian souls of any and every contemporary Christian tradition.

Callahan's format allows for both a devotional and studious usage. One can permit one's soul to savor every spiritual nuance the author uncovers, verse by verse, mark the passage, and return later for further nourishment. Or one can linger from text to text, gleaning with the author both theological and spiritual insight for enhancing personal discipleship, equally applicable in the arena of church and society.

The author draws on an array of insightful theological and spiritual wisdom, garnered from scholars and saints alike, theologians and missionaries. Calvin's Institutes guide Callahan's expositions, as well as the work of Markus Barth—known for his commentary on Ephesians and his delineation of Pauline theology. The author cites frequent and astute observations from Barth's exegesis of this nature. In addition, Callahan makes wise usage of Martyn Lloyd-Jones' emphasis on "experiencing the living Christ." For Lloyd-Jones, as well as the author, mere intellectual knowledge of the Christ fails to undergird one's faith or discipleship, when life's journey truly becomes sore bestead. Callahan also draws from the great 17th century theologian William Gurnall's delightful work: The Christian in Complete Armour. Perhaps students of Church history remember how both John Newton and Charles Spurgeon prized Gurnall's approach and piety and preferred it to many perspicacious studies available in their time. Gurnall's Complete Armour is known for its pithy, fervent, and wise counsel that confronts human vagaries with the truth about the self. In that respect, so too does Robert Callahan's gentle but firm counsel enrich the Christian heart and inspire one to a higher level of discipleship. No one can fail to sense this in Walking with Jesus. Whether encouraged to venture this methodology owing to his own years as a Presbyterian elder, or as an avid member and participant of the bi-annual Calvin's Colloquiums for the past 30 years, or as a fond reader of Ruth Paxson's The Wealth, Walk and Warfare of the Christian, the result is the same: a powerful, inspirational, and theologically heart-warming guide to discipleship today.

Ministers, Christian educators, seminary students, laypersons, and lovers of Jesus' life will find Callahan's work immensely valuable. His volumes deserve our grateful and sincere attention, as we too seek to walk with Jesus.

Benjamin W. Farley
Younts Professor Emeritus of Bible, Religion, and Philosophy
Erskine College, Due West, South Carolina

Preface

Paul's Epistle to the Ephesians shows us the joy and challenge of being united to Christ in his death and resurrection. It takes us from being seated with Him in the heavenlies (chapter 2), down to the battles we must wage, in His armor, with powers of evil (Eph. 6). In a balanced and judicious manner, longtime Presbyterian elder, Bob Callahan, exercises remarkable insight in opening to believers the vital truths of Ephesians; truths that once taken in, transform the attitude towards life, and often set the soul singing!

As a professor of theology, I have carefully worked through one of his multivolumed series, and found it to be theologically sound: evangelical and scholarly at the same time. It has spiritual depth and is extremely practical; it is accessible in good, clear English. It is neither a commentary, nor a series of sermons. In some ways it reminds me of some of the ancient Patristic engagements with a series of texts of Holy Scripture. It brings the reader into the presence of the Most High, and—if considered thoughtfully and prayerfully, is likely to cause him to sit down under the canopy of God's love.

The journey of Christians in today's world is very demanding indeed, and Bob's work is intended to be a guide to help every pilgrim 'Walking with Jesus.' It will be a rich resource for Sunday Schools, Bible studies, as well as for individual devotions.

Douglas F. Kelly
Reformed Theological Seminary
Charlotte, NC

Acknowledgments

The crafting of Walking with Jesus was not a "one man show" but numerous people working together to present a formidable work. Three guiding lights have been paramount in the minds of those making significant contributions: one, presenting the theology in accord with the tenets of the Reformed Faith; two, employing language that presents the Gospel in a meaningful and understandable light; and, three, expounding upon Scripture in a clear, concise, and forthright manner.

It has been God's blessing that the following ministers and theologians have enthusiastically and willingly provided their time and talents to enhance this work. They are:

- Dr. Frank Barker, Founder and Pastor Emeritus of the Briarwood Presbyterian Church, Birmingham, AL
- Dr. Benjamin W. Farley, Younts Professor Emeritus, Bible, Religion, and Philosophy, Erskine College, Due West, SC
- Dr. James C. Goodloe, IV, Executive Director, Foundation for Reformed Theology, Richmond, VA
- Dr. Todd Jones, Senior Minister, First Presbyterian Church, Nashville, TN
- Dr. Douglas Kelly, Richard Jordan, Professor of Theology, Reformed Theological Seminary, Charlotte, NC
- Dr. Norman McCrummen, Senior Pastor, Spring Hill Presbyterian Church, Mobile, AL
- Dr. Mark Mueller, Senior Pastor, First Presbyterian Church, Huntsville, AL
- Dr. Richard Ray, Former Managing Director of John Knox Press, Montreat, NC

Acknowledgments

Without the knowledge, wisdom, and encouragement of these individuals this work would neither have become a reality nor available to individuals seeking a better understanding of the teachings of the Scripture and the joy of walking daily with the Lord Jesus.

Several others have labored diligently to create this work, and to produce the finished product. Our daughter, Karen Callahan Myrick, made significant contributions during the drafting process through her knowledge of grammar. Ms. Lynn Sledge, as the copy editor, judiciously reviewed the manuscript and made valuable contributions for improving it. Four ladies, Helen Marshall, D'Anne Dendy, Kelly Comferford, and Elizabeth Annan, worked tirelessly, with dedication, to prepare draft after draft and to make positive contributions to the project. In addition, Wick Skinner made invaluable contributions through his attention to details, grammar, and vocabulary.

It is not possible to thank them sufficiently for their dedication to making this volume a desirable repository of Christian truths, and in so doing to cheerfully work on draft after draft, to recommend enhancements, and to make appropriate changes in the text. Their unselfish contributions are too many to enumerate. May God bless them.

The Question of Authorship

Recent scholars have questioned the authorship of the letter to the Ephesians and have been less convinced that it was the Apostle Paul. However, for the sake of simplicity of expression we will abide by the traditional view and refer to Paul as its author.

Introduction

The creation of this work was the result of unusual developments which some would attribute to happenstance and others to God's providence. You may be the judge after considering the following.

During May 2000 a friend invited my wife and me to visit the Spring Hill Presbyterian Church in Mobile and hear their new minister, Norman McCrummen. We accepted his invitation.

The following March, Dr. McCrummen was preaching on anything but Ephesians when he interrupted his sermon, paused long enough to slowly scan the congregation twice, and said, "I want everyone to read the first and second chapters of Ephesians by next Sunday" and promptly returned to his sermon. The next day I called him and said, "I can't do it" a few times. Finally, his light went on and he said, "What can't you do?" I said, "I can't read the first and second chapters of Ephesians by next Sunday." He asked, "Why can't you? It will only take ten to fifteen minutes." I responded, "I have fifty-eight to sixty expository messages on the first two chapters of Ephesians that took thirty to thirty-five minutes to present." His response was, "I want to read all those and everything else you have on Ephesians." Thus began the long, arduous, and heart-warming journey of converting handwritten notes along with printed ones into the written word. It has been a joyful, though demanding experience.

Paul's Letter to the Ephesians has been described as "The holiest of the holies." My love affair with it began in the 1980's when I read a book containing great sermons of the twentieth century. The most impressive one was written by Martyn Lloyd-Jones. As a result, I read other works of his including his exposition of Ephesians. Thereafter, unexpectedly, I was asked to teach an adult Bible Study Group. They said they would provide the material, but I demurred and said, "I would gather my own material." This set in motion the process of acquiring knowledge through the best expository works available at the time on Ephesians including Martyn

Lloyd-Jones, William Gurnall, Ruth Paxson, Markus Barth, John Calvin, Otto Weber, and others.

The objective was to present the essence of Paul's letter as it was presented to him by the Lord Jesus and the Holy Spirit. Further, to mine the gold available in the fruitful works of those fertile minds that God had cultivated and enabled to expound upon the truths that His only begotten Son had revealed to His apostles and disciples. Therefore, it was a paramount obligation to express God's truths in a simple, straightforward manner according to the dictates of the Holy Spirit so that the reader may grasp it and interpret it according to the will of our Lord and Saviour Jesus Christ.

The need for the truths of the Gospel is as great today as it was in the first century. The conditions are similar and the challenges facing our culture reveal the need for knowing the living God and His Son. Today, the people of faith require the same spiritual nourishment as those brave souls of the early days after the Resurrection, who would rather face death than deny their Lord and Saviour.

There are people in responsible positions in Christ's church who deny Him by: their passivity; seeking secular acceptance; and failing to honor Him in public. These apostasies negatively impact members of organized Christian churches as well as non-believers.

They create an environment in which unrighteousness flourishes. This results in irreverence as aptly described by R.W. Dale, "Where there is irreverence for the divine law the vision of God becomes fainter; as the vision of God becomes fainter the restraints of the Divine Righteousness are lessened and at last the vision of God is lost altogether." May God enlighten us regarding His infallible Word so that we will hunger and thirst for righteousness, and for the vision of God to shine brighter and brighter as we serve Him with courage, wisdom, justice, and self-control.

This expository commentary is designed to bring individuals, whether they are spiritually children, adolescents or adults into a closer, more mature relationship with the Lord Jesus Christ. It begins with the Triune God; presents the doctrines of the Christian faith; reminds us "that we henceforth be no more children, tossed to and fro . . . but speaking the truth in love, may grow up into Him in all things, . . . even Christ." It continues by emphasizing the importance of being renewed in the spirit of your mind; putting on the new man, which after God is created in righteousness and true holiness; using the whole armor of God to thwart the manifold attacks of Satan; and concluding with the admonition to conduct ourselves as Christ's ambassadors.

The spiritual food contained ranges from milk and honey to tough meat. The flavor of this exposition encompasses all varieties—sweet, sour, pleasant, bitter, tart, tasteless, dry, burned, and succulent. Do not reject the nourishment because of its texture or flavor, but seek to understand it despite your preferences, since it provides food for good health and strength for joyful living. May God's truths flourish in your heart and mind, and enable you to withstand the tests, trials, and tribulations that come your way as you are "Walking with Jesus."

In presenting this work, I realize everyone has different challenges. The fascinating part of God's Word is that it meets us where we are. The question is, will we meet Him there, hear what He has to say, and accept the nourishment He offers?

The words of William Gurnall are appropriate and enlightening in contemplating God's Word. He said prior to expounding upon Ephesians, "The fare that I shall be serving during the coming weeks will be from God's own table. If perchance it does not go down well or should not have the flavor that you desire, please do not despise the provider of the food, but blame the cook who has prepared it and is serving it." To that I say, Amen!

The courses being served by this cook are described herein. May they provide the taste and nourishment you are seeking.

Robert B. Callahan, Sr.

1

Children, Obey Your Parents

> CHILDREN, obey your parents in the Lord: for this is right.
> HONOR THY FATHER AND MOTHER; which is the first commandment with promise;
> THAT IT MAY BE WELL WITH THEE, AND THOU MAYEST LIVE LONG ON THE EARTH.
> And, ye fathers, provoke not your children to wrath: but bring them up in the nurture (training) and admonition of the Lord [Eph. 6:1–4].

Children, obey your parents. What a wonderful phrase! How many people through the ages have made that statement! However, as happens so often, people only quote a portion of a statement, taking it out of context.

The full statement is CHILDREN, *obey your parents in the Lord: for this is right* [Eph. 6:1]. That is the complete statement. This command has both a qualification and an admonition. The qualification is *in the Lord.* That is how the children are to obey their parents. The admonition is *for this is right.* When considering this statement, bear in mind the context in which it is presented. It proceeds naturally from

> Walk worthy of the vocation (calling) wherewith you have been called, . . . [Eph. 4:1].
> Be filled with the Spirit [Eph. 5:18].
> Submitting yourselves one to another in the fear of God [Eph. 5:21].

After examining the teachings about Christ and the church, and husbands and wives in marriage, it is time to proceed to the other important members of the family—the children.

Paul is writing to the children who are members of Christ's body and have undoubtedly been baptized. Otto Weber says this particular verse [Eph. 6:1] "makes plain that there were children in the community assembly, although their ages are not precisely given."

In these verses, the children are to obey their parents, but their fathers or parents are to *bring them up in the nurture* (training) *and admonition of the Lord* [Eph. 6:4]. There is a definite responsibility for both parties. The children are to obey. They are to listen, attend, and submit to their parents. But the parents have a definite responsibility regarding how they are to raise them.

Why does the Apostle use this word *obey* instead of other words such as "listen," "attend," or "honor"? Calvin supplies the answer when he says, "Obedience is the evidence of that honor which children owe to their parents," and obedience is much "more difficult; for the human mind recoils from subjection and only with difficulty suffers itself to be forced under the control of another." This is true of children as well as adults.

"Obey—no stronger word could be used to show that God's command to parents is to exercise parental authority, and to children to practice implicit obedience. In two places in Scripture God reveals His estimate of the heinousness of disobedience to parents when he places in the list of the most degrading sins of the godless, heathen world . . ., and of the sins of lawlessness that characterize the perilous times of the last days. . . . The child that has never learned to obey parents in the home will not find it easy to obey the law of his government or the commands of his God. The obedience God requires is not merely that of action, but also of attitude, which makes a child ready to listen to his parents, willing to heed their advice and to follow the guidance of more mature minds," as described by Ruth Paxson.

We should remember that children are in the same category as adults. They are new creatures in Christ. They are to be reminded that there is a distinct difference between those who are in Christ and those outside His body, regardless of their age. Further, we are not talking merely about ethics or morality. The Apostle is discussing a right relationship with God. He is referring to righteousness, obedience, and doing the will of the Father.

Two reasons for a lack of harmony in the home are disobedience and the lack of discipline. All of us have heard much, read much, and seen much about the unruliness, recklessness, and uncontrollableness of children, especially teenagers, and some young people who will not submit to their parents, how they do not want anyone to interfere with their plans, how they want to do their own thing, and do not want to be encumbered by authority, listening to parents, and hearing the counsel of adults.

Children obeying their parents is not merely a phenomenon today. It has been evident for more than two thousand years. That is why Paul wrote about it and undoubtedly preached about it. Paul's wisdom enabled him to know that both the obedience and the instruction of the children should be according to the will of God. Therefore, Paul uses the phrases *in the Lord* and *of the Lord* when telling the children to obey their parents, and the fathers to nurture and admonish their children.

Why did Paul direct his teaching to children and parents? He knew full well that a breakdown in the home had negative effects in the family, which is the basic unit of society. Also, it sent shockwaves to other young people. The people hearing these things would emulate them or try to outdo them, and the entire process would repeat itself.

Paul describes in his letter to the Romans what happens when people ignore God, do not acknowledge Him, and do not obey His commands. He says,

> *And even as they did not like to retain God in their knowledge, God gave them over to a reprobate* (debased) *mind, to do those things which are not convenient* (fitting) [Rom. 1:28].
>
> *Being filled with all unrighteousness, . . . haters of God, despiteful* (violent), *proud, boasters, . . . disobedient to parents,*
> *Without understanding, . . . without natural affection, implacable (unforgiving), unmerciful:*
> *Who knowing the* (righteous) *judgment of God, that they which commit such things are worthy of death, not only do the same, but have pleasure in* (approve of) *them that do them* [Rom. 1:30–32].

Paul amplifies upon this in his second letter to Timothy saying,

> THIS know also, that in the last days perilous times shall come.
> For men shall be lovers of their own selves, covetous, (money lovers) ... proud, ... disobedient to parents, unthankful, unholy,
> ... despisers of those that are good,
> ... lovers of pleasures more (rather) than lovers of God;
> Having a form of godliness, but denying the power thereof: from such turn away [2 Tim. 3:1–5].

The last days refers to the period from the birth of Christ until He returns in full glory. Both passages contain the phrase *disobedient to parents*.

Recall that the passages from Paul's letter to the Romans began with the statement: *And even as they did not like to retain God in their knowledge, God gave them over to a reprobate* (debased) *mind to do those things which are not convenient* (considered to be fit) [Rom. 1:28]. And in Timothy it says, *Having a form of godliness, but denying the power thereof: from such turn away* [2 Tim. 3:5]. Paul reminds us that one of the striking factors during periods of godlessness and apostasy is children being disobedient to their parents. This is true regardless of the ages of the children or parents.

It is interesting to note that Paul specifically talks to both the parents and children when he talks about children being disobedient. There is a connection between disobedience to parents, ungodliness, and indecent behavior. *For the wrath of God is revealed from heaven against all ungodliness and unrighteousness of men, who hold* (suppress) *the truth in unrighteousness* [Rom. 1:18]. When you have ungodliness you have unrighteousness. The two go together like ham and eggs.

If you want righteous conduct, it must be preceded by godliness. People tend to confuse morality with righteousness. They are not the same. Morality relates to the principles of right or wrong behavior. Righteousness is being in a right relationship with God, the Father.

When you have righteousness, you have discipline and obedience. However, when you have unrighteousness you have a lack of discipline, you have a dearth of proper instruction resulting in lawlessness, disrespect, and deteriorating conditions.

Many people cannot remember when they began to love, trust, and obey Christ, just as they cannot remember when they began to love, trust, and obey their parents. "Children may obey their parents in the Lord, before they are able to understand any Christian doctrine; they may discharge every childish duty, under the inspiration of the Spirit of God, before they have so much as heard whether the Spirit of God has been given," as expressed by R.W. Dale. However, that is the exception. If it does exist for a period of time, then there are usually occasions when obedience is lacking or authority needs to be exercised.

When thinking of the relationship between children and parents, we must realize that children go through different phases as they enter the new age groups through which they must pass before becoming adults and parents. The different stages of development can be trying, taxing, difficult, and even heartrending. That is why Paul says,

> CHILDREN, *obey your parents in the Lord: for this is right* [Eph. 6:1].
>
> *And, ye fathers, provoke not your children to wrath: but bring them up in the nurture* (training) *and admonition of the Lord* [Eph. 6:4].

Parents have a divine obligation to teach their children, instruct them, direct their paths, and elicit obedience from them, but they are to do it according to the will of God. They are to nurture and admonish their children as Christ does the church.

Ruth Paxson provides additional light regarding parents, discipline and children obeying their parents. She says, "though the headship of the family resides in the father, yet the plural form of the noun implies that Christian parents should be agreed and united in the discipline of their children, so that the child knows that there is no possibility of appeal from one to the other, or for interference on his behalf, the mutual support and strengthening of parents in discipline is absolutely essential if obedience from the child is expected."

On the other side of the coin, the children have an obligation to obey their *parents in the Lord: for this is right.* The child who does not learn to obey his or her parents will have difficulty obeying rules and regulations no matter where he or she may encounter them. Probably they will have trouble obeying the laws of the land and the commandments of Christ.

The obedience of which Paul speaks is more than blind action. "What God requires is not merely that of action, but also of attitude, which makes a child ready to listen to his parents, willing to heed their advice, and to follow the guidance of more mature minds," as stated by Ruth Paxson.

Children's obedience to their parents is something that Christ requires from them. It is something that He manifested in His life toward His parents as revealed in Scripture. *And he went down with them, and came to Nazareth, and was subject unto them: . . . And Jesus increased in wisdom and stature, and in favor with God and man* [Luke 2:51–52]. Jesus was twelve years old when this happened. He was about to enter His teens. He was the Son of God, but He was subject to His earthly parents, and He humbled Himself, was obedient, was doing the will of His Father, and set a proper example.

There is a significant point contained in Luke's Gospel regarding that episode. Jesus had been

> *. . . in the temple, sitting in the midst of the doctors, (teachers) both hearing them, and asking them questions.*
>
> *And all that heard him were astonished at his understanding and answers.*
>
> *And when they saw him, they were amazed: and his mother said unto him, Son, why hast thou thus dealt with us? behold, thy father and I have sought thee sorrowing (anxiously).*
>
> *And he said unto them, How is it that ye sought me? wist (know) ye not that I must be about my Father's business?*
>
> *And they understood not the saying which he spake unto them* [Luke 2:46–50].

It is after that that Scripture says he *came to Nazareth, and was subject unto them* [Luke 2:51]. Even though Jesus was about His Heavenly Father's business, He was obedient unto His earthly parents.

Children of all ages have a difficult time with respect to parental authority, especially when there is a question involving listening, hearing, attending, and being subject to their parents and doing their Father's business. Jesus set the ultimate example.

Children are to discharge certain duties and responsibilities toward their parents. They are to be truthful, honest, kind, temperate, and industrious. These characteristics are to be displayed whether their parents request, demand, or practice them. They are to be exhibited regardless of their parents' authority.

The test comes when the parents require obedience and the child does not know what is right or wrong, or when the child believes he or she is doing the will of their Heavenly Father. Also, the test comes when parents require obedience for the child's welfare, the child's health, the child's spiritual development, and the benefit of the family.

Of course, it is not easy for parents to point out to their children or for children to accept the fact that the parents have the responsibility for making the rules, and the children are not the most competent judges.

Yes, it is true that parents may be unwise in imposing certain rules and may wish they had never tried to do so. However, it is more unwise for the children not to abide by them. To say the least, there is the opportunity for both parents and children to witness to others about the Apostle's command. In so doing, they may bring someone to a knowledge of the truth.

Jesus said to the scribes and Pharisees,

> *For God commanded, saying, Honor thy father and mother: and He that curseth father or mother, let him die* (be put to death) *the death.*
> *But ye say, Whosoever shall say to his father or his mother, It is a gift (dedicated to the temple), by whatsoever thou mightest be profited by me;*
> *And honor not his father or mother, he shall be free. Thus have ye made the commandment of God of none effect by your tradition* [Matt. 15:4–6].

Why did Jesus present this teaching? The Pharisees and scribes were distorting the law and the Ten Commandments. Further, children who were adults were not discharging their responsibility to honor their parents. They were saying that they had dedicated their time and money to the Lord; therefore, they could not care or provide for their parents.

Unfortunately, it is those in authority in the church who distort the teachings of God and thereby mislead those listening to them. John Calvin appropriately declared, "For when once men have given themselves the freedom to command, they demand a strict observance of their laws and will not bear the least letter of the law to be left out either by contempt or oversight. The world is impatient of legitimate rule and especially stubborn against bearing the yoke of God. Yet it will quickly and willingly ensnare itself in empty traditions; nay, many seem to desire such slavery. And so the worship of God is vitiated, for its principle and head is obedience. The authority of men is preferred to His rule."

It should be evident from this that God wants His Word taught, understood, and applied. He wants the Word expounded. He does not want men initiating their own ideas. You will recall that it was the Pharisees and scribes who initiated the false teachings.

Young people become caught up in false teachings. Consequently, they are deluded by Satan and mistreat their parents and others by exhibiting false witnesses. This results in their being a stumbling block to others instead of being a light to their pathway. Paul says, *CHILDREN, obey your parents in the Lord, for this is right* [Eph. 6:1]. He adds the phrase *for this is right* to solidify his statement and to provide a definite stamp of approval that according to the Old Testament and the New Testament it is right for children to obey their parents. Further, when they show forth obedience they are glorifying God. Remember, Jesus says, *If ye love me, keep my commandments* [John 14:15].

How are children to obey their parents? They are to: honor their fathers and mothers; respect them; obey them according to the letter and spirit of the commandments; revere them; and regard it as a privilege to do so.

What are the reasons for this exhortation? For it is right, it is righteous. It is being in a right relationship with God. The person who is a member of Christ's body does not mind this explanation or reason. Other people may not accept it.

You will find not only among humans but also among the animals that the young will obey their parents. This is true of the birds teaching the young to fly and of the animals teaching the young to walk and to obtain food.

A second reason for obeying parents is that it is one of the Ten Commandments and the first one with a promise. What does this mean? Yes, it has a promise connected to it, but it is the first commandment directly related to our relationships with one another. The first four are concerned with our relationship to God. The Ten Commandments were given to the people to impress upon them and to state clearly what they were to do or not to do.

The Fifth Commandment has a promise attached to it. As an unknown commentator notes, "It is not just a promise to individuals but it is a promise to the nation Israel." It was a national promise. God was not saying that every obedient child would live to a ripe old age. But He was saying that the nation's prosperity, its stability and continuance, depended upon the respect and reverence the children exhibited in their attitude and actions toward their parents. Further, the life of the family, family life, had a direct impact upon the state. How true!

What does the Fifth Commandment mean in its full context? The Church of Scotland's Youth Committee catechism provides valuable insight to the divine importance of the family. It embraces courtship, marriage, the setting up of a home, the coming and the bringing up of children. Human society could not exist if it were not for these things.

We owe our very existence to our fathers and mothers because God has endowed them with His own life-creating power. This is one of the most sacred gifts we possess. The birth of a child is a powerful force in binding together a man and woman already united in marriage. The husband and wife have the joyous and responsible task of nourishing and bringing up a child.

It is in the family that children learn what love means. They learn to be unselfish, to cooperate with others, discipline, sharing, and that they cannot always have their way. It is in the family that children are educated; guided in selecting friends; gain their earliest knowledge of God; see the meaning of sacrifice; and know the real blessings, the blessings of the Spirit as compared to the material ones.

Family life should be filled with love, understanding, peace, joy, harmony, compassion, and trust to such a degree that Christ would be at home there. If that is the case then the children will love, honor, and obey their parents.

Remember, we belong not only to our own family, but to the family of God. The family is to train children to be worthy members of God's family. To disobey parents and to treat them with disrespect is to break one of God's laws and to dishonor Him.

When children honor and obey their parents seeds are sown that will produce order and obedience in adults. These traits are the bulwark of maintaining and securing the public peace, and enabling people to resist the vices and vulgarities causing the corruption and ruin of society or elements within it.

A third reason for Paul's exhortation is that they are to do it *in the Lord*. Remember Jesus was subject unto His earthly mother and father. Children should follow His example. Also, parents should *bring them up in the nurture* (training) *and admonition of the Lord* [Eph. 6:4].

> May children and parents of all ages *be filled with the Spirit* [Eph. 5:18].

Amen!

2

Discipline

CHILDREN, obey your parents in the Lord: for this is right.
  Honor thy father and mother; which is the first commandment with promise;
  That it may be well with thee, and thou mayest live long on the earth.
  And, ye fathers, provoke not your children to wrath: but bring them up in the nurture (training) *and admonition of the Lord* [Eph. 6:1-4].

Probably, all of us have heard the statement that the coming of our Lord two thousand years ago was an event that turned the world upside down. God sent His only begotten Son to earth, born of a virgin, raised by earthly parents. He was an obedient son, worked in Nazareth, attended the synagogue, and embarked upon His ministry. He taught according to the spirit of the law as well as the letter of it, according to the will of His Father, and He was obedient to His father in Heaven.

He did all these things and more. He went to the heart of daily living. He touched the hearts of people. He changed their attitudes, their customs, their prejudices. He taught His disciples. He prepared the apostles so they could write the Epistles. He penetrated the shields people erected around themselves.

He addressed each person's priorities with respect to worldly and spiritual matters, He addressed every relationship a person can have between self and self, self and spouse, self and parent, self and child, self and employer, self and employee, self and friends, and self and God. He addressed all these relationships. Can we do less? I realize our situations, interests, and associations change as God bestows upon us additional years in which to toil in His vineyard. However, while this is happening there are other developments occurring or opportunities presenting themselves where we can be of assistance, or witness to those in need for various reasons.

As members of Christ's body it is important to be knowledgeable regarding divine teachings, the principles and truths contained in Scripture. Paul writes to the Ephesians not directing his message to one segment of believers, but to all members. He wanted them to know that God provides for their every need, no matter what their position is in life. The Lord Jesus Christ is to be their primary focal point in providing guidance for their conduct.

Once a person accepts the Lord Jesus Christ as his Lord and Saviour, he is to obey Him. This means not only learning about Him and His teachings, but knowing Him as *the way, the truth, and the life*. This is not easy. It is difficult. Why say that? Because we are called to a living relationship and a living faith. We are called to practical living situations, not theoretical ones.

Think of the children who were told to obey their parents in the Lord. Scripture does not qualify this statement and say obey only those parents who have accepted Christ. No, it does not. It tells the parents not to provoke their children to wrath. It does not provide for any exceptions or establish any qualifications. However, it does say to *bring them up in the nurture* (training) *and admonition of the Lord* [Eph. 6:4].

From a human perspective, I imagine there were times when the Master may have been tempted to provoke His disciples. But when I think about it and as I grow closer to Him, I realize that He would never do that. The only thing He would do was help them to develop *in the nurture and admonition of the Lord*.

The two commands given in these four verses apply to most people and are directed toward the core of human existence, the family. People are to learn how to live in this most intimate and complex relationship, so they may enjoy all other relationships and have life more abundantly.

The real emphasis in these four verses is in the phrases *in the Lord* and *of the Lord*. Our lives are to be lived unto the Lord. We are to live to the glory of God no matter what conditions or situations may befall us. If parents are too demanding or unreasonable the children are to obey *in the Lord* and to know the teachings of the Master.

If the children are not responding *in the Lord*, regardless of their ages, the parents are to extend and exhibit the qualities of instruction, in love, required in the command to *bring them up in the nurture* (training) *and admonition of the Lord*. In this verse, *nurture* means "training." Oh, how children need it! And parents!

"The atmosphere of a Christian home (in the Lord), which is surcharged with the mother's loyalty to and reverence for the father, and the father's love for and tender care of the mother, will inspire within the child the desire to emulate their example of mutual submission by an obedience that does not spring from compulsion or fear, but from love and respect. '*For this right*.' From the standpoint of both the human and divine, such obedience is right. Obedience is a fundamental law in all God's universe, so of course it must be in the most intimate of relationships. From every angle it is right for God's glory, the home's harmony, and the child's good.

"Obedience may be given grudgingly and ungraciously because there seems nothing else to do to avoid the penalty of punishment. So another command is given which calls the child to still higher ground: "*Honour thy father and thy mother; which is the first commandment with promise*."

"To honour parents implies genuine deference to their wishes, respect for their judgment, and trust in their love. Willing; heartfelt honour is instinctively given. Such obedience and honour are enjoined first, because they are right, and then because they reap a rich reward of definite blessings," as expressed by Ruth Paxson.

These relationships, though they may not be ideal, though they may have differences, are to be conducted *in the Lord* and *of the Lord*. This requires knowledge of the Lord's teachings; much prayer for strength, understanding, unity, holiness, love, light, wisdom, praise, and harmony; and denying oneself.

Paul's teaching with respect to children and parents can be applied to their other relationships, whether they are in the church, or the social sphere, wherever they may be and whatever they may be doing. Why do I say that? Because they are called to be in a right relationship with God. They are to be righteous.

The people who are in Christ are to act according to the teachings of the Master. They are to *be filled with the Spirit* and they are to submit themselves *one to another in the fear of Christ*. This is not easy. Why? Because often they let self get in the way and do not think or act *in the Lord*.

You may wonder why Paul directs attention to the different family institutions. Markus Barth provides illumination, saying, "The man-woman relationship stands at the head of all other discussions. In addition, we did not choose our parents nor can we determine the character of our own children, nor the path they shall follow; and we live in an economic framework having a real impact upon our thinking and conduct."

Paul, following in the footsteps of the Lord Jesus, wants Christ's followers to know the broad arena of life in which they are to live and have their being. Further, in each of these areas, they are to *walk worthy of the vocation* (calling) *wherewith ye are called*. They are to walk *in the Lord*, and their conduct is to be *of the Lord*.

Scripture reveals that no matter what our position may be, we are under the same high authority, the Lord Jesus Christ and God His Father. Further, each of us is subject to the discipline, teachings, and the commands of the Lord.

Paul not only commands the children as to how they are to conduct themselves regarding their parents, but commands the fathers and mothers to *provoke not your children to wrath: but bring them up in the nurture* (training) *and admonition of the Lord*. This is not easy. Why? Because it requires parents to dedicate the necessary time and effort to establish the proper priorities. Why? Because God requires it. The children and parents have their individual responsibilities and they are to exercise them day in and day out, not neglect them. "What additional requirements are placed on parents? To bring up children in a Scriptural way implies a serious and enlightened assumption of responsibility for their spiritual, moral, mental and physical well-being. This requires wise counsel and guidance in regard to the books they read, the pleasures they seek, the friendships they form, the school or college they attend, and all other matters that relate to character-building. Children are God's gift to parents, and they are also a trust. Will not God one day require Christian parents to give an account of their stewardship of parenthood and of the guardianship of the their children? Will you have failed in this most sacred trust?

"The parent needs to be taught and trained (*in the nurture and admonition*) of the Lord for the task of teaching and training the child. Many parents, feeling their own incompetency, shirk their responsibility and entrust the spiritual nurture of their children to the minister and

Sunday School teacher. But here in Ephesians, God places squarely upon parents the responsibility for the instruction and training of the child in those things which make for a well-rounded, full-orbed Christian character and service. Such bringing up will include discipline, warning, admonition, correction, above all the teaching of God's word and fellowship in prayer around the family altar. God tells clearly how it is to be done and to what end," as appropriately described by Ruth Paxson.

There is a significant point that should not be overlooked at the close of the fifth chapter and the beginning of the sixth one. Paul writes to each and every type of person. He is not writing just to the male members of the community, he is writing to them all.

What does he say? He wants them to know that all members of Christ's body are to share in performing their duties and responsibilities according to the Lord. He tells each and every one that he or she is responsible for making contributions to others according to Christ's commands and teachings, regardless of their position. He is not telling them that they will have a perfect society, or marriage, or family, or work situation. But he is telling them that they are to have knowledge of the Lord Jesus Christ's authority and that they are to conduct themselves as members of His body. They are to remember that the Lord said to Paul, *My grace is sufficient for thee: for my strength* (power) *is made perfect in weakness* [2 Cor. 12:9]. That is what the Lord Jesus said.

Paul adds his conclusion after years of ministering to others by saying, *Most gladly therefore will I rather glory in my infirmities,* (weaknesses) *that the power of Christ may rest upon me* [2 Cor. 12:9]. Think of that! May our prayer be, *That the power of Christ may rest upon me* as we walk through life, as we face challenges and obstacles, and as we seek to witness to others.

Paul conveys another thought to the Ephesians (and us) in these verses saying, think of the long term, develop good practices, and learn what the Master teaches. Do not be subject to: impulses and short-term reactions or emotional decisions. He tells them to: accrue knowledge and understanding; educate themselves in the Lord; recognize that their actions and attitudes are being transmitted not only to others, but to future generations; realize that the good a person is not something he or she produces by him or herself, but is a gift from God; and accept the fact that *in the Lord* different groups can get along according to the teachings of the Master. Paul had seen how the Jews and Gentiles could become one people as members of Christ's body.

These teachings are provided not only for our instruction but also to: help us grow in the faith; have a right relationship with the Lord Jesus Christ; and do the will of the Father. Remember, we are to be a light unto the world and salt to society. Therefore, understand the teachings contained in the Word of God, and apply them to your daily living. It is a tough requirement. It is not easy to learn Scripture, to come into a meaningful relationship with our Lord Jesus, and to obey His commands. But, as the saying goes, no one ever said that life would be easy.

What is a key element and teaching in these verses? Probably several answers could be given. However, what about discipline? The exhortations to the children and parents require discipline. So do the instructions to the husbands and wives. It requires discipline to do things in the Lord, to study the Word, to read the Word, and to apply the teachings of the Master.

Why bring this up? Because discipline, or the lack of it, impacts all aspects of our lives and living. Some of us remember and many have heard or read about people raised during the Victorian period, World War II, and the Great Depression. During all those periods there was discipline no matter how difficult the times were. However, there has been a reaction to discipline. This has been accompanied by opposition to the idea of justice, righteousness, wrath, truth, and punishment. These terms are not popular today. They are disliked. The terms we have been hearing in recent years are peace, happiness, love, enjoyment, ease, tolerance, and rights.

People today react against the accepted norms and practices of the nineteenth and early twentieth centuries. However, what makes the situation so serious in one respect, ludicrous in another, is that the prevailing attitude in the last thirty-five to forty years is presented as being the teachings of the New Testament. The people espousing these ideas will say there is a difference between the Old Testament and the New Testament. That the God of the Old Testament is different from the God of the New Testament. Therefore, as Lloyd-Jones says, these people say "they are not interested in justice and righteousness, wrath and punishment. Nothing matters but love and understanding."

So what do we have? People both within and outside the church who agree with one another but do not present an accurate exposition of

Scripture. They present the thesis that discipline is neither an essential ingredient nor an important matter in either the Old Testament or New Testament. What else has become evident?

First, there is a basic premise that human nature is essentially good. Therefore, you must develop a child's personality and allow him or her to express themselves. There is not to be any real control, or punishment, or corrective action on the child or teenager because it might have a negative impact upon them and their development.

Second, you should allow children to choose for themselves, to decide what they are going to study and to do. This is in direct contrast to learning the three R's because you were supposed to learn them whether you wanted to or not. Today, there is the thought that if you make children learn it may have a negative effect upon their personalities. Therefore, people are not supposed to learn in a mechanical manner, but only when reasonable explanations are given.

Third, there has been a strong school of thought that you are not to punish children. If not, what are you to do? You are to appeal to them; you are to set a positive example; and you are to reward them. But you are not to rebuke or punish them. The approach being presented, echoed, and re-echoed, is that human nature is essentially good. Therefore, all you have to do is appeal to them, and they will respond. But you are not to punish them.

What does the Bible reveal with respect to discipline and to the nature of people? It reveals that the harsh, authoritarian approach characterized by the Victorian period and the modern period of permissiveness with its lack of discipline are both wrong.

There are several factors to consider. An opinion or attitude has been developed and nurtured that if the wrong type of discipline has been practiced then you should not have discipline. That is not the answer. What needs to be implemented is the right type of discipline.

The discipline of which Paul speaks, Calvin says, "conveys the idea of gentleness and friendliness." Yet, it also conveys the idea of correcting the individuals with resoluteness and not allowing them free rein.

The discipline *in the Lord* and *of the Lord* is not to be kept in a closet where one has to search for it. Rather, it is part of the normal living environment, just as the sidelines are part of a football game.

Second, there are groups that say they are under the Lord; therefore, they are under grace. According to both the Old Testament and the

New Testament there is both the law and grace. God provided for grace in the Old Testament when He said He would accept burnt offerings and sacrifices. On the other hand, it cannot be said since we are under grace that the law does not apply and we are free to do as we wish or to act according to the ways of the world or flesh. Paul said,

> *For sin shall not have dominion over you: for ye are not under the law, but under grace.*
> *What then? shall we sin, because we are not under the law, but under grace? God forbid* (Certainly not) [Rom. 6:14–15].

Then he adds, with direct, pointed emphasis,

> *Know ye not, that to whom ye yield* (present) *yourselves servants to obey, his servants* (slaves) *ye are to whom ye obey; whether of sin unto death, or of obedience unto righteousness* [Rom. 6:16]?

We are to remember that the only part of the law which does not apply to those who are members of Christ's body is the curse. Why? Because we are subject to Christ's grace. If we are subject to His grace then we are to be obedient *unto righteousness*. We are to know and do the will of the Father.

We are to obey His commandments, and that requires discipline. As members of Christ's body we need to realize there is more discipline required under the New Testament than under the Old Testament. Paul says we are not to dismiss or to ignore the law when he proclaims, *Wherefore the law was our schoolmaster to bring us unto Christ* [Gal. 3:24].

Third, there is a prevailing misconception and misunderstanding about God and His teachings in today's world. There is the idea that God is love, and since He is, I can go merrily on my way. What those people should really say is that "God is permissive," because that is the way they are acting.

Unfortunately, most people form their picture of God not from Scripture but from the teachings of the world. The populace has created God in their own image and according to their own desires, just like people have for centuries.

What traits of God are revealed in Scripture? God is holy, righteous, just, love, our Father, a consuming fire, all these things and many more.

However, He does not turn His back on sin or disobedience and pretend they do not exist. No! That is the reason He sent His Son. That is why we are members of His body. Remember Jesus telling His disciples about the goats and the sheep, the wheat and the chaff, *I never knew you: depart from me, ye that work iniquity* [Matt. 7:23].

God punishes sin. This is evident in both the Old and New Testaments. What does God want from us? He wants us to *be filled with the Spirit; submit ourselves one to another in the fear of Christ; obey His commandments; and be in a right relationship with Him.* People do not realize what sin has done to man and to the world. They want to attribute the problems of the world to everything but sin and disobedience to the will of God. Man dislikes the light of God. He dislikes *I am the way, the truth and the life* [John 14:6]. Genesis strikes at the heart of the matter when it says, *And God saw that the wickedness of man was great in the earth, and that every imagination* (intent) *of the thoughts of his heart was only evil continually* [Gen. 6:5]. "There is a complete misunderstanding of the Doctrine of the Atonement and of redemption, and . . . of regeneration," as Martyn Lloyd-Jones declares.

What does the atonement tell us? On the Cross the holy, just, righteous God punished sin. How? In His Son. Does that sound like a loving, permissive, weak God? No, it does not!

Why the atonement? That we might be justified, made righteous, and have our sins forgiven. Paul states with clarity,

> *For he hath made him to be sin for us, who knew no sin; that we might be made the righteousness of God in him* [2 Cor. 5:21].

Peter confirms this, adding with emphasis what God through Christ has done for sinful man, saying,

> *BY WHOSE STRIPES* (WOUNDS) *WE ARE HEALED* [1 Pet. 2:24].

Paul and Peter remind us that God's justice and righteousness demanded it, His wrath against sin required it, and His love for us dictated it.

There is much more than emotion or sentimentality in the Cross. What we see in the Cross is that God punishes sin. Throughout the Bible it is evident that discipline is required and it is to be exercised.

When the law was broken, the consequences of so doing were applied and carried out. When God gives a law or a commandment He is not doing so for the fun of it or to play games. He expects it to be carried out. He gives us the wherewithal to do so. Obedience matters to Him and so does disobedience.

The Bible teaches that man has fallen in sin. Therefore, he is subject to the wiles of the flesh and the lusts of the world. He must be governed, he must have commandments, and he must know them and follow them.

The Lord Jesus Christ came to fulfill the law, carry our burdens, redeem us, enlighten us, and discipline us. In addition, He came that we might know the Father, obey the Father's commandments, please the Father, discipline ourselves, and follow Him.

Christ came to fulfill His duties and responsibilities, and He did that! We have been called to fulfill our duties and responsibilities as His disciples, and may it be said of each of us did that!

Christ's victory over sin and death on the Cross enables you and me to be clothed in His righteousness, to be in a right relationship with God, and for God the Father to be glorified.

Amen!

3

Man's Relationship to God

> *Servants, be obedient to them that are your masters according to the flesh, with fear and trembling, in singleness* (sincerity) *of your heart, as unto Christ;*
> *Not with eyeservice, as menpleasers; but as the servants of Christ, doing the will of God from the heart;*
> *With good will doing service, as to the Lord, and not to men* [Eph. 6:5–7].

The Apostle Paul, under the influence of the Holy Spirit, delves into life's critical areas. What can be more difficult to understand and to do correctly day after day and year after year than the marriage relationship between husband and wife, the family relationship between parents and children, and the relationships between servants and masters, and employers and employees?

Recently, I was told in a very loving way that the life of the Christian is not to become caught up in deep theological terms, or technical terms that are difficult to *grasp*. However, we are called to a living faith that centers around the Son of God, the Lord Jesus Christ. We are to know Him, know His teachings, and apply them in our daily living. Therefore, we are to grasp pastoral expositions of the Triune God by hearing and reading God's Word.

Some say, that is fine for you to say, but you do not know or understand my peculiar situation. You do not know the type of person to whom I am married; you do not know what my parents are like or how my children behave. You do not know what type of boss I have, or you do not realize how my employees act.

Christ knew about those conditions then and now. He ministered unto people. He went into their homes. He heard their complaints. He observed their conduct, and as a result of His love and understanding, He taught not only His disciples, but His enemies. He taught the people—husbands and wives, parents and children, masters and servants, employers and employees.

What is more, He prepared the apostles to address these matters, effectively and forcefully, in which people find themselves, by providing them with God's teachings, which were not always what they wanted to hear.

Think about how Paul treated the Ephesians. He did not just tell them how good they were, how much God loved them, how happy they were to be, and how pleasant life was. No! What did he say in his letter to the Ephesians? He reminded them that he was . . . *an apostle of Jesus Christ by the will of God,* and that he was writing *to the saints which are at Ephesus, and to the faithful in Christ Jesus: . . . who hath blessed us with all spiritual blessings* [Eph. 1:1, 3].

He expands upon this saying,

- that God has adopted them as children, and that in Christ Jesus they have an inheritance;
- that the eyes of their understanding may be enlightened, in order that they may know *the riches of the glory of his inheritance in the saints, . . .* [Eph. 1:18];
- *For by grace are ye* (you have been) *saved through faith; and that not of yourselves; it is the gift of God!* [Eph. 2:8]; and
- for by Christ *we both have access by one Spirit unto the Father,* and we *are no more strangers and foreigners, but fellow citizens with the saints, and of the household of God* [Eph. 2:18–19].

Paul prayed for the Ephesians,

That he would grant you, according to the riches of his glory, to be strengthened with might by his Spirit in the inner man;
That Christ may dwell in your hearts by faith [Eph. 3:16–17].

. . . that ye . . . may know the love of Christ, which passeth knowledge, that ye might be filled with all the fullness of God [Eph. 3:19].

Paul tells the Ephesians those truths. He glorifies God. He tells them about Christ's love and God's unsearchable riches.

Then what does he do? He shifts gears, gets personal, and starts to meddle. He tells them not to focus on themselves but on the *One Lord, one faith, one baptism, One God and Father of all*. He tells them that grace has been given to them and that *apostles, prophets, evangelists, pastors and teachers* have been given to them.

Why are these things provided? Scripture says they are provided for the perfecting of the saints, the work of the ministry, and the edifying of the body of Christ: you and me. All these blessings were bestowed upon the Ephesians, and they are bestowed upon us as well.

What does Paul say next? We are to grow. He has told us all these wonderful things that God in Christ has done, but he has the audacity to say we must grow in Christ. We must grow in our character, conduct, and conversation as Christ would have us to do. He follows that by saying, you are not to walk as your neighbors walk or as the world walks.

Then he adds something monumental to his statements. He says we are to learn Christ. It is not enough that *ye have heard him, ye have been taught by him*, and *the truth is in Jesus*. There is more to it than that. We have to learn Christ Himself, Christ the Master, Christ the Son of God, Christ the Saviour, Christ the companion, and Christ the Person.

That is not all. With our learning we are to do something. We are to become new creatures, new people, and our tenor of life is to be different. We are to grow, learn, and become new creatures. The emphasis is on what we are to become. It is a process. It is ongoing.

Paul describes how we are to conduct ourselves in different situations: we are to become kind, tenderhearted, and forgiving; we are to be followers of God; and we are to walk in love, not according to our ways, or background, or experience, or definition of love, but as Christ hath loved us.

As if that were not enough, Paul tells us we are to *walk as children of light*. We are to *be filled with the Spirit*. We are to submit ourselves *one to another in the fear of Christ*.

What does Paul say to the Ephesians (and to us)? He states what God has done; he exhorts us to learn Christ; he tells us to become new creatures; and he says we are to apply the teachings of the Master in our daily living. He describes in detail how we are to act in the three basic relationships we experience during our lives: husbands and wives, parents and children, and employers and employees.

What is required in order to appreciate, understand, and apply the teachings the Apostle has been proclaiming? We must recognize that man loves darkness rather than light; that individuals succumb to sin; that we do the things we would not and do not do the things we should; and that sin, self-centeredness, and selfishness affect relationships. Martyn Lloyd-Jones accurately describes the results of such conduct, saying "While man is in sin, and while, as a result of that, he is always primarily and essentially selfish and self-centered, there will of necessity be tensions in different relationships."

What is significant about the Apostle's message? First, it is unique. It cannot be found anywhere else. Other teachings may plagiarize or lift certain aspects of this teaching, but they stop short of the key, vital ingredient, which is the Lord Jesus Christ Himself. They may borrow from His teachings, but they do not accept Him.

Second, these teachings assume that the people to whom they are addressed are members of Christ's body and that they are new creatures. Therefore, they have new priorities, new objectives, and have been regenerated. The people to whom Paul is writing have been called, and they have responded in faith. They have grasped the impact of the Apostle's teachings.

Third, Paul assumes that the people to whom he is writing have a basic understanding of the Master's teachings and of the Lord Himself. Paul spent three years in Ephesus, and he taught from house to house, expounding upon Christ's teachings. Consequently, the individuals accepted the teachings and doctrines he presented.

However, there is a point that cannot be dismissed or overlooked. As members of Christ's body we do not receive a list of do's and don'ts to learn and apply to specific situations. It does not say as a master or employer you are to do 1, 2, and 3, or as a servant or employee you are to do 8, 9, and 10. In the New Testament we are given a doctrine and told to apply it to our personal lives and to our relationships with other people, no matter who they may be.

What must we do in order to apply a doctrine? First, we must be told about it. Then we must learn it, accept it, and realize we are to apply it in our daily living. If we do not learn about it, we cannot apply it. If we do not apply it, we will not do the will of our Father, and we will not obey His commands.

Knowledge of the basic teachings is necessary as well as believing that different doctrines apply to real life situations. Of course, belief may not come at first as we try to apply the basic principles, but it will by trusting Him and persevering.

Last, Scripture always maintains a balance. This is revealed in the fact that the Apostle describes the duties and responsibilities of both the husbands and wives as well as those of the parents and children. God shows the proper perspective with each situation. He does not play favorites.

Then Paul focuses attention on servants and masters, on employees and employers, as well as their respective duties and responsibilities. What does Scripture say about these meaningful and important relationships? How does it apply to the world of reality compared to abstract ideas? Certainly, these can be highly charged areas. The Apostle commands obedience on the part of servants, but in so doing it is to be in accord with *doing the will of the Lord from the heart*, saying,

> *Servants, be obedient to them that are your masters according to the flesh, with fear and trembling, in singleness* (sincerity) *of your heart, as unto Christ;*
> *Not with eyeservice, as menpleasers; but as the servants of Christ, doing the will of God from the heart;*
> *With good will doing service, as to the Lord, and not to men.*

The term for *servant* is interpreted from the Greek word *doulos* which means "bond servant" or "slave." He is not addressing hired servants or employees directly. However, the message applies to these people. Also, there were slaves who had accepted Christ. Undoubtedly, Paul taught and preached to the slaves or bond-servants as well as the free men of the day.

The Apostle does an interesting thing. He exhorts these servants to be obedient to their masters according to the flesh. In so doing, he realizes the burden they are bearing and that they may be troubled and bitter about their condition. As we all know, it is very difficult for anyone to yield himself or herself completely to the control of another person.

Many of these slaves knew that they had been bought, that they were to perform nasty, undesirable tasks, and that their masters had the right under the law to take their lives or to spare them.

Paul knew that some of the slaves exhibited obedience on the surface but not with their hearts and minds. He tells them to be obedient with a right and positive attitude from the depth of their being, and he urges them to do it with singleness of heart. What does this mean? It means without duplicity but sincerely with simplicity, liberality, and respect.

That is quite a command to those people, especially when they have been told that they are new creatures in Christ and that they have a new freedom in Him. Paul tells them that their surface obedience, which is seen of men and may be pleasing to them, is not enough. God looks upon their heart and requires them to act with sincerity and in truth.

Do you see what the Apostle is doing? He is focusing attention upon God and their relationship to Him. As Calvin says, "When they serve their masters faithfully, they obey God."

How are they to show this obedience? With good will, not with obstinacy, nor dislike, nor unwillingness, nor reluctance. They are to perform their tasks honestly, conscientiously, and with sincerity. In these verses, Paul tells them to be obedient to their masters as unto Christ, *As the servants of Christ, doing the will of God . . . as to the Lord, and not to men.*

What does this mean? When they render faithful service it is accepted by Christ as being performed unto Him. Further, since God is the One controlling society, their real service is performed unto Christ. The Lord Jesus addresses the question of rendering faithful service in His encounter with the Pharisees and the Herodians who were seeking to trap Him by asking,

> *Is it lawful* (permitted) *to give tribute* (pay taxes) *unto Caesar, or not?*
> *But Jesus perceived* (knew) *their wickedness, and said, Why tempt* (test) *ye me, ye hypocrites?*
> *Show me the tribute* (tax) *money. And they brought unto him a penny.*
> *And he* (Jesus) *saith unto them, Whose is this image and superscription* (inscription)*?*
> *They say unto him, Caesar's. Then saith he unto them, Render* (Pay) *therefore unto Caesar the things which are Casear's; and unto God the things that are God's* [Matt. 22:17–21].

Jesus listened to their question and went directly to the heart of the matter. The Pharisees and Herodians wanted to focus on paying tribute to Caesar, or being disobedient to Him. However, our Lord responded with those famous words, *Render therefore unto Caesar the things which are Caesar's*, and He added something they had not been expecting. He told them *and unto God the things that are God's*.

That statement changed the whole complexion of the situation. Though they were in the world and subject to the laws of the world, they were to be obedient unto God, and they were to serve Him.

Peter says that we are to do the *will of God* and *put to silence the ignorance of foolish men* [1 Pet. 2:15]. When people are deprived of understanding and reason concerning the will of God and His teachings, then they cannot conduct themselves according to His commands. "The unbelieving may be satisfied with their own acuteness, and may even seem to others to be wise and prudent, yet the Spirit of God condemns them for their folly, in order that we may know that, apart from God, we cannot be really wise, as without Him there is nothing firm," as John Calvin proclaimed under the influence of the Holy Spirit.

Peter continues by telling the servants to *be subject to your masters with all fear* [1 Pet. 2:18]. They are to perform their tasks sincerely and willingly, with a fear that is based on the desire to do the right thing. However, it should be noted that obeying earthly masters does not diminish one iota God's authority and control. The Lord Jesus says with his incomparable wisdom, *Render* (Pay) *unto Caesar, the things that are Caesar's; and unto God the things that are God's* [Matt. 22:21]. Further, Peter says that the servants are to be subject *not only to the good and gentle* (masters), *but also to the froward* (harsh; the crooked and perverse ones) [1 Pet. 2:18].

Someone may ask, why is there relatively little teaching in Scripture on the subject of servants and masters, employers and employees? What is the primary thrust of the Bible? Man's relationship to God. That is its message. That is of primary importance.

Certainly, there are many questions that can be raised concerning economics, politics, social relationships, and society. They are all based upon man's relationship to man. That is also basically true of how people look at marriage, family, children, and work.

What Christ was saying to the Pharisees and Herodians and what the apostles are stressing in the Epistles is man's relationship to God. It is acting according to Christ's teachings and commands. The first item of importance is man's relationship to God. A scribe asked the Lord Jesus,

> *Master, which is the great commandment in the law?* Jesus answered immediately,
> THOU SHALT LOVE THE LORD THY GOD WITH ALL THY HEART, AND WITH ALL THEY SOUL, AND WITH ALL THY MIND.
> *This is the first and great commandment.*
> *And the second is like unto it,* THOU SHALT LOVE THY NEIGHBOR AS THYSELF.
> *On these two commandments hang all the law and prophets* [Matt. 22:36–40].

"Human relationships do not come first; they never come first in the Bible, it is always man's relationship to God first," as emphasized by Martyn Lloyd-Jones.

Remember what Jesus said to the Pharisees and Scribes in that oft-forgotten and neglected twenty-third chapter of Matthew,

> *Woe unto you, scribes and Pharisees, hypocrites! for ye pay tithe of mint and anise and cummin, and have omitted* (neglected) *the weightier matters of the law, judgment* (justice)*, mercy, and faith: these ought ye to have done, and not to leave the other undone* [Matt. 23:23].

Man's relationship to God comes first.

What is the chief function of the church as the body of Christ? It is to open the Word, expound upon Scripture, and through the Holy Spirit enable people to learn, grow, and become new creatures in Christ by God's grace.

It is not the church's primary function to deal directly with conditions in this world but rather with the people who are members of Christ's body, to have them understand and accept the fact that their primary responsibility is to be in a right relationship with God. Then the members of Christ's body are to go into the world and do as Christ would have them to do.

Scripture emphasizes how Christians conduct themselves in existing conditions and that they are to be in a right relationship to God. They are to examine themselves in the light of Scripture. Then they are to go forth and do according to the teachings and commands of our Lord.

In closing, I wish to share with you a situation described by Ruth Paxson, who was a missionary to China. "A mission station and hospital in China had problems, unrest, and disobedience. Then there was a revival as a result of preaching and teaching the Word and the Holy Spirit working among the people. The missionary wrote our hospital is no more like it used to be. There is perfect harmony among all the hospital workers from servants up. All do faithful work. I never have to reprove any of them. I even never have to tell servants what to do. All know their work and do it faithfully."

Oh, the power of the Word and the teachings of the Master. "Filled with the Holy Spirit, both the manner and the motive of every servant's work will be such as to make for harmony," as recorded by Ruth Paxson after observing the impact of the Holy Spirit where she was a missionary working in China.

Amen!

4

Priorities

> *Servants, be obedient to them that are your masters according to the flesh, with fear and trembling, in singleness* (sincerity) *of your heart, as unto Christ;*
>
> *Not with eyeservice, as menpleasers; but as the servants of Christ, doing the will of God from the heart;*
>
> *With good will doing service, as to the Lord, and not to men* [Eph. 6:5–7].

Do you ever think about priorities? Do you ever think about all the things you have to do? Do you ever think about the demands placed upon you? Do you ever get so wrapped up in doing, whether for your self or others, that you allow your thoughts to become lopsided, warped, and negative?

Do you ever ask, what can I learn about living, about my relationship to God, about the teachings of Christ? Do you spend time learning? When you receive a new recipe, you make something. When you get a new sweater, you wear it. When you get a new tool, you use it.

Although the grace of God makes us clean and whole in His sight through the atoning blood of our Lord Jesus Christ, does that mean there is nothing else for us to do? With respect to our salvation the answer is *yes*. With respect to our sanctification and daily living the answer is *NO!*

Where does our daily living take us? Family relations, work places, market places, and church activities. It takes us into the midst of things. However, it does not take us into an ideal environment. So, what are we to do?

Consider Paul's words to the Ephesians. He told them when they went into those situations to do what?

> *. . . be filled with the Spirit;*
> *Speaking to yourselves in psalms and hymns and spiritual songs, singing and making melody in your heart to the Lord;*
> *Giving thanks always for all things to God and the Father in the name of the Lord Jesus Christ* [Eph. 5:18–20].

These are the things we are supposed to do in the face of difficulties and obstacles as we go about our daily tasks. One thing is certain, it is not easy.

However, did you notice how many times the Apostle refers to and includes God and the Lord Jesus Christ in his exhortation to the Ephesians? Twenty-seven times the Apostle refers to God and Christ in the twenty-five verses from Ephesians 5:18 through Ephesians 6:9.

Think of that, twenty-seven times. They were to take God and Christ with them wherever they went. They were to do so in all the basic relationships of life. Their awareness of God the Father, and His Son, the Lord Jesus Christ, was to permeate every facet of their living. The same is expected of you and me.

This teaching should have a significant impact on all professing Christians. The primary task of the church is to preach the Gospel, evangelize others, bring people to a knowledge of God, reach people under the dominion of sin, and strengthen all those longing for a purpose that only the Lord can give.

What has been required of most church members during much of the twentieth century and into the twenty-first century? Make a profession of faith, join the church, attend services on Sundays, let the full-time minister take care of most matters, and perform worldly tasks according to human standards.

What does the Apostle say to the members of Christ's body? Wherever you go, whatever you do, *your standard of conduct is to be the Lord Jesus Christ* and your relationship with Him. Therefore, if that is the standard, you must learn about Him, you must assimilate His teachings, and above all you must come to know Him.

What principles emerge from the teachings contained in this portion of Ephesians? First, it is obvious that accepting Christ and becoming one of His followers does not do away with participating in the existing social, political, and economic affairs with which we come into contact. Some early Christians thought that once they accepted Christ their relationships with other people or institutions would change radically. Also, some thought if they accepted Christ and their spouse did not, then they were no longer bound by their marriage vows.

Paul reminds them of what the Lord commands. For the covenant entered into by the husband and wife was consecrated by God. Therefore, it is not to be terminated by the whim of either person. The union of a man and woman in marriage is in the name of God. Therefore, if one person accepts Christ, but the other does not, that does not mean the Christian partner can dissolve the marriage. They are not free to break the knot and go their own way.

Paul informs the true believers, as Calvin states explicitly, "that the sanctity of the marriage vow depends upon God." Therefore, "what further need is there for a believing wife to remain with an unbelieving husband?" As Scripture says, *For the unbelieving husband is sanctified by the wife, and the unbelieving wife is sanctified by the husband; else were your children unclean; but now are they holy* [1 Cor. 7:14]. What does the Apostle say in this verse? He states that the godliness of either the husband or wife does more to *sanctify* a marriage than the ungodliness of the other can do to mar or distort it. It shows that the children of the believers are set apart and they are deemed to be holy in the body of Christ. *For if the first fruit be holy, the lump is also holy; and if the root be holy, so are the branches* [Rom. 11:16].

We are to walk according to the grace given unto us. When we do, we are to remember that Christ said to Paul, *My grace is sufficient unto thee*. Also, we are to walk worthy of the vocation to which we have been called. These two things are to be remembered as we go about our daily tasks. We are to think upon them.

God has made us His servants. He has made us worthy and capable of being His servants, and in each and every situation His grace is sufficient. Our calling should enable us to serve Him even under difficult or trying circumstances.

Paul's teaching, under the influence of the Holy Spirit, states that even though you accept Christ and become His follower that does not mean the relationships which have been in existence cease to exist or that you are to withdraw from all political, social, and economic activities. Bear in mind that the Apostle is teaching us how to conduct ourselves and live in marriage, in the home, in the workplace, and under less than ideal situations or circumstances.

There is no difference with respect to people concerning salvation. However, that does not eliminate the orders and functions of society. Membership in the body of Christ does not do away with the differences between people as they function in marriage, the home, or the workplace.

Becoming a Christian does not automatically dissolve social conditions or require a person to change jobs or occupations. Paul, under the influence of the Holy Spirit, states what the person called by God should do, saying,

> *Let every man abide in the same calling wherein he was called* [1 Cor. 7:20].

> *For he that is called in the Lord, being a servant, is the Lord's freeman: likewise also he that is called, being free, is Christ's servant.*
> *Ye are bought with a price, be not ye the servants of men.*
> *Brethren, let every man, wherein he is called, therein abide with God* [1 Cor. 7:22–24].

Scripture says each person should not be eager to change his calling or his occupation because he has accepted Christ. He or she is to serve the Lord in their existing conditions. However, it does not mean that people cannot change their position or occupation. But they are not to act impulsively or to do something without proper reasoning.

Calvin points out that the Apostle does not say "that each person must remain in a certain way of life once he has adopted it, but he condemns the restlessness which prevents individuals from remaining contentedly as they are."

He wants the people who have accepted Christ to serve God where they are and to witness unto Him in their existing conditions. Note how Paul states it: *For he that is called in the Lord, being a servant, is the Lord's freeman: likewise, also, he that is called, being free, is Christ's servant* [1 Cor. 7:22]. Paul, following the example of His Master, always addresses both sides of the coin.

He tells them straightforwardly that they are now part of Christ's body; therefore, they are not to serve men or other people in a way that brings shame or dishonor to God. They are not to perform wicked or shameful deeds. Paul wants them to *abide with God*. Therefore, he wants them to exercise self-control and bring their impulses under rein.

A person's occupation does not make any difference to God, but his or her conduct does. Differences in a person's occupation should not produce a negative in their daily living or faith.

Second, certain aspects of the Christian faith are difficult for many people to grasp. The Christian faith is not controlled by a list of do's and don'ts, nor does it provide a series of prescriptions as to what we are to do or not to do.

The Scripture being examined neither condemns nor condones slavery. This is difficult for some people to recognize and to accept. Consequently, they say since something is wrong, such as slavery or apartheid, that the Christian churches must denounce it and make official pronouncements about different social conditions. They argue that if something is wrong according to man's moral standards then the various governing bodies of the different denominations should make appropriate statements condemning the wrong that exists. However, the fact remains that the Bible neither condemns nor condones slavery.

What does the Bible say? It teaches that one's reason for being is to have a personal relationship with God. No matter what one's status in life may be, when they are in a right relationship to God then the manner in which they conduct themselves is changed and the most important thing is how they serve the Lord. The slave becomes Christ's freeman, and the freeman becomes Christ's slave.

"What Christianity is interested in is the way in which a Christian slave behaves towards his Master, and, how the Master behaves towards his slave. It does not deal directly with the questions of slavery per se," as Martyn Lloyd-Jones explains.

A great problem today is that so many people want to take direct action. They want to have preachers preach about them, to have protests sent to governments, and to take part in processions. They want direct intervention.

What does the Bible present? It is concerned with how the people on both sides of a situation or issue conduct themselves. Scripture does not denounce different types of governments, whether they be democratic or communistic. Nor do they denounce drinking, but they denounce drunkenness, revelry, and unrighteousness.

What does the Bible stress? A right relationship to God, walking with the Lord Jesus Christ, and learning the teachings contained in Scripture. When people accept and believe on the Lord Jesus Christ, then they will be changed. They will act differently, and they will exhibit the proper conduct towards one another. The important thing is to: know the Lord Jesus Christ; be obedient unto Him; and be in a right relationship with God, the Father.

Third, another principle is involved. How is a member of Christ's body to react to these teachings, and how is he or she to live in the real world?

> *Servants, be subject to your masters with all fear; not only to the good and gentle, but also to the froward* (harsh; the crooked and perverse ones) [1 Pet. 2:18].

The slaves are urged not to rebel. Both sides are urged to serve the Lord and are reminded that their duty is to God.

The primary concern of the person accepting Christ is to do the will of God, regardless of his or her occupation or social position. They are to submit themselves to God and be His servants. The servant should endeavor to serve his master diligently and positively. Likewise the master should be concerned with the welfare of the servant.

John Calvin, the renowned theologian, provides additional light regarding masters and servants saying, ". . . that no distinction is to be made between a slave and a free man. The world is wont to set less value on the labours of slaves. He says that it is not so with God, but they are as precious to Him as the duties of kings. For the outward station is set aside and each is judged according to the integrity of his heart."

Fourth, someone may say you just want to protect the status quo, you are not exhibiting concern for undesirable situations, and you are not concerned about social conditions. We are addressing a delicate situation. In some areas it is an emotional issue. Therefore, it is important to express myself clearly and concisely.

It is the church's business to espouse God's themes that are evident throughout Scripture, such as justice and righteousness. Certainly, justice is part of God's righteousness. Wherever there is injustice, the church is to go on the offensive. If it does not, it becomes a participant in evil.

It is the church's responsibility to proclaim the full Gospel, not just milk and honey or the Advent season or Easter morning. Preachers and teachers are to proclaim the tough meat provided in God's commandments, the wisdom and commands of the Lord Jesus, and the pertinent teachings of the apostles and prophets. Professing Christians are to continuously acquire knowledge and increase in their faith as they encounter the tests, trials, and tribulations of life.

What does this mean? Biblical truths are to be proclaimed in their full glory and majesty. The hearers of the Word are to pray for enlightenment, understanding, and strength. Professing Christians have a responsibility to respond positively when the Gospel is preached and taught. They are to know that Christ's blood was shed for them, that He atoned for their sins, and that the Holy Spirit works within them and changes their minds and hearts. When He does, they become new creatures in Christ. Their values change, their focus changes, their priorities change, and as a result, their attitude and conduct change. Why? Because of the Triune God, Father, Son, and Holy Ghost.

Then what happens? The people are affected; their personalities, minds, thinking, attitudes, and understanding become changed. When that happens people see things in a different light and they begin to approach their daily living with different thoughts.

I might note that for a period of approximately fourteen years the Stated Clerk of the General Assembly did not issue statements about social, political, and economic matters. This occurred during the late 1950s and 1960s.

Are you aware of the conditions existing in England at the time of John Wesley? There was rampant illiteracy and immorality, along with pitiful living and working conditions. What did Wesley do when he went into one of the poorest of the poor districts? He preached from Isaiah 53. The text was *He was wounded* (pierced through) *for our transgressions, he was bruised* (crushed) *for our iniquities: the chastisement of our peace was upon him; and with his stripes* (blows) *we are healed* [Isa. 53:5]. He preached to them about their Saviour and their spiritual condition, but not about the social, political, and economic conditions.

What happened? People were converted; they were changed. They were awakened spiritually. They started using their minds. They learned to read so they could read the Bible. They became enlightened. They began to realize the truth about themselves, about man and his need for God, and about their own personalities and conduct. Then they began to look at the conditions existing around them. Then they began to ask questions as individuals. Then they became involved as individuals, and conditions began to change.

Scripture neither condemns nor condones certain things in the social, political, and economic area. Martyn Lloyd-Jones explains it this way, "It does not expect men to rise up and change it; neither does it simply maintain the status quo. It deals with man himself first, and then under the influence of this teaching, the man himself begins to examine the position and to deal with it."

The church does not command changes to be made and then they occur. Scripture does not deal with some things directly. However, when people come into a right relationship with Christ, they look at things differently.

Dr. Robert Ferguson, a Presbyterian minister, tells about Dr. Barnardo, who founded homes for destitute children in London and brought about significant social changes. The church brings about changes when it converts people and produces members of Christ's body.

When the church produces Christians, conditions change for the better. However, if the churches are not producing enlightened Christians, then the conditions will not improve.

Preachers and teachers are to be concerned with the souls of people and to present the Gospel of the Lord Jesus Christ. Then there will be more people under the influence of Christ. These people, in turn, will have an impact on social, political, and economic situations.

Remember, it is the Spirit of God that produces Christians, and they are to be a light unto the world. This means they are charged (commanded) to do in the world as Christ would do and bring His kingdom to all people, that they might know not only the love of Christ, but His mercy, truth, righteousness, and justice.

In conclusion, is your primary area of concern society, politics, and economics, or a right relationship with God and the Lord Jesus Christ? The Christian's primary concern should be his or her relationship to God and to Christ. He or she should be able to say, "My Master is in heaven; whether I am a servant or master, whether I am an employee or an employer, I am to submit myself to the Lord and to be obedient to His commands."

The work of the church is presenting the full Gospel, not just selected portions. Further, it is not to be directly involved in social, political and economic affairs. However, individual members can be and may be involved in different issues.

The primary work of the individual member is to acquire knowledge about God and His teachings. Then he or she may participate in social, political, and economic affairs.

"The Christian teaching realizes that it cannot transform society as a whole; it must go on trusting that gradually the teaching will act as a leaven, and that men will become more and more enlightened. The time lag is not to be explained in terms of the failure of biblical teachings; it is to be explained in terms of the blindness of the world to Christian teaching. Christians have been given wisdom by God and the power to be patient and to wait until the right time for action has arrived," as summarized and expressed by Martyn Lloyd-Jones.

Amen!

5

Christ's Slaves

Knowing that whatsoever good thing any man doeth, the same shall he receive of the Lord, whether he be bond (slave) *or free.*

And, ye masters, do the same things unto them, forbearing (giving up) *threatening: knowing that your Master also is in heaven; neither is there respect of persons with him* [Eph. 6:8-9].

An interesting trait of Scripture is that it always presents two sides of a coin, never just one. You will note that in verses 5-9 of this sixth chapter that the Apostle Paul is speaking to servants and masters, and to employees and employers. You know something? At one and the same time he is telling them something different as well as the same thing.

He tells the servants to be obedient unto their *masters according to the flesh* and as *servants of Christ, doing the will of God from the heart* [Eph. 6:5-6]. Imagine the impact of those words on disgruntled workers, people unhappy with their positions or jobs. Imagine the reaction this exhortation would receive from union members about to go on strike or who were on strike.

Then look at the other side of the coin. Scripture says, *And, ye masters, do the same things unto them, . . . knowing that your Master also is in heaven* [Eph. 6:9]. The masters or employers are to be obedient unto their Master, Christ Jesus. Imagine the impact this command would have on people in authority when exercising control if they recognized their relationship to Christ, were knowledgeable about His commandments, and were obeying them. Certainly, it would make a difference in relationships!

There is a principle in these passages that should not be overlooked: both the servant and the master are to learn not only how to conduct themselves, but to realize that their relationship to Christ Jesus takes precedence and must be the controlling factor.

Both the servant and master, or the employee and employer, are to perform their assigned tasks, and to realize in so doing that Christ is the Master. They may be required to perform tasks they may not like to do, but if those tasks do not transgress their relationship to God then they are to do them.

Each is to be obedient in performing his or her tasks and function as part of the economic system. One should be obedient to the work rules and his or her assignments. Some may not like to work on Sunday mornings, Christmas Day, or Easter Sunday, but when required to do so, *be obedient . . . as unto Christ.*

If a person is a member of a union and a Christian, then he or she is to function according to the will of the majority as long as they perform their work to the best of their ability and are not disobedient to the will of God.

The person who is a member of Christ's body is not to be a rebel or malcontent or do anything producing a negative impact on the body of Christ. Yet he or she is to conduct himself or herself according to the teachings of Christ. This may mean taking a stand, but it is to be on that solid rock, Christ Jesus.

When is the member of Christ's body to take a stand? When one is asked or expected to do something that will effect their personal relationship to Christ and to God the Father. This may sound easy or cut and dried, but it is not. It requires understanding and discernment. It requires being in a right relationship with God, knowing the teachings of Christ, and applying them. It requires knowing what Scripture says, not what people say, or experience says, or philosophy says, or other organizations say. This means reading and studying Scripture. It means getting self out of the way and letting the Holy Spirit speak.

What does this portion of Scripture say? What type of conduct are both the servants and masters to exhibit? Scripture says,

> *Servants, be obedient to them that are your masters . . . in singleness* (sincerity) *of your heart, as unto Christ;*
> *Not with eyeservice, as menpleasers; but as the servants of Christ, doing the will of God from the heart* [Eph. 6:5–6].

The servants are to obey their masters from the heart, *Not with eyeservice*.

They are not to keep one eye looking for the master and only doing their job half-heartedly. They must work wholeheartedly as unto the Lord. They are not to do the minimum or to be looking to see if their master is coming. They are to work dutifully whether the master is present or not.

Actually, Scripture, in these verses, condemns the attitude or outlook that is interested in just getting by or doing the least amount possible. This is not the way in which the Christian disciple is to work. How then are the servants to perform their tasks? The statement may seem a little unusual, but Scripture says,

> *Servants, be obedient to them, that are your masters, . . . with fear and trembling, in singleness* (sincerity) *of your heart, as unto the Lord* [Eph. 6:5].

What is meant by the phrase *with fear and trembling*? Scripture says,

> *I was with you in weakness, and in fear, and in much trembling* [1 Cor. 2:3].

> *And his inward affection is more abundant toward you, whilst he remembereth the obedience of you all, how with fear and trembling ye received him* [2 Cor. 7:15].

Paul says to the Philippians,

> *Wherefore, my beloved, as ye have always obeyed, not as in my presence only, but now much more in my absence, work out your own salvation with fear and trembling* [Phil. 2:12].

The *fear and trembling* described in these verses is not that of being terrified or cowering in the face of something terrible. Rather it is a reverential fear that wants to please God, do His will, have Him control one's daily life, and avoid the wholesome dread of displeasing Him. There are situations in our lives where we want to do well, to turn in an outstanding performance. Why? Because we do not want to displease someone or disappoint Him.

Too often, I have wanted to do well for self-satisfaction, for my own ego. There are other times I have wanted to do well to please my parents, my grandmother, my family, my school, my team. Then, thank God, came the revelation to do well so that I would not disappoint or displease Him, the Lord Jesus Christ. This represents a shift of emphasis, a change of direction, and establishing of the right priorities. Oh, that we may have the *fear and trembling* that Scripture describes in these verses. May our obedience be unto the Lord. May we be submissive and humble according to the teachings of Christ.

This *fear and trembling* comes from obtaining *a right knowledge of duty* [1 Pet. 2:18]. Paul's words to the Philippians should be enlightening and comforting when he says, *Wherefore, my beloved, as ye have always obeyed, not as in my presence only, but now much more in my absence, work out your own salvation with fear and trembling* [Phil. 2:12]. Calvin says in referring to these words that it comes from knowing, "How wretched we are, and devoid of all good without the power of the Holy Spirit working within us and bringing us into a right relationship with God."

Fear and trembling enables one to get rid of their own pride and self-importance, to put their confidence in God's strength, and to depend upon His grace. These are difficult steps to take. It makes me think of my children and grandchildren learning to walk. We are to be like the little child. We are to take those first few steps with the arms of a loving Father around us to support us, keep us from falling, watch over us, prepare us, protect us, and enable us to grow and mature as Christians.

There is a significant difference between adults in Christ and a little child. The child will soon go about walking on his own and will not want the loving arms about him, but the person in Christ will want the loving arms of the Father about him or her forever and ever.

Did you notice the other phrase the Apostle uses when exhorting the servants? He says, *Servants, be obedient to them that are your masters according to the flesh, . . . in singleness* (sincerity) *of your heart, as unto Christ* [Eph. 6:5]. This phrase, *in singleness* (sincerity) *of your heart*, is most interesting. It describes an attitude, an approach to living, and the performance of one's responsibilities.

What does it mean? First, it means freedom from duplicity, deception, dual speech, and evil action. It does not stop there. It means bounty or bountifulness. It denotes liberality in a positive sense, a sincere simplicity, an unaffected but generous giving of oneself.

Are we able to give with singleness of heart? Are we able to concentrate on being obedient, doing the will of our Father, learning and accepting the teachings of Christ? Are we able to work and to perform in an unaffected manner and in a generous way, with sincere simplicity? Are we able to exhibit a bountiful approach? Are we able to do all these things in our daily living as we go about our everyday tasks?

These are not characteristics with which we are born. They are acquired and developed through learning and practice. The more I learn about Scripture and the more I try to apply its teachings to my daily tasks, the more I realize the need for God's grace. The truth is, I am just not capable of doing as I should. Thank God, the Lord Jesus said, *My grace is sufficient unto thee*. A servant is to give himself or herself unreservedly to working for his or her earthly master as long as he or she does not disobey God's commands.

A third phrase the Apostle uses in telling the servants to be obedient is to do it from the heart. Probably this phrase could be translated "from the soul." Then the Apostle says, *be obedient . . . with good will doing service, as to the Lord, and not to men* [Eph. 6:5, 7]. This statement refers to the mind and understanding. The person who is a member of Christ's body is to show that he or she has thought about the situation and the right thing to do. One must examine it, obtain a clear understanding, and proceed to use the mind.

Have you noted what the Apostle says to the Ephesians in these verses? He tells them to obey the Lord and to do that which is pleasing to Him; conduct themselves *in singleness* (sincerity) *of your heart* to exhibit love liberally, bountifully, and generously; to do the will of God from the heart; and to do so *With good will, . . . as to the Lord, and not to men* [Eph. 6:7]. What is expressed here? The heart, soul, and mind, along with love and obedience, are contained in this command. Yes, it is a command, and we are to obey it.

What is the first and great commandment?

> THOU SHALT LOVE THE LORD THY GOD WITH ALL THY HEART, AND WITH ALL THY SOUL, AND WITH ALL THY MIND, AND WITH ALL THY STRENGTH [Mark 12:30].

The Apostle Paul emphasizes the whole person. He says the whole person is to do these things and do them heartily, bountifully, sincerely, and liberally. They are to do them from the depth of their being in a positive, beneficial manner, not in a grudging or hesitant way. They are to do them with all their heart, mind, soul, and strength.

You may ask, why does the Apostle exhort the servants, slaves, and employees to act this way toward their masters or employers? In order to understand his teaching and consider it in its entirety. So far we have considered some strong medicine. We are to be obedient with *fear and trembling, in singleness* (sincerity) *of your heart, and good will.*

What else does Scripture say? We are *not* to be obedient *with eyeservice, as menpleasers.* The servant, or the member of Christ's body, is not to be occupied by keeping his or her eye on others and being concerned with personal opinions. For example: What do they think of me? How will this affect me? How will this benefit me? How is my appearance? What do they think of my ability? What does this group or that one think? We are not to focus on these questions and similar ones. We are not to seek the praise of men. We are not to conduct ourselves as menpleasers. These things are difficult. They may seem easy, but they are not. Also, they affect our priorities and they affect how we act.

What does the Apostle tell us to do?

> . . . *be obedient to them that are your masters according to the flesh, . . . as unto Christ;*
> . . . *as the servants of Christ, doing the will of God from the heart;*
> *With good will doing service, as to the Lord, and not to men* [Eph. 6:5–7].

When a person becomes a member of Christ's body, he or she begins to see things differently and to place them in a different perspective. *Old things are passed away; behold, all things are become new* [2 Cor. 5:17].

How does this teaching impact those who are members of Christ's body? *PAUL, an apostle of Jesus Christ by the will of God, to the saints which are at Ephesus, and to the faithful in Christ Jesus* [Eph. 1:1]. The first question and answer in the Shorter Catechism is, "What is the chief end of man? The chief end of man is to glorify God and to enjoy Him forever."

Who is the Christian saint, or faithful person, in Christ Jesus? Someone "who has come to the realization that he is a sinner," as stated by Martyn Lloyd-Jones. I like that! Recall that Andrew was one of the two who heard John the Baptist speak when he said, *Behold the Lamb of God* [John 1:29]! Andrew followed Jesus and then went to tell Peter about the Master. We do not know what the other person did. First,

Andrew was found by the Master, and it was revealed to him that Jesus was the Messiah. Later, he realized he was a sinner.

The Apostle Paul thought he was a righteous person when he started down the road to Damascus. The Lord Jesus Christ revealed Himself to Paul, and Paul accepted the Master. Then he realized that he was a sinner. As Paul said to Timothy, *And the grace of our Lord was exceeding abundant with faith and love which is in Christ Jesus. This is a faithful saying, and worthy of all acceptation, that Christ Jesus came into the world to save sinners; of whom I am chief* [1 Tim. 1:14–15].

What is a sinner? It is not merely someone who does not abide by acceptable moral codes or does not do what he or she should do. It is someone who does not live to glorify God, who does not live according to God's will, who does not learn God's commandments and seek to obey them. It is someone who has not been living to serve the Lord seven days a week, fifty-two weeks a year, who puts himself or herself first and foremost, and lives to please himself or herself, not others.

There is a difference, a big difference. Andrew and Paul were found of God through Christ Jesus. They acknowledged who He was. Then they came to realize that they were sinners. They were in need of God's grace and love. They were not living to please God and to do His will but they were living to please themselves and possibly their associates. There is a big difference between abiding by certain do's and don'ts as compared to finding out what pleases God, and doing it.

What is to be the first consideration of the saint, the faithful person in Christ Jesus? To know and to do the will of God. Not to continue as I am, satisfied with myself. It is to seek to change, to move into a closer relationship with Him, and to obey His commands.

Am I a servant rendering *eyeservice as menpleasers*, or am I becoming an obedient servant with *fear and trembling*, and *singleness of heart*? Am I performing the will of God from my heart, mind, and soul? Am I sincerely exhibiting goodwill in doing service as to the Lord, not to men?

Don't you love Scripture the more you delve into it? Don't you love the teachings of the Master as you are exposed to them? He not only tells us what not to do, but He provides positive instructions enabling us to understand ourselves and our shortcomings. Through Paul's words, He tells us how we are to act and how we are to apply the teachings: *As unto Christ; As the servants of Christ; Doing the will of God from the heart, and Doing service . . . as to the Lord, and not to men* [Eph. 6:5–7].

Remember, as *ye walk worthy of the vocation* (calling) *wherewith ye are called* that the arms of the loving Father, who is just, righteous, merciful, forgiving, and full of grace, are enfolded about you.

Remember, although we are members of Christ's body, we live and work and have our being in the real world. We are to be good witnesses. We are to use our capabilities to the best of our ability.

As servants or masters in the world, we are to be honest, industrious, truthful, reliable, helpful, and trustworthy. We are to conduct ourselves in a manner that is first and foremost pleasing to God, the glorious Father.

Everything we do as saints and as the faithful in Christ is to be done joyfully unto the Lord. We are to be obedient servants, obeying His commands.

Amen!

6

Knowing Your Master in Heaven

And, ye masters, do the same things unto them, forbearing (giving up) threatening: knowing that your Master also is in heaven; neither is there respect of persons with him [Eph. 6:9].

We are now coming to the conclusion of this portion of Ephesians, which some scholars refer to as "Life in the Spirit." It began with the exhortation to *be filled with the Spirit*. It concludes with the admonition, *And, ye masters, do the same things unto them, forbearing (giving up) threatening: knowing that your Master also is in heaven; neither is there respect of persons with him* [Eph. 6:9].

That is quite an exhortation! Paul proceeds to the heart of the matter. The masters, the bosses, the managers, the officers, the officials had been hearing or reading about what the servants were supposed to do and agreeing with it. These masters who are in positions of authority whether great or small are told to *do the same things unto them*, the servants.

They are to treat them with *fear and trembling* in a reverent way and act with singleness of heart toward the servants, without duplicity or deception. They are to sincerely exhibit bountifulness, liberality, and generosity in the giving of themselves to the needs and concerns of the servants. Further, they are to act unto the servants as if they were discharging their responsibilities *unto Christ*.

Next, the masters are not to treat their servants with *eyeservice, as menpleasers*. They are not to conduct themselves so that they will please some men, their contemporaries or peers, or so that they will have something to talk about in a boastful or derogatory manner.

The masters are to do *the will of God from the heart*. They are to perform their responsibilities with good will, *as to the Lord, and not to men*. This may be a difficult task for masters to do. Also, it may be difficult for servants to understand and to accept. The people who are masters, as well as those who are servants, are to conduct themselves according to the teachings of Scripture.

The Apostle not only tells the masters that they are to do these things, but under the influence of the Holy Spirit adds three important items to the list. When he does, it reminds us of when the preacher really starts presenting the Gospel and making the people in the pews realize their need of forgiveness because they sin against God. That is when a person is most apt to say, "The preacher has gone from preaching to meddling." Oh, how many times we hear that from not only the occasional and regular churchgoer but from the officers and even from ministers. Who was the greatest meddler of all time? There is no question that it was, is, and will be forever the Lord Jesus Christ.

What are the additional things that earthly masters are to do? First, they are to conduct themselves by *forbearing* (giving up) *threatening*. Okay, I can do that. Well, I can do it most of the time. However, the ability to threaten is one of the tools of the master.

Second, the Apostle hits the masters with a blow to the solar plexus. He tells them that their master is in heaven. No matter what your holdings are, Mr. or Mrs. Earthly Master, your Master is in heaven, your Master is the Lord Jesus Christ. Remember, Paul is writing *to the saints*, and *to the faithful in Christ Jesus*. Scripture says,

> *Blessed be the God and Father of our Lord Jesus Christ, who hath blessed us with all spiritual blessings in heavenly places in Christ:*
> *According as he hath chosen us in him before the foundation of the world, that we should be holy and without blame before him in love* [Eph. 1:3–4].

Paul reminds the Ephesians, as he begins his letter, of the majesty, power, and love of God toward us. He prayed,

> *That the God of our Lord Jesus Christ, the Father of glory, may give unto you the spirit of wisdom and revelation in the knowledge of him:*
> *The eyes of your understanding being enlightened; that ye may know what is the hope of his calling, and what (are) the riches of the glory of his inheritance in the saints,*

> *And what is the exceeding greatness of his power to us-ward who believe, according to the working of his mighty power,* . . . [Eph. 1:17–19].

Paul reminded the Ephesians of the Master's glory: that from the Father you receive wisdom, revelation, and knowledge; that your understanding may be enlightened through the call of the Lord Jesus Christ; and that you are the recipient of the exceeding greatness of the Master's mighty power through His abundant grace. Paul calls attention to the Master and to the great difference between them.

Third, he adds the *coup de grace*. He tells the earthly masters that in their Master *neither is there respect of persons with him* [Eph. 6:9]. Think of that! We all love to go places where we are treated with respect. The Greek word for *respect* means "acceptance of face." When we are known by our faces for our accomplishments, our position, or our possessions, we are pleased with ourselves.

When considering these three points, is it safe to say that the Apostle has our attention? Do you see the complete fairness of Scripture? There is nothing else like it. Certainly, there is not any other literature like it. Where do most of the troubles, disagreements, clashes, and discords occur? In marriage, the home, and the workplace! Scripture addresses these in detail because people living according to the Master's proclamations can practice His teachings in every phase of their daily living.

Therefore, the Apostle laid down basic principles to guide our conduct. *Forbearing* (giving up) *threatening*. We are not to exhibit a wrong spirit or wrong actions toward others because we happen to be in a position of authority, or control. Threatening is not to be displayed by either overt or subtle actions.

Your Master also is in heaven. Whether we are a master or servant we are accountable to the Lord Jesus Christ, accountable for our actions, our conduct, and our words. "Paul here reminds them, that while masters rule over their servants, they have the same Master in heaven, to whom they must render an account," someday as appropriately expressed by John Calvin.

Accountability to the Master is a different thought. Different from being accountable "to our own standards, or to our peers, or to the world and different from what the scholars or philosophers say. We are to live and be accountable to goodness, beauty, and truth," as further stated by Calvin.

What does scripture say about being accountable to the Master? In his Gospel, Luke records how the Lord will hold accountable both the faithful and unfaithful stewards. The Lord Jesus in this parable asks, who is the faithful steward? He is the one doing the will of the Master. What shall he receive? The Master *will make him ruler over all that he hath* [Luke 12:44].

The steward is to be diligent and attentive. He is not to be lax, forgetful, or uninterested. What happens to the steward who is not doing the will of the master? Three answers are given about those not doing the will of the master. They are:

> . . . *will cut him in* (two) *sunder.* (The Greek word used for *sunder* in this verse means "to scourge severely", "to whip," or "punish severely.")
>
> . . . *that servant, which knew his lord's (master's) will, and prepared not himself, neither did according to his will, shall be beaten with many stripes.*
>
> *But he that knew not, and did commit things worthy of stripes, shall be beaten with few stripes.* [Luke 12:46–48]

Christ's servants are to be attentive and perform their tasks, whatever they may be, with diligence.

However, many people think the day of giving an account will never come, that it will pass them by. These people should remember the day of the Crucifixion: when Christ was scourged, when He climbed Calvary's Hill, when He was crucified, when He shed His blood and died. Yes, we are to remember that day. But thank God the third day came when He rose from the dead. *The day of giving an account will come.*

Paul reveals in 1 Corinthians that there is only one foundation on which we can build, and that is the Lord Jesus Christ. He says, *Every man's work shall be made manifest* (become evident) [1 Cor. 3:13]. Later, he tells us that . . . *we must all appear* (made manifest) *before the judgment seat of Christ; that every one may receive the things done in his body, according to that he hath done, whether it be good or bad* [2 Cor. 5:10]. That is specific! That is the New Testament teaching!

Yes, there are rewards for good works, but this teaching does not replace or supersede the teaching that salvation, a right relationship to God, is by grace and the free gift of God. "Evil deeds are given the punishment they deserve, but in rewarding good deeds, God does not have regard to their merit or worth. No work of ours is so full and complete in all its parts as to deserve God's approval . . . ," as discerned by John Calvin. Remember, God accepts people by *not imputing their trespasses unto them* [1 Cor. 5:19]. This is achieved through His Son, our Lord Jesus Christ.

Yes, good works may be rewarded, but we must recognize and accept the fact that eternal life is obtained by the free grace of God. Justification is by faith alone. There is no other way. Yes, that is true. But, Scripture makes it clear that there will be a full accountability to the Lord Jesus Christ, and our words and deeds will be assessed. There will be judging for the rewards that are available.

These teachings are to be known by the members of Christ's body. Note what the Holy Spirit says through Paul, *Knowing that whatsoever good thing any man doeth, the same shall he receive of the Lord, whether he be bond* (slave) *or free* [Eph. 6:8]. The slaves or servants are to know that their good conduct and comments will be well received of the Lord.

The Apostle uses the same word *knowing* when he addresses the masters and says, *knowing that your Master also is in heaven* [Eph. 6:9]. The word *knowing* in these two verses means *to see* or *to perceive*. What are the earthly masters to know? That they are accountable for their actions and their words.

The beginning of this section says, *But be filled with the Spirit* and *Submitting yourselves one to another in the fear of Christ* [Eph. 5:18, 21]. The other verses amplify on these two commands and tell us how we are to conduct ourselves. It tells us what we are to do, and how we are to do it, *as unto Christ, even as Christ, subject unto Christ, of the Lord,* and *according to the will of God.* That is how we are to perform the various and sundry tasks assigned to us. So we say, fine, that is nice, and it is good to hear about it. I will do these things, or some of them, or a few of them, that are defined as being "life in the Spirit."

Then the thought comes, "Some of my peers may know about these teachings, so I better do them, or a few of them, or put on a good appearance." That is not what the New Testament teaches. That is not what Paul says. They are to know that they are accountable to their Master, who is in heaven. They will be graded for their good deeds and their bad ones. There will be a review of the acts of commission and those of omission.

Now what do you think of *PAUL, an apostle of Jesus Christ by the will of God* [Eph. 1:1]? He begins the fourth chapter by telling us to *walk worthy of the vocation* (calling) *wherewith ye are called.* Then he tells us how to act and how not to act. To emphasize these teachings he gives illustrations of what we are to do and not to do. Then everyone says "How nice," or "Wouldn't it be wonderful." Paul will have none of that. He tells us we are accountable. You know what? He means it; he is dead serious.

I remember the first time I played marbles for fun, to have a good time, to be with the other boys. When it was time to go home, I would take all my marbles with me. I would count them, and when I got home I would wash and clean them. Then one day I got into a game of keepers with the older boys. Guess what? They played for real. When it came time to go home, I did not have all my marbles. They played keepers, and they kept some of my marbles. Why? Because I did not perform as well as I should have in those circumstances. When it is time for us to go to our final home, we need to remember that we will receive rewards according to our conduct. Paul tells us it is a game of keepers. What do you want to receive? To be placed over more and more by your Master, or to receive many stripes or few. These are the alternatives. The choice is yours.

When considering the Apostle's teaching, it is well to bear in mind these wonderful words from the hymn "Nearer Home," penned by James Montgomery,

> Here in the body pent,
> *Absent from Him I roam,*
> *Yet nightly pitch my moving tent,*
> A day's march nearer home.

The Apostle makes it clear that the saints are accountable to the Master. Then he adds the phrase, *knowing that your Master also is in heaven* [Eph. 6:9]. That is to remind us where our eternal home is. He emphasizes the realm of the Spirit. He wants us to know that there is someone "who is over all, and above all, the one who controls everything and changes not," as observed by Martyn Lloyd-Jones. He is the Master and the Lord.

The Apostle concludes this portion of Scripture by saying *neither is there respect of persons with him*. What does this phrase mean? When people consider others, they have their eyes blinded by factors that do not have a significant value in God's sight. They are impressed by and ready to judge others based upon family, wealth, attractiveness, friendship, and similar qualities. These qualities or the lack of them produce human judgments.

God does not "accept the face" or what is on the surface. He is not concerned with the exterior, with the nationality, or the position in society. He is concerned with certain things, like, do we realize we are sinners in the sight of God and need His forgiveness? Do we realize that each individual needs to be in a right relationship with God? Do we put our faith and trust entirely in the Lord Jesus Christ, who died for our sins? Do we know that it is only God's grace that can save miserable sinners such as we? Do we realize we are to become new creatures in Christ, and that we are to put off the old and put on the new?

This is difficult. It means looking at ourselves honestly, looking at our shortcomings and our needs. Yes, it is an individual question. It also affects the relationship between masters and slaves, employers and employees, and among family members. We must realize Scripture says, *neither is there respect of persons with him.*

Basically, it does not matter what we are in this world, or what we may accomplish, or whether our face is accepted by many or few. The real significance of our living is whether or not we are in a right relationship with God, have become new creatures, and conduct ourselves *as unto Christ.*

When these things are true then our actions and conduct have an impact upon the people outside the body of Christ. We may still be a master or a servant, there still may be differences socially and economically, but our words and deeds will be noticeable because they will be according to the *will of God.*

Unfortunately, many truths contained in the New Testament are not preached or taught. Many people think, "God is love," and that is all. Therefore, nothing is required of them, not even faith or obedience. Others think that if they believe and are saved that nothing else matters. These people ignore the teachings about rewards in Scripture, and obeying Christ's commands.

Consequently, they continue to do the minimum in God's kingdom and do not seem to understand their true relationship to the Lord Jesus Christ and His Father. They conveniently forget that records are kept and that we are accountable unto Christ. We shall see Him face to face. *For we must all appear before the judgment seat of Christ* [2 Cor. 5:10].

In conclusion, recall a parable told by our Lord that is often forgotten. It is the parable of Lazarus and the rich man.

> *There was a certain rich man, which was clothed in purple and fine linen, and fared sumptuously* (lived in luxury) *everyday:*
>
> *And there was a certain beggar named Lazarus, which was laid at his gate, full of sores*
>
> *. . . And it came to pass, that the beggar died, and was carried by the angels into Abraham's bosom: the rich man also died, and was buried;*
>
> *And in hell he lift up his eyes, being in torments, and seeth Abraham afar off, and Lazarus in his bosom* [Luke 16:19–20, 22–23].

Lazarus received favorable consideration whereas the rich man was severely scourged. The rich man realized he had not done as he should have and begged for mercy,

> *He cried and said, Father Abraham . . . send Lazarus, that he may dip the tip of his finger in water, and cool my tongue; for I am tormented in this flame.*
>
> *But Abraham said, Son, remember that thou in thy lifetime receivedst thy good things, and likewise Lazarus evil things: but now he is comforted, and thou art tormented* [Luke 16:24–25].

The rich man sought for himself. He wanted Lazarus to minister to him.

Next, he expressed concern for his five brothers. The response was that *Abraham saith unto him, they have Moses and the prophets; let them hear them* [Luke 16:29].

We are to listen to God speaking in His way through His prophets, His apostles, and His Son. That is sufficient. Then the rich man pleaded with father Abraham, saying, *Nay, father Abraham: but if one went unto them from the dead, they will repent* [Luke 16:30]. And what did Abraham reply? *If they hear not Moses and the prophets, neither will they be persuaded, though one rose from the dead* [Luke 16:31].

Tough words! Tough meat! Oh, that we search the scriptures, study them, learn from them, and apply them. These teachings cast a different light. They are provided for our edification and our uplifting: may we ponder them; give thanks for them; realize the game of life is played for keepers; and act accordingly, knowing we are held accountable.

Thanks be unto God!

Amen!

7

Finally My Brethren, Be Strong . . .

> *Finally, my brethren, be strong in the Lord, and in the power of his might.*
> *Put on the whole armor of God, that ye may be able to stand against the wiles* (schemes) *of the devil* [Eph. 6:10–11].

God blesses the reading and studying of His Word in Ephesians. Take a moment to reflect upon the material covered in Walking With Jesus.

The first three chapters contain the great doctrines of the Christian faith. They are addressed to the saints and the faithful in Christ Jesus. They are the backbone to presenting and describing the character of the life available to those who are or who become members of Christ's body. These initial chapters describe what God in Christ has done for us. *That we should be holy and without blame before him in love, . . .* [Eph. 1:4] and *That ye might be filled with all the fullness of God* [Eph. 3:19].

These verses describe how to become members of His body, or Christians. How does this happen? In a way that we should always keep in the front of our minds: by the blood of Christ! Romans says, *THEREFORE being justified by faith, we have peace with God through our Lord Jesus Christ* [Rom. 5:1].

> *But God commendeth* (demonstrates) *his* (own) *love toward us, in that, while we were yet sinners, Christ died for us.*
> *Much more then, being now* (having been) *justified by his blood, we shall be saved from wrath through him.* [Rom. 5:8–9].

During the Advent season, we remember and focus on the babe born in Bethlehem, the Deliverer. We must not lose sight of the fact that the babe went to the Cross in obedience to His Father's will to deliver us so that we might be in a right relationship to Him. When we understand these things we more deeply appreciate Paul's prayer that

> The eyes of your understanding being enlightened; that ye may know what is the hope of his calling, and what (are) the riches of the glory of his inheritance in the saints.
> And what is the exceeding greatness of his power to us-ward who believe, according to the working of his mighty power [Eph. 1:18–19].

Then, beginning at the first verse of the fourth chapter, the Apostle appeals to the saints and faithful to live their individual and collective lives worthy of being members of Christ's body. How can we forget Paul's trumpet call, *I THEREFORE, the prisoner of the Lord, beseech you that ye walk worthy of the vocation* (calling) *wherewith ye are called* [Eph. 4:1]?

Following that, Paul provides an excellent exposition of what is to be the nature and composition of the church, Christ's body. He points out that we are members of that body. Though there may be different offices, we are all members. There is no such thing as a laity.

This leads to stating boldly that we are to become new creatures. We are to *put off* the old and *put on* the new. The Apostle describes how the new creature is to conduct him or herself, how the new creature is to walk in unity, holiness, love, light, wisdom, praise, and harmony. Paul reminds us of what we are, who we are, and how we are to act. He describes the type of life that we are to live in the everyday world.

He talks about lying, anger, the devil, stealing, truth, working, corrupt communications, bitterness, wrath, clamor, evil speaking, and malice. He also talks about becoming kind, tenderhearted, and forgiving; about walking in love; about uncleanness, covetousness, foolish talking, filthiness, disobedience, darkness, and walking *circumspectly* (carefully), *not as fools, but as wise* [Eph. 5:15].

The Apostle tells the saints and faithful to be filled with the Spirit and how they are to act in marriage, the home, and the work place. The Apostle covers just about everything imaginable from the beginning of this Epistle through family life and working relationships. Why does he continue his letter? What remains to be presented?

It almost appears that the Apostle could close his letter at this point. Note I said, "almost appears." Why do I say that? There are vivid descriptions of how the saints and faithful are to live. There are poignant exhortations directed toward us. There is the call to be up and about, to do something, and to perform as Christ would have us to act.

There is the recognition that the saints and faithful have a difficult task facing them, if they are to faithfully represent their Lord day in and day out as they go about their tasks. God knew that something else was needed. Therefore, the Holy Spirit worked through the Apostle to provide additional insight, understanding, and strength.

It is as if everything in this magnificent letter that precedes the last fifteen verses was leading up to this blessed culmination. Everything that has gone before is to illuminate, enlighten, and prepare one to *walk worthy of the vocation* (calling) *wherewith ye are called* [Eph. 4:1].

Reflecting on these passages makes me think of the young people who go off to college, or the service, or to work for the first time and are no longer surrounded by the security blanket of their own homes and friends. However, I must admit the one thought that permeated my mind was the Apostle Paul himself as I considered his meaningful, modern, up-to-date letter.

He has written succinctly, logically, compassionately, energetically, and lovingly as *an apostle of Jesus Christ*. He has shared these great truths. Then he says, *Finally, my brethren, be strong in the Lord, and in the power of his might* [Eph. 6:10].

This is Paul, who was converted on the road to Damascus and had to be let down in a basket to flee the city. Paul, who went to Jerusalem to go before the council. Paul, who confronted Peter. Paul, who studied and prepared himself after his conversion. Paul, who was sent to the Gentiles, not to the Jews. Paul, who was beaten, rejected, and jailed. The Apostle Paul said,

> *Nevertheless I live; yet not I, but Christ liveth in me: and the life which I now live in the flesh I live by the faith of* (by faith in) *the Son of God, who loved me, and gave himself for me* [Gal. 2:20].

Paul could relate to our going out into the world. He could relate to not only hearing the teachings of Christ but also to applying them. Therefore, he says *Finally, my brethren, be strong in the Lord, and in the power of his might*. He exhorts them, he issues a call to arms, and he tells them that what he is about to say is most important. The word *finally* indicates that the letter is coming to a close and that the rest of the letter is based upon what has preceded it. As Martyn Lloyd-Jones beautifully states, "It is not enough to know all that he has already told us about the Christian life; we must also realize and accept what he is now about to say. It is still part of the whole picture, and his essential teaching."

Paul says, *Finally, my brethren*. He does not say my fellow apostles, or prophets, or evangelists, or pastors and teachers. He is directing his exhortation to each and every one of the saints and faithful. All of us are included, for we are all members of Christ's body. All of us are involved in the conflict. Therefore, Paul calls the brethren to *be strong in the Lord, and in the power of his might. Put on the whole armor of God, that ye may be able to stand against the wiles* (schemes) *of the devil*. Why does Paul make this strong statement to the *brethren*?

> *For we wrestle not against flesh and blood, but against principalities, against powers, against the rulers of the darkness of this world* (age), *against spiritual* (hosts of)*wickedness in high places . . . that ye may be able to withstand in the evil day, and having done all, to stand* [Eph. 6:12–13].

Ruth Paxson provides additional illumination, saying, "The arch enemy of Christ is attacking His body of which the 'brethren' are members. Therefore, no one is exempt from the conflict. God has no place for a spiritual pacifist."

Can you imagine that the General Assembly would expunge the hymns, "Onward Christian Soldiers," "The Old Rugged Cross," and others because they are too war-like? They do not realize we are in a war with Satan and all his evil forces. They do not understand what Scripture teaches. They are ignorant. Paul's message is for each and every one of us. There are no omissions. It is all available. Therefore, we are to partake of every morsel.

There are difficulties, obstacles, rationalizations, and pressures to keep us from applying the teachings of the Lord Jesus Christ to the events and situations encountered in everyday living. Each of us experiences days when everything seems to go wrong, when there are subtle and overt temptations, when questions permeate our minds such as, "What difference does it make?" In addition, we experience feelings of having to get it done, of being rejected, of why God would let that happen, especially to me and to mine. At a given time, any one of us may ask, "Where is God when I need Him?"

The Apostle Paul encountered these questions and these difficulties. He had wrestled with the forces opposing the Gospel of the Lord

Jesus Christ. He had first hand knowledge of what was required to live in the world, to earn a living, and to endeavor to live as Christ would have him to live.

Therefore, as Paul was drawing this letter to a close, I believe he reviewed the contents, edited the materials, made some changes, and probably reflected upon his life as the chief persecutor of the Lord Jesus Christ, upon his conversion, and upon the trials and tribulations that followed him throughout his ministry. Then he thought about who had sustained him, who had strengthened him, and who had enabled him. Undoubtedly he thought about those people in Ephesus among whom he had ministered for three years. He knew their problems, concerns, and needs.

With these thoughts in mind, Paul said, . . . *be strong in the Lord, and in the power of his might. Put on the whole armor of God.* He did not tell them to do their own thing or to support one another because they had listened and studied Christ and His teachings. Nor did he tell them they could go it alone. No! He did not say any of those things. He said, . . . *be strong in the Lord and in the power of his might. Put on the whole armor of God.* Paul was showing his complete dependence upon God. He wanted to share with the saints and faithful the great truths of the Gospel and his understanding of how to live successfully as one of Christ's disciples.

The renowned John Calvin expounds upon Paul's words saying, ". . . first he bids them to be strong, to summon up courage and vigour; for there is always much to enfeeble us, and we are ill fitted to resist. But because we are weak, an exhortation would be cold unless the Lord were present, and stretched out his hand to give help, in fact, unless he supplied the whole power; and therefore he adds, *in the Lord.* As if he had said, 'you cannot reply that you lack the ability; for I only *require you to be strong in the Lord.*' And then in explanation he adds, *in the power of his might,* which greatly increases our confidence, particularly as it shows the help which God is accustomed to bestow on believers. If the Lord aids us by His extraordinary power, we have no reason to be irresolute in battle. But someone will say, 'What purpose did it serve to bid the Ephesians be strong in the Lord's power which was certainly not at their command?' I answer, there are two clauses here which must be considered. He exhorts them to courage, but then reminds them to ask from God's supply what in themselves they lack; and at the same time promises that, if they ask for it the power of God will be displayed."

The question may be asked: what is the difference between what Paul has been presenting, especially from telling them to *walk worthy of the vocation* (calling) *wherewith ye are called* to closing his enlightening statements on personal relationships with those meaningful, penetrating words *knowing that your Master also is in heaven; neither is there respect of persons with him* [Eph. 4:1, 6:9]?

Previously, Paul had been dealing with conflicts: those encountered in the world; those experienced through the lusts of the flesh and mind, and those initiated by knowing how we should live as members of Christ's body. He also observed how people live outside Christ's body. All of this is spelled out clearly and succinctly, beginning with Paul's command, *That ye henceforth walk not as other Gentiles walk, in the vanity* (futility) *of their mind* [Eph. 4:17]. Paul continues to enlighten the Ephesians (and us) with his ineffable wisdom, as he begins to draw this letter to a close with the words: *Finally, my brethren, be strong in the Lord, and in the power of his might.* We are not to walk as the Gentiles walk. However, we are to learn Christ; we are to become new creatures; and we are to conduct ourselves *as unto Christ* and *doing the will of God from the heart*. That is what he presents in these passages!

There is a slight shift in emphasis in verses 10–20. Paul identifies the enemy outside of us. He says we are to *be strong in the Lord, and in the power of his might. Put on the whole armor of God, so that ye may be able to stand against the wiles* (schemes) *of the devil.* The Apostle now deals with that formidable outside enemy, the devil and his forces.

This last section of Ephesians contains a wealth of material applicable to everyday living. It is vitally important with respect to sanctification and becoming holy. The truths contained in these last verses are to be grasped and examined, and they are to become part of us.

When beginning to study these verses there are a few significant observations to share. First, *we wrestle*. As previously stated we are engaged in a struggle, in a war. Note the Apostle says, *we wrestle*. He did not say, "I have wrestled," or "You will wrestle." He uses the personal pronoun *we* and the active present tense of the verb *wrestle*. That presents a different picture than the one presented by people who say that the life in Christ is one of ease and does not have its share of battles and struggles.

Paul acknowledges that there are struggles and difficulties when he says *we wrestle,* and when he says, *be strong in the Lord, and in the power of his might. Put on the whole armor of God, that ye may be able to stand against the wiles* (schemes) *of the devil* [Eph. 6:10-11]. Does that sound like a life of ease? Does that sound like we have nothing to do? No, it does not. We have to realize and accept the fact that even though we are the saints and faithful, we are engaged in a struggle when we are obedient servants of the Lord. We do not live in Utopia. The path we are walking is not smooth and easy.

Second, the warfare described in Scripture, which we face in reality, is one that we have to fight individually. Please note that the exhortations are to . . . *be strong in the Lord, and in the power of his might. Put on the whole armor of God, that ye may be able to stand* [Selections from Eph. 6:10-11]. Neither, does it say, "Hand it over to the Lord; He will fight for you," nor does it say, "Let go and let God." Martyn Lloyd-Jones confirms the fact that we will not have a life of ease and that we have certain responsibilities as Christ's disciples, saying, "I do not find the Apostle telling me to hand it over to the Lord and that He will fight my battles for me while I just sit back and enjoy the fruit of His victory. It is not here! I have to fight!"

We are in the world, we are members of His body, we are separated unto Christ, but we still have to exert ourselves. We have to enter the fray and do our part. How true!

However, we are to remember our strength lies in the Lord, not in ourselves. He will provide the strength and power, but we have to do it. It was the Lord who was the strength of David's heart. The Lord Jesus says,

> *I am the vine, ye are the branches: He that abideth in me, and I in him, the same bringeth forth much fruit: for without me ye can do nothing* [John 15:5].

Further, Scripture says,

> *Not that we are sufficient of ourselves to think any thing as of ourselves; but our sufficiency is of God;*
> *Who also hath made us able* (sufficient) *ministers of the new testament* (covenant); *not of the letter, but of the spirit: for the letter killeth, but the spirit giveth life* [2 Cor. 3:5-6].

William Gurnall provides sage counsel to all believers with the following words: "We saints that have habitual grace, yet this lies like water at the bottom of a well, which will not ascend with all our pumping till

God pour in his exciting grace, and then it comes. To will is more than to think, to exert our will into action more than both." These are of God: *For it is God which worketh in you both to will and to do of* (according to) *his good pleasure* [Phil. 2:13].

Third, note how Paul issues this call to battle and his exhortation to the brethren. He exhorts them to be strong and of good courage and to exhibit vigor in performing their tasks. He tells them that the Lord will supply the power to support and strengthen them. There is nothing sentimental, apologetic, or weak about Paul's words to the saints and faithful. Anything that exhibits those particular traits is not scriptural.

Paul's words are a call to action, but it is to be action in a defined way according to the Master's teachings. We are to *be strong in the Lord, and in the power of his might*. This knowledge should increase our confidence. "If the Lord aids us by His extraordinary power, we have no reason to be irresolute in battle," according to Calvin's penetrating words.

Of course, someone may ask, what purpose does it serve to urge the saints and the faithful to *be strong in the Lord* when they cannot command the Lord to do as they wish? Paul says, be of courage but remember to ask God to provide what you lack, and bear in mind that if you ask for it, then, as Calvin notes, "the power of God will be displayed." The call of the Lord in these verses is strong and infectious. We are called to go forth and to do.

Lastly, we are to keep on doing. We are not to do it for a few years or many and then retire or take it easy. We are to keep going, to keep fighting the conflict, and to

> *. . . be strong in the Lord, and in the power of His might.*
> *Put on the whole armor of God, that ye may be able to stand against the wiles* (schemes) *of the devil.*

This will enable us to face the difficult tasks of life, to walk worthy of the vocation to which we have been called, and to be victors against Satan and his evil forces.

May we ponder the beautiful, meaningful words of a hymn written long ago ascribed to Andrew of Crete. They are as pertinent today as they were then:

> *Christian, dost thou see them On the holy ground,*
> *How the powers of darkness Rage thy steps around?*
> *Christian, up and smite them, Counting gain but loss,*
> *In the strength that cometh By the Holy Cross.*

Christian, dost thou feel them, How they work within,
Striving, tempting, luring, Goading into sin?
Christian, never tremble; Never be downcast;
Gird thee for the battle; Thou shalt win at last.

Christian, dost thou hear them, How they speak thee fair?
"Always fast and vigil? Always watch and prayer?"
Christian, answer boldly, "While I breathe I pray!"
Peace shall follow battle, Night shall end in day.

"Well I know thy trouble, O My servant true,
Thou art very weary—I was weary too;
But that toil shall make thee Someday all Mine own,
And the end of sorrow Shall be near My throne."

Amen!

8

Separating Ourselves

> *Finally, my brethren, be strong in the Lord, and in the power of his might.*
> *Put on the whole armor of God, that ye may be able to stand against the wiles* (schemes) *of the devil* [Eph. 6:10–11].

Questions arise when the Word of God is opened, when it is approached, and when it is contemplated. Thank God for questions. Yes, and thank Him for the proper answers. But mostly, thank Him for providing His Word and the desire to pursue answers.

Usually, there are questions regarding Paul's statement, *Finally, my brethren, be strong in the Lord, and in the power of His might.* This exhortation should stimulate two things: to know, therefore to learn; and to contemplate, therefore to apply. It is *not* an exhortation to sit back and to enjoy a good book or good music. We are entering an area of personal involvement, personal conflict, personal doubts, desires, and demands.

We are going to re-examine ideas, mindsets, plus accepted thoughts and teachings from the world that have impacted people for many years. When beginning to do these things we are to pray for God to keep our eye (really the eye of our mind) focused on the Lord Jesus Christ and the truth found in Him.

> *I am the way, the truth, and the life, no man cometh unto the Father, but by me* [John 14:6].

> Jesus prayed that we *might be sanctified through the truth* [John 17:19].

The truth is in Him! He is the truth!

The Apostle Paul wants us to come closer to the Lord Jesus Christ. However, he knows to do this, we have to contend *against the wiles* (schemes) *of the devil. . . . against principalities, against powers, against the rulers of the darkness of this world, against spiritual* (hosts of) *wickedness in high places* [Eph. 6:11-12]. He wants us to consider various impediments and to develop the strength to *be able to stand*.

Therefore, we are to remind ourselves constantly of the advice given by that great Puritan preacher, William Gurnall, "The fare that I shall be serving during the coming weeks will be from God's own table. If per chance it does not go down well or should not have the flavor that you desire, please do not despise the provider of the food but blame the cook who has prepared it and is serving it."

When partaking of this sumptuous feast the Lord provided we need to prepare our hearts and minds by communing with God. We need to prepare and discipline ourselves in order to benefit from the nourishment provided and to savor every morsel. We need to provide the time to get ready, to attend, to know all the different foods available for our consumption and welfare. Then we are to take the time to sample, to eat, to digest, and to reflect on each morsel with pleasure and a strong desire to participate in each and every feast offered by the Lord.

The truth available from God through the Lord Jesus Christ helps prepare us for the conflicts we must face. The Apostle wants us prepared, so that success may be attained against the enemy. The Apostle's exhortation is directed primarily to the saints and faithful in Jesus Christ. However, it also applies to those who are outside Christ's body.

They may not realize it, but the truths contained in Christ are applicable to understanding the conflicts evident in the world. People outside Christ cannot understand why the world is as it is. They can neither comprehend the wiles of the devil nor the sinfulness of man.

What is the Apostle doing in these final verses of Ephesians? He is describing the way the saints, the faithful, and the nonbelievers can successfully fight the evil forces employed and deployed against them. Further how they are to prepare themselves regarding matters such as modern morality, evil in society, national and international affairs, a living faith in Christ, and the Bible.

Some say the church, whatever they mean by "the church," should take a more active role in moral matters, sex, drugs, greed, and other evils. Of course, they really want pronouncements conforming to the solutions offered by the world or worldly people. They want to say that Scripture is only one of the various alternatives available.

The Apostle says the only way to overcome the conflicts besetting man individually and collectively is to *be strong in the Lord, and in the power of his might.* Failure to do this results in defeat. When providing this positive response in accord with the teachings of Scripture, some will say we are narrow-minded, stubborn, and shortsighted. However, I suggest that the failure to use a logical, knowledgeable remedy is not being narrow-minded. Just ask the person who has been told, "You are going into surgery tomorrow at 7:00 a.m." There is no arguing that it is a narrow-minded or shortsighted remedy. Yet surgery and surgery alone could deal with the person's multiple problems.

What does Scripture say? That it and it alone can deal with the problems confronting the saints and the faithful as well as those outside the body of Christ. The teachings of Scripture are not one of several or many books; the Bible is God's book. "It is a unique book, it is the book, standing apart from all the others," as Martyn Lloyd-Jones said. The church is not one institution of many. What is the church? She is the body of Christ and subject to her Head, the Master.

Why does Paul expound Christ's words unto the Ephesians and exhort them to practice these teachings? Why? Paul provides the answer saying,

> *How that by revelation he made known unto me the mystery* (hidden truth); *(as I wrote afore in few words,*
> *Whereby, when ye read, ye may understand my knowledge in the mystery of Christ.)*
> *Which in other ages was not made known unto the sons of men, as it is now revealed unto his holy apostles and prophets by the Spirit;*
> *That the Gentiles should be fellow heirs, and of the same body, and partakers of his promise in Christ by the gospel* [Eph. 3:3–6].

Paul does not say he studied under Gamaliel, or the law, or different books, or the philosophers. All of which he could have said. No! He said it was revealed to him by revelation. It is not his message. It was given to him by the Lord Jesus Christ, by divine revelation and communication. The authority for the teaching is none other than the Lord Himself. Peter says, *For there is none other name under heaven given among men, whereby we must be saved* [Acts 4:12]. Please note it says *none other name.*

There are no second, third, or fourth ones. There is only one. Therefore, we are not to say that it is one of a few or many alternatives. There is only one!

Some may say that that is a dogmatic statement. However, a review of history books, the Old Testament, Romans 1:18–32, the Greek philosophers, and the Decline and Fall of the Roman Empire will reveal that "As nations, and peoples in supposed 'wisdom' have turned their backs upon God the Creator, they have always become fools," as appropriately observed by Martyn Lloyd-Jones. Paul puts it this way, *Professing themselves to be wise, they became fools* [Rom. 1:22].

What about modern times? Certainly, moral problems have increased. So have the educational and cultural opportunities as well as the expenditures and participation in these areas. Yet what has happened? The moral standards have deteriorated. Consequently, some say the church must do something. However, it wants the church, as stated earlier, to conform to the world.

Also, it is well-known that church attendance and membership has declined, as has participation in Sunday School and in learning the teachings of Scripture, especially in the New Testament. Interesting, is it not? As religion has gone down, other things have gone up, which fall into the categories of immorality and godlessness.

Others say that the way to correct the problems of the day is education, clubs, and cultural programs. People want to consider these alternatives, but ignore or sidestep the teachings of the Master. They want to consider man only as having a mind and an intellect. Therefore, if you tell him what to do and give valid reasons, he will do it.

They do not want to accept the fact that man also has an evil spirit and an evil nature. Man is just not a mind and an intellect. He is much more, and that must be addressed. It cannot be ignored.

When you think about it and really probe into this matter, it becomes evident that man is governed by more than his mind, intellect, and understanding. He is controlled by his desires, impulses, and instincts. These are what really control him! That is why the Apostle tells us that, *we wrestle not against flesh and blood, but against principalities, against powers, against the rulers of darkness of this world* (age), *against spiritual* (hosts of) *wickedness in high places* [Eph. 6:12].

That is why more is needed than moral schemes and teachings. We need to reclaim the emphasis the Apostle placed in previous verses:

- *As unto Christ;*
- *As to the Lord;*
- *In the fear of Christ;*
- *Even as Christ;*
- *As the servants of Christ;*
- *Doing the will of God from the heart.*

   [Selections from chapters 5 and 6 in Ephesians]]

These commands are positive. They are the standards we are to attain and by which we are to abide. Scripture does not merely tell us to be good, clean, nice people and to conduct ourselves in a respectable manner. These things can be achieved outside the church by people who are not members of Christ's body. But that is not living according to the teachings of the Master. Why do I say that? Because the Christian is not someone who does not do certain things or who tries to live by certain do's and don'ts.

A member of Christ's body is called to hunger and thirst after righteousness, live according to the two great commandments, be pure in heart, be perfect even as your Father in heaven is perfect, be like Christ, and live as He lived. These standards are entirely different than a list of do's and don'ts. It is difficult to live according to these teachings and commandments.

Consequently, that is the reason the Lord Jesus came into the world. There was no other way! Nothing else would do. There had to be the incarnation, the road to Calvary's Hill, the Crucifixion, the shedding of Christ's blood, and the resurrection. Why? Because it was necessary for Christ to come, to seek, and to save the lost. He came because it was a necessity! There was no other way.

When considering the conflicts existing between members of Christ's body and those outside of it, it is understandable that the Apostle says, *Be strong in the Lord, and in the power of his might.* Why does he say that? Before considering the details of this exhortation it is well to examine the factors having an impact upon us.

Today, people within and outside the church misunderstand the message contained in these teachings and, above all, in the life of the Lord Jesus Christ. They want the church to play a role in society and have an impact upon its moral life. Therefore, they equate the Christian faith or faith in Christ to a moral teaching they must apply. They say that it is one of several teachings which if followed will allow people to live a good, moral life. Further, in order to achieve this, there are certain things that one must do. Their basic premise is that faith is a list of do's and don'ts, basically a teaching that is just and moral. This school of thought lists Jesus as one of the great teachers of all time, if not the greatest. However, their emphasis is on Jesus as a teacher.

Of course, there are those who consider Jesus Christ as the Jesus of history! They eliminate or ignore the miracles, the supernatural events, and His atonement for our sins. They say, since He was such a great teacher and person in history you should listen to Him, follow Him, and try to do as He did. Their whole emphasis is on moral and ethical codes and what we as individuals, or as a group, are to do. They do not go into the details of Christ's being, God incarnate, the Son of God,

> . . . *the exceeding greatness of his power to us-ward who believe, according to the working of his mighty power,* . . . [Eph. 1:19]

> *Far above all principality, and power, and might, and dominion, and every name that is named, not only in this world* (age), *but also in that which is to come* [Eph. 1:21].

Nor do they consider the essence of His being, the basic truths contained in Him, and the power available from Him and through Him to change us, to make us new creatures, and to enable us to do His will.

We cannot imitate Christ. It is ludicrous for people to say go and do as He did. We can only ask Him to have mercy upon us, to forgive us, and to strengthen us, as we endeavor to do and say as He did, and commands us to do. We are to ask Him for the *power of his might*, not just once in a while, but continuously. We must learn that his power is available. Then we must avail ourselves of it. When we do, we will be able to obey His commands and teachings, rather than fall prey to the wiles of the evil one, Satan. This is cause for rejoicing in *the power of his might*.

When thinking about the teachings promulgated and prevailing during this century and the last it is not surprising that church membership has declined and that there has been moral degeneration and collapse. Why? Because the emphasis has been on what man (you and me) should and can do, and what we are capable of doing. It has not been on Christ, the Son of the Living God, and what He can do in and through us.

Scripture stresses the weaknesses of the flesh:

> *But I see another law in my members, warring against the law of my mind, and bringing me into captivity to the law of sin which is in my members* [Rom. 7:23].

Then the Apostle adds,

> *O wretched man that I am! Who shall deliver me from the body of this death* (this body of death) [Rom. 7:24]?

He also says,

> *I thank God through Jesus Christ our Lord* [Rom. 7:25].

It is not moral and ethical teachings that deliver us. It is the Lord Jesus Christ and the shedding of His blood. Do not get me wrong. There is a place for teaching moral codes and ethics. But more is needed than that teaching. It is the power to implement, to do.

There is great emphasis today about sex, especially in light of the moral decline and the threat of AIDS. Therefore, some want to know what the church has to say or to teach about it. What additional knowledge can the church impart? It is not more knowledge or more teaching that is needed. What is needed is the power to deliver people from being controlled and driven by their desires and peer pressure. Where does that power come from? It comes from the Lord Jesus Christ. That is the power that is needed. Not just moral and ethical teachings.

This leads to another point. Some say the pressure is too great. Therefore, the thing to do is to get away from it all and remove yourself from the temptations surrounding you. Consequently, for these and similar reasons, people started monastic orders. There are people today who enter monasteries. They are concerned about their souls, their lives, their daily living and serving others. Therefore, they enter the monastery to live a religious life. Probably their thinking was to get away from the enemy, Satan, and the temptations of the secular world. There is something commendable in that.

However, it is not according to the New Testament and the teachings of the Master. You can leave the world with all its faults, pressures, and temptations, but you cannot leave yourself. You have to take your own sinful nature with you when you enter a monastery. You cannot leave on the outside the evil thoughts and imaginations that are part of your mind and nature. Nor can you leave on the outside *the wiles of the devil.* Paul says, *we wrestle not against flesh and blood, but against principalities, against powers, against the rulers of the darkness of this world* (age), *against spiritual* (hosts of) *wickedness in high places* [Eph. 6:12]. These things against which we wrestle can penetrate walls and doors. They can enter into your heart and mind no matter where you are. You cannot eliminate them, but you can overcome them *in the power of his might*.

Think about Martin Luther: what did he discover? He was a knowledgeable, intelligent monk well-versed in the teachings of the church. There he was, fasting, praying, studying, and sweating: wrestling with spiritual enemies. Then, at last, it was revealed unto him by the Holy Spirit that faith in Christ was not separating oneself from the world, *it was separating oneself unto Christ*. Talk about changing the mindset: Luther did. He realized a person could be separated to Christ even though he was in the midst of the world. As Luther put it, "You could be a Christian sweeping the floor."

Luther, according to Martyn Lloyd-Jones, "suddenly saw that the monastic way was not God's way, and that was the beginning of the great Protestant Reformation. Thank God that that which Luther had to unlearn is not the Christian teaching, for the logical end of the monastic argument is that you cannot be a true Christian and still live in the world."

We are all members of Christ's body, though we may have different assignments and callings. There is no division between the priesthood and laity. That development occurred within the Roman Church and has been perpetuated through the ages and the different denominations.

The witness to the Gospel of the Lord Jesus Christ is provided not only by the clergy, but by husbands, wives, parents, children, ordinary and gifted people in every walk of life. It is to them that Paul is saying, *Finally, my brethren, be strong in the Lord, and in the power of his might.* Without these people there would be no witness to the Lord Jesus Christ in the world.

What then is the method proposed by Scripture? To imitate Christ? To adopt His moral and ethical teachings? To get away from worldly lusts and temptations? *No, a resounding no, it is not!* But it is "to bloom where you are planted." To realize that wherever you are in this world, no matter what deceits, evils, wiles, lusts, or temptations besiege you, no matter what is discouraging or troubling you, heed and remember that the Apostle says, *be strong in the Lord, and in the power of his might.* Put *on the whole armor of God, that you may be able to stand against the wiles* (schemes) *of the devil.* It is not easy, it is difficult, but it is possible by *the power of his might.*

Why is it possible? Think on the words of Paul:

> *Nay, in all these things we are more than conquerors through him that loved us.*
>
> *For I am persuaded that neither death, nor life, nor angels, nor principalities, nor powers, nor things present, nor things to come,*
>
> *Nor height, nor depth, nor any other creature, shall be able to separate us from the love of God, which is in Christ Jesus our Lord* [Rom. 8:37–39].

Think during the remainder of today and in the days to come about that power! And may we, like Luther, separate ourselves unto Christ wherever we may be.

May we follow Christ our King as we travel along life's pathway. May the words of that immortal hymn by Ernest W. Shurtleff guide us as we march along day by day:

> *Lead on, O King Eternal, the day of march has come;*
> *Henceforth in fields of conquest thy tents shall be our home:*
> *Through days of preparation Thy grace has made us strong;*
> *And now, O King eternal, we lift our battle song.*
>
> *Lead on, O King eternal, till sin's fierce war shall cease,*
> *And holiness shall whisper The sweet amen of peace;*
> *For not with swords' loud clashing, Nor roll of stirring drums,*
> *With deeds of love and mercy, The heavenly kingdom comes.*
>
> *Lead on, O King eternal: We follow not with fears;*
> *For gladness breaks like morning Where'er Thy face appears;*
> *Thy cross is lifted o'er us; We journey in its light:*
> *The crown awaits the conquest; Lead on, O God of might.*

Amen!

9

Strength, Power, and Might

> *Finally, my brethren, be strong in the Lord, and in the power of his might* [Eph. 6:10].

When you think, say, or hear "God is Love," or "Jesus loves me," there is one thing to keep in the forefront of your mind and heart: the love stated in those two statements is an all powerful, all consuming, and almighty love. It is a strong, vibrant, tireless, and ineffable love. Nothing less, nothing more, nothing else.

There are additional details to consider about this tenth verse. First, there are three key words, *strong*, *power*, and *might*. *Be strong in the Lord, and in the power of his might.*

What do they mean? The definition of the Greek word for *strong* is "to strengthen inwardly" or "to make or become powerful inwardly."

Second, the Greek word for *power* is *kratos*. It is a very interesting word. It means "dominion" or "to have complete or perfect power." This particular word is used only six times in Scripture. One other time is in Ephesians, where it says, *According to the working of his mighty power* [Eph. 1:19]. This can be interpreted, "According to the working of his mighty, complete, or perfect power." Remember, in these particular verses we are talking about God's almighty power, which is complete and perfect.

The third word is *might*. It is translated from the Greek word *ischus*, which means "strength." However, in this verse and in the first chapter of Ephesians, it means "the strength God bestows upon believers." It indicates strength afforded by the power of His might.

When considering these three words we cannot ignore the word *Finally* that begins this verse. Paul wants us to recall what he has presented in this magnificent letter and to focus upon the truths it contains. Therefore, I suggest that this verse be interpreted, "Bearing all these teachings and truths in mind, my brethren, become strengthened and powerful inwardly in the Lord, and in the complete, perfect power of His strength which He bestows upon believers."

When considering this exhortation reflect and meditate upon the material contained in the previous chapters. Why? Because there is a definite relationship to them. Why does the Apostle want us to become strengthened inwardly with a complete, perfect power? Because he knows that a person possessed by fear or weakness is not capable of a positive approach or accepting counsel as to how he or she should conduct themselves. When people think they are outmatched or opposing a stronger, more numerous opponent, it is difficult for them to be self-confident or to muster the necessary strength.

Calvin by the grace of God and clarity provided by the Holy Spirit offers additional insight into the Apostles formidable statement, "adding . . . these words, 'of the mighty power of God', (*be strong in the Lord, and in the power of his might*) is to make us overcome all distrust, for we find ourselves inclined to be discouraged, inasmuch that if we cannot manage to do what he commands us as we would wish, we conclude that in the end we are bound to falter. But on the contrary, St. Paul says that God will display a mighty and victorious power, according as it is said that he who is on our side is stronger than all the world. Seeing then that God takes our part and upholds us with his power, let us not fear of being surprised by Satan and all he can ever devise against us. Whatever distresses happen to us, in the end we shall overcome all, even by resting upon God's invincible power. For it is true that God perfects his power in our weakness. That is to say, he does not work in such a way that we go without limping and stumbling, and being hindered. At times we find ourselves taking a wrong step, and now and then we backslide.

"You see then how our Lord assists us by His Holy Spirit. We find that he still keeps us in check, in order to give us occasion to humble ourselves. Our weakness therefore is mingled with the strength of God's assistance, and that is in order that we should know what need we have to call upon him and to flee to him for refuge. For we are ready enough of ourselves to darken God's glory. And therefore God has to waken us and to say to us, "Wretched creatures, would you not be lost a thousand times, if I did not hold you in my hand?" Now then, our Lord's leaving of infirmities is to draw us to himself, and to subdue us to meekness that we may have matter for which to praise him, in that he does not permit our falls to be deadly; and again, that we should seek him every minute of time, knowing that if he did not lift us up again when we have fallen, and keep us on our feet, we should perish without any mercy.

"That then is the reason why Paul's former saying we must also join this other sentence, that God leaves some weakness in us as long as we live in this world. But be this as it may, he does not cease to display his invincible power in making us victorious. And we must arrive at this conclusion, that when Satan has done all that is possible to him, we must march on nevertheless, and keep on our way to journey's end. And why? Because it is not only said that God will humble us and that he will take pity upon us, but also that his power will show itself in succouring us, and that not with a simple and common power, but with a mighty power, that is to say, with a power that shall overcome all the hindrances from the world." May these truths be firmly implanted in our hearts and minds, so that we will boldly walk with Jesus knowing that His mighty power undergirds us."

Paul wants us to go forward on this difficult path not only with courage and confidence, but in full reliance upon the Lord God of hosts. He wants us to be fully dependent upon God for our resources and strength. Yes, the Apostle wants us to be knowledgeable about what he has presented, but also he is preparing us for a daily, ongoing battle *against the wiles* (schemes) *of the devil*, and he wants us to stand victoriously.

If we are to stand, it is necessary to know and to remember that the strength the Apostle describes does not come from within, but from without. It comes from the Lord Himself, through His Son and the Holy Spirit. It is this strength, and this alone, that can "fortify the saints, and the faithful," according to Markus Barth.

The saints and faithful are to take the following steps in applying this teaching. In the true sense of the words, the Christian needs courage and resolution. Hear what the Lord said to Joshua,

> [A]s I was with Moses, so I will be with thee: I will not fail thee, nor forsake thee [Josh. 1:5]

> *Only be thou strong and very courageous, that thou mayest observe to do according to all the law, which Moses my servant commanded thee: turn not from it to the right hand or to the left, that thou mayest prosper* (have success) *whithersoever thou goest.*
>
> *This book of the law shall not depart out of* (be constantly in) *thy mouth; but thou shalt meditate therein day and night, that thou mayest observe to do according to all that is written therein: for then thou shalt make thy way prosperous, and then thou shalt have good success* [Josh. 1:7–8].

By being prosperous and having good success He means being in a relationship to God Himself and being an obedient servant.

Think how much more courage and resolve it takes to faithfully obey than to command people to do this or that. If I may be so bold: are not the qualities of courage and resoluteness required to enter into God's presence in prayer when fully aware of one's sinful nature and disobedience to His will? These qualities are required if one not only seeks forgiveness, but asks the Father to bestow His blessings upon him or her.

We are not to flee from God in fear, weakness, or shamefulness, but we are to go to Him with a humble boldness beseeching Him to strengthen us with His complete might. Though we may lose a battle, we are to prepare to win the war and to stand victoriously.

When walking with the Lord Jesus Christ, and endeavoring to serve Him, one needs to realize that the road is not always smooth. There will be difficulties. The enemy will try to snare you or make you stumble and fall.

What is the saint and faithful follower to do when exhibiting courage and resolution? Exert every possible effort against the sins that have become resident within one's heart and mind. We are to be strong in the Lord. Think of Abraham when he offered up Isaac. What sins do we have within our breasts that both control us and give us pleasure? What about the lusts of the flesh and mind? Are we willing to identify them and then to slay them? I am not talking about the characteristics of one's personality, whether one is an extrovert or introvert, but those traits opposed to the will of God.

Some people confuse personality and individuality. "The characteristics of individuality are independence and self-assertiveness. It is the continual assertion of individuality that hinders our spiritual life more than anything else," as poignantly observed by Oswald Chambers.

He added to that: "Individuality never can believe. Personality cannot help believing."

Individuality keeps one from surrendering to the will of God and from being reconciled to his or her brother or sister. If we are in a right relationship with God, then we must deny ourselves and our individuality.

On the other side of the coin is personality. It may distinguish us from others, but it allows us to be transformed and to be merged into the Father. Jesus said, *I and my Father are one* [John 10:30]. When God takes hold of someone that person no longer thinks of himself or herself as an individual, but as a member of Christ's body and as being subject and obedient to Him.

Second, the saint or faithful follower is to do as Romans states very succinctly: *And be not conformed to this world: but be ye transformed by the renewing of your mind, that ye may prove what is that good, and acceptable, and perfect, will of God* [Rom. 12:2]. This ties in with the command to *be strong in the Lord, and in the power of his might.* We are not to be conformed to this world. We are to be knowledgeable about the principles that Christ taught and to stand firmly on them.

Third, the Christian must continue to follow the road to heaven. The hill may become steep, or the way may proceed through treacherous country strewn with obstacles. When this happens, we are to be obedient unto the Lord, no matter what we may encounter. Traveling along the road to heaven requires obedience to the road signs and directions.

Fourth, the saint or faithful follower is to persevere along this road to heaven as long as he or she has the ability to think and to do. Many start down the road, but few finish the trip. Some turn off or turn back after traveling only a short distance. Others travel for a while, become discouraged and give up. Then there are others who travel quite a distance before they become weak and weary, and allow distractions to get the best of them.

Persevering in service to the Lord is difficult. Praying diligently day in and day out requires courage and resolve. One significant trait of walking with the Lord Jesus Christ is that there are no holidays or vacations, nor is there a desire to take one. If a believer takes a holiday or vacation, he also takes with him the resoluteness to serve the Lord and to be obedient to Him. This personality trait identifies the person who is a member of Christ's body.

These four commands (i) exert every effort against the sins in one's heart and mind; (ii) be not conformed to this world; (iii) obey Christ's road signs and directions; and, (iv) persevere on life's journey are placed upon those who are members of Christ's body or profess to be. Many start on the road at one time or another, but few finish the course. When they do, the gates of heaven are opened to them.

Why is this true? One reason is that so many people desire to be what they define as happy as compared to being joyful. William Gurnall beautifully and forcefully describes this saying, "Few have courage and resolution to grapple with the difficulties that meet them in the way to their happiness." There are those who profess the Gospel, but they grow weary of the task and are not able to perservere for Christ. Their individuality takes over, and their commitment fades.

Then there are those who profess wanting to travel the road to heaven, but find that they must deny themselves, that they must do the will of the Father, and that they must give up the lusts of the flesh and mind. Though they desire heaven, they are loath to pay the price and subject themselves to the will of God. Christ's open arms appeal to many, but they require opening one's heart to . . . *be strong in the Lord, and in the power of his might.*

From whence does the saint and faithful follower receive his strength? From the Lord God omnipotent, not from himself. God is referred to as *the strength of Israel* [1 Sam. 15:29]. God was David's strength during his times of adversity. The Lord Jesus says, *For without me ye can do nothing* [John 15:5]. Paul says,

> *Our sufficiency is of God* [2 Cor. 3:5].

> *For it is God which worketh in you both to will and to do of his good pleasure* [Phil. 2:13].

> *For that which I do I allow* (understand) *not: for what I would* (want to do), *that do I not; but what I hate, that do I* [Rom. 7:15].

These portions of Scripture make it perfectly clear that our strength comes from the Lord and not from within ourselves. God's strength is needed to sustain and to renew us as we proceed along the heaven-bound pathway.

This is further emphasized in our Master's high priestly prayer when he prays, *Holy Father, keep through thine own name those whom thou hast given me, that they may be one, as we are* [John 17:11]. How is this strength acquired from the Lord? First and foremost by praying to the Lord boldly, frequently, continuously, energetically, positively, and expectantly. A verse from Hosea is most appropriate. *Take with you words, and turn to the Lord: say unto him, Take away all iniquity, and receive us graciously* [Hos. 14:2].

What happens in prayer and as a result of it? The Spirit will come and melt any iciness that is in one's heart. However, it does not mean that a person can pray himself into a position of strength or, by himself, can weaken a corrupt power that has controlled him or her. Hear what David has to say: *In the day when I cried thou answeredst me, and strengthenedst me* (made me bold) *with strength in my soul* [Ps. 138:3]. There is a significant point here. David prayed and received strength. True! But from whence did he receive his strength? God strengthened him. God acted, God imparted, and God bestowed. David did not strengthen himself. May we understand this truth and embrace it.

Second, we are to listen and to hear the word taught and preached. It is God who opens the heart to receive and to understand His Word. The Lord opened Lydia's heart, then she was able to attend and give heed to the Word. When a person's heart is opened, and they give heed to the Word, what happens? As Paul prays,

> *That the God of our Lord Jesus Christ, the Father of glory, may give unto you the spirit of wisdom and revelation in the knowledge of him:*
> *The eyes of your understanding being enlightened; that ye may know what is the hope of his calling,*
> *And . . . the exceeding greatness of his power to us-ward who believe, according to the working of his mighty power* [Eph. 1:17–19].

Why should we receive strength from God? First, we are the creatures, the created ones. He is the Creator. When Jesus was on earth He worked, He ministered unto others, and He preserved and empowered them with His strength. He enabled them to be and to do. He laid hold of many souls with whom He came into contact. Christ is at the right hand of God. He continues to make intercession for us with the Father and also to impart His strength to us.

Second, we need to recognize that we are not only creatures, but weak ones needing God's strength if we are to overcome the enemies that permeate the walls of our minds and hearts. The wiles of the devil beset us; therefore, the grace of God and His strength is required to empower us, if we are to have the victory. We need to progress to the point where we are the bond-slaves of Christ Jesus and willingly submit ourselves unto Him in everything, not rebelling in anything.

Third, God's grand design is to bring us into a right relationship with Himself that we should eventually be with Him in heaven through eternity. Therefore, He provides His love, mercy, and grace, and the power to receive them. God knows we are weak creatures and need His strength. Jesus says, . . . *and your Father knoweth that ye have need of these things* [Luke 12:30].

God knows we need His strength to pray, to hear, to suffer, and to do. It is not our own strength that enables us to do, but the strength God provides. This strength is provided on a continuing basis. It is needed daily, just as we need food and drink to sustain and strengthen us. *Our strength is in the Lord.*

What type of strength is this? It is His almighty power. God is almighty. Some people may be mighty in some things, but God is almighty. As the people of God, it is important for us to know, as an enlightened William Gurnall states, "That this almighty power of God is engaged for its (or our) defense; so as to bear up in the midst of all trials and temptations. Undauntedly, leaning on the arm of God almighty, as if it were his own strength."

What does Paul want us to do? Not depend on our own power, but to lean on God's almighty power. The saints and faithful have a responsibility while traveling along the road to heaven. What is it? To not only believe God is almighty, but to carry it further. We are to depend upon His almighty power and to appropriate it during our trials and tribulations. *Trust ye in the Lord for ever: for in the Lord Jehovah is everlasting strength* [Isa. 26:4].

Why are we to depend upon the power of the Lord? Very simply because God is almighty. It is something we forget or ignore in the time of our woes, or when we are self-centered, or downhearted. This is the God of Abraham, Isaac, and Jacob. The God who led Moses and the Israelites out of Egypt and fed them in the wilderness. The Lord Jesus Christ who raised Lazarus from the dead, who fed the five thousand with a few loaves and a few fish.

God loves us and cares for us. He willingly provides His power and strength if we but turn to Him and ask Him to come in. We are to acknowledge His almighty power and believe that He is able to sustain and strengthen us, just as He did with the Israelites and the apostles.

Oh, how often we doubt the power of God. Think of Zechariah when the angel told him to *Fear not . . . for thy prayer is heard; and thy wife Elisabeth shall bear thee a son, and thou shalt call his name John* [Luke 1:13]. Zechariah responded, saying, *Whereby shall I know this? For I am an old man, and my wife well stricken* (advanced) *in years* [Luke 1:18]. He doubted; he exhibited unbelief. He was struck dumb for a period of time, but after that his faith was strengthened. God wants us to believe His Word, but He does not want us to dispute His power and might.

As Martin Luther said, "God loves the obedient, not the caviling." Abraham responded in faith, believing in the power of God. Paul states it simply and forcefully:

> *He* (Abraham) *staggered* (wavered) *not at the promise of God through unbelief; but was strong* (strengthened) *in faith, giving glory to God;*
> *And being fully persuaded* (convinced) *that, what he had promised, he was able also to perform* [Rom. 4:20–21].

Therefore, let us remember what an unknown author wrote: "Bearing all these teachings and truths in mind, my brethren become strengthened and powerful inwardly in the Lord, and in the complete, perfect power of His strength which He bestows upon believers."

Amen!

10

To Fall or To Stand

Put on the whole armor of God, that ye may be able to stand against the wiles (schemes) *of the devil* [Eph. 6:11].

There is one question common to everyone. The question may surprise you, but it applies to each of us. Am I going to fall or stand? The question is *not* whether someone else will fall or stand, *but will I?*

What is my position going to be in marriage, in the home, in the workplace, in the church, in the community, with friends, with associates, in social circles, in the eyes of others? The question also applies in health or sickness, in loneliness or the company of others, in despair, in plenty, and in want.

David had his victories and defeats. He had acclaim and he had enemies. Have we not had our triumphs and our failures, our supporters and our detractors, our torment and our praise? David was confronted by many of the same things that surround us, and except for a few lapses, he kept his eye on God. He continued to travel the road to heaven, though it was not an easy one.

David depended upon God. He knew He would be with him on the journey and would be waiting for him at the end of the road. We all have fears that enter our hearts and minds as we travel on the road of life encountering temptations and tests, but may we trust God as David did. Remember David said, *What time I am afraid, I will trust in thee* [Ps. 56:3]. Oh, pray God that we can do the same! It is a difficult lesson to learn, to renounce our own self-reliance and to cast our dependence upon God. However, that is what we must do!

We are to *be strong in the Lord and in the power of his might*. We have considered several truths pertaining to this teaching that God provides abundantly for our needs. He bestows His complete, perfect strength upon believers when they sincerely ask Him and open their hearts. He wants us to become strengthened inwardly. God said unto Abram, *I am the Almighty God; walk before me, and be thou perfect* (blameless) [Gen. 17:1]. Abraham responded with much faith and was strengthened by God as he proceeded on the road to heaven.

The author of Hebrews says, *For he* (the Lord) *hath said, I WILL NEVER LEAVE THEE, NOR FORSAKE THEE. So that we may boldly say, THE LORD IS MY HELPER* [Heb. 13:5–6]. When we are certain of God's helping hand then we will overcome the fears besetting us at different times and in different circumstances. "Anyone who has the firm conviction that he will never be forsaken by the Lord will not be unduly anxious because he will depend on His providence," as John Calvin appropriately stated. How do we obtain that firm conviction? By knowing God's Word; by trusting Him to be faithful; by knowing God's will; and by depending upon Him. God will help. He has done so through the ages, through the Old Testament, the New Testament, the Apostolic Age, the Dark Ages, the Reformation, and ever since.

Receiving this truth requires two things, among others. First, obedience. Abraham was obedient when God called. God said unto Gideon, *Go in this thy might* (strength of yours), *. . . have I not sent thee* [Judg. 6:14]. Second, the saints or faithful increase or decrease in strength according to their faith in the power of God Almighty.

Their faith is fixed upon God, His power, and His promise, not upon their own capabilities. They look to God as their protector, defender, and shield, and they hear Him call. Also, they claim and accept God's promises.

William Gurnall stated an important truth for each believer, "The way of the Lord is strength." We, as the saints and faithful, are to partake of God's strength on a daily basis, not just when we face great tests, temptations, or calamities. We are to go to Him often with our prayers and petitions. Isaiah says, *Surely, shall one say, in the Lord have I righteousness and strength* [Isa. 45:24]. Our righteousness is in God's righteousness and our strength is in God's strength.

These teachings contain the seeds of comfort and blessings, as well as the seeds of unrest and distrust. What a dichotomy! Some will say, I have prayed for strength again and again, but I remain weak in the face of certain enemies or temptations. Others bemoan their condition and say, if God is a God of love, or if He is really with man, then why am I suffering, or why has this happened to me?

Consider certain relevant factors. First, when we do not receive that for which we are looking, do we receive some other strength? God does not always answer us in the manner we ask. Our vision is weak and narrow compared to God's broad, all-encompassing vision that looks upon the whole person.

Though the answer for which we have been praying has not been forthcoming, it is good to consider the benefits that have been received. This is not easy. It is difficult, especially when our minds have been set and we may be disappointed.

Probably, the person has continued to pray earnestly and sincerely. As a consequence, his or her prayer life has been strengthened, and they have become more dependent upon God in other areas. Though the weakness remained, or the condition was not changed, the spirit of prayer increased, and so did the desire to serve God. Think of Paul and his thorn in the flesh. What about David? He began to improve when he devoted himself to prayer and repented again for his sin against God.

When we pray to God, it is not just to ask, but to listen and to observe what God is doing within us. The question is not whether God has specifically dealt with a particular weakness or sin, but whether God is being heard and the capabilities He is providing are used to good advantage, whether they are being used to further His kingdom, and whether they enable the saints and faithful to walk more closely with Him.

What are our thoughts when we believe we have pleaded our cause before God, but have not received the answer we have been seeking? What is our natural inclination when this happens? To charge God foolishly with not responding or not providing according to our requests?

How soon we forget or ignore earlier lessons or teachings. God may withhold the blessing we are seeking. He may want us to search more diligently, or He may want us to become more aware of what He is trying to do within us. What does a caring mother or father do with a child? Yes, they try to strengthen weaknesses, but they also try to help a child in areas that are being ignored or need strengthening.

At times, it may appear that a person prays for strength in the face of certain temptations, and what happens? The temptations increase in power and attractiveness. Further, it appears that no aid or support is forthcoming. What then? The person must learn to exercise care and diligence with the capabilities available. He or she may learn to be more careful and observant, not to succumb to temptations or weaknesses. Sometimes it is a case of making do with the resources available. When a person has limited talents or resources, then he or she must learn to live within them.

God may withhold His strength from a person in order to eventually show His love. Sometimes, a person will pray for strength while facing a certain adversary or combating a specific weakness only to find that the adversary becomes stronger, or the weakness becomes greater and gives way to the onslaught. Yet God may exhibit both His grace and mercy by continuing to show forth His love even when we succumb to weaknesses.

We may better understand this thought by turning again to David. He was better able to understand and accept God's mercy because of His own weaknesses and infirmities. If he had previously received such strength so as to free him from his infirmities, then David may have congratulated himself instead of thanking God for His mercy.

It is helpful to realize that there are two types of strengths available from God. One is what we call the "assisting" or "making possible" type of strength. It is the "can-do" type. It is active! It does something. On the other hand, there is the "passive alternative" or "supporting strength." It is when a loved one must perform a task. You want to actively help them, but you cannot. Yet they draw strength from your presence. How much more God supports us with His presence.

There is another factor significantly affecting our ability to receive strength from God. What is it? We may pray fervently and long for something but not receive it. The hindrance may rest within ourselves. We may erect obstacles that prevent receiving assistance from the Master. People may think they have certain duties to perform or ordinances to follow instead of seeking God's help. It is not duties or ordinances that strengthen us. It is the Lord Jesus Christ!

We are to seek Him, find Him, ask Him, talk with Him, and listen to Him. John tells us that there were certain Greeks who said to Philip, *Sir, we would see Jesus* [John 12:21]. Philip told Andrew and they went to see the Lord. Those Greeks wanted to see Christ. Should we want anything less?

There is an area that is often neglected. Do we thank God for the little strength that we have? The parable of the talents [Matt. 25:14–30] reveals that we are to use the talents that have been given to us. We are to be thankful for the talents we have, and we are to use them.

The saint is to focus on God and how he or she can best serve Him. Though weaknesses may be present, the question is, what is God doing or going to do? Therefore, we are to stay in touch with God, we are to thank Him for what we have, and we are to use the talents we possess whether they be many or few. If weak, do we thank God for life? If we fail, do we seek God's mercy? If we succumb, do we ask God's forgiveness and accept it?

Do we truly recognize the assistance and strength God gives us? Or are we filled with pride about our own accomplishments? Where do we focus our attention? "A proud heart and a lofty mountain are never fruitful," as William Gurnall sagely observed. Pride overvalues itself and undervalues others. When thinking of pride, we do not like to think of ourselves. Yet pride in some form or shape finds a safe harbor in the best of us. However, when it becomes evident, it stands between Christ and ourselves. Think of Peter. In his boldness he stated what he would do. Yet he denied his Master.

Pride also impacts the saints and faithful by allowing them to neglect those areas or things God uses to nourish them through Christ and the Holy Spirit. Pride in one's own ability keeps him or her from receiving God's manna. Remember: we are vessels. We can be filled with our own pride, or we can allow God to fill us with His own strength. *Be filled with the Spirit* [Eph. 5:18].

Probably one of the hardest things any of us has to do is to wait. Most people do not like to wait. It is difficult to petition God when pursuing our desires and wants, then wait expectantly and not receive them. However, God provides for our needs when we let Him. We are to pray, *Thy will be done.*

At the end of Luke's Gospel, Jesus tells His disciples, *But tarry ye in the city of Jerusalem, until ye be endued with power from on high* [Luke 24:49]. The disciples were to persevere in waiting. Are we to do less? The disciples were to exhibit faith and patience; so are we!

By studying Scripture we learn that God's strength fills the saints and faithful when they humbly and obediently open their hearts and seek to do His will. The strength comes in God's way and time. When the temptation is great, when the weakness is evident, if we call upon the Lord, He will bestow His strength upon us.

These thoughts lead us to the next command, which is *Put on the whole armor of God*. However, before proceeding it is appropriate to consider Paul's words to the Romans regarding love and how it is to be expressed:

> *Owe no man any thing, but to love one another: for he that loveth another hath fulfilled the law*
> *... If there be any other commandment, it is briefly (summed up) comprehended in this saying, namely, THOU SHALT LOVE THY NEIGHBOR AS THYSELF.*
> *Love worketh no ill* (does no harm) *to his neighbor: therefore love is the fulfilling of the law* [Rom. 13:8–10].
>
> *... The night is far spent, the day is at hand: let us therefore cast off the works of darkness, and let us put on the armor of light.*
> *Let us walk honestly* (properly), *as in the day; not in rioting* (revelry) *and drunkenness ... not in strife and envying.*
> *But put ye on the Lord Jesus Christ, and make not provision for the flesh, to fulfill the lusts thereof* [Rom. 13:12–14].

These verses say, *love is the fulfilling of the law* [Verse 10]; *put on the armor of light* [Verse 12]; and *put ye on the Lord Jesus Christ, and make not provision for the flesh* [Verse 14]. "Paul's design is to reduce all the precepts of the law to love, so that we may know we are duly obeying the commandments when we are maintaining love," as stated by John Calvin with appropriate insight.

When Paul speaks of night and darkness he is talking about being ignorant of God and not knowing His teachings. When he speaks of the light he is speaking of the divine truth as revealed in Christ Jesus. *The armor of light* means those things that can be performed in the light of day.

Further, *to put on the Lord Jesus Christ* means to be defended by Him and the Holy Spirit in everything and in every way. It is in this way that we are renewed. It is by putting on Christ that we become new creatures in Him.

Putting on *the whole armor of God* means putting on the Lord Jesus Christ. *And that ye put on the new man, which after God is created in righteousness and true holiness* [Eph. 4:24]. The only way the new man can be created in righteousness and true holiness is to be in Christ, to be in His righteousness and His holiness.

What is the person's condition who does not have *the armor of God*? First, he or she is alienated from God. Paul says to the Ephesians, *That at that time ye were without Christ, being aliens from the commonwealth of Israel, and strangers from the covenants of promise, having no hope, and without God in the world* [Eph. 2:12].

Next, the person without this armor is ignorant of God's power, love, strength, mercy, and grace. *For ye were sometimes* (once) *darkness, but now are ye light in the Lord* [Eph. 5:8]. A person cannot have light in the darkness except he or she becomes a member of Christ's body and a new creature in Him.

Further, without the *whole armor of God*, a person is impotent. He or she is subject to the power of Satan. The Spirit of God fills a person with love, joy, and the power of the Spirit, whereas the spirit of Satan fills one with pride, lust, lying, and other weaknesses.

Last, when a person is without *the whole armor of God* they are in a state of unregeneracy. The unregenerate soul is at enmity with God and in friendship with Satan. When people know what it is like to be without the whole armor of God, hopefully they will open their hearts to receive the Word and to practice it.

There is something unique about this armor: it is the *armor of God*. Not only that, it is *the whole armor of God*. It is the full and complete armor from God. It was instituted by God and appointed by Him for the protection and preservation of the saints and the faithful in Christ Jesus. However, though it is *the whole armor of God*, our confidence is not to be in the armor, but in the Lord our God who provides the armor.

What are the characteristics of *the whole armor of God*? It covers every part of the body. Satan is all around us looking for an opening; therefore, it is to completely cover for every part of the saint. This armor contains several different graces: faith, knowledge, charity, temperance, patience, and godliness. In this instance, godliness is the inward and outward worship of God. To these characteristics should be added brotherly kindness. Why? Because if Satan can cause divisions and bitterness, then he will cause damage to one's godliness.

The saints and faithful are to *put on the whole armor of God*. What are they to do with it? They are to use it, keep it in good repair, and exercise it on a continuing basis. Paul says, *And herein* (this being so) *do I exercise* (strive) *myself, to have always a conscience void of offense toward God, and toward men* [Acts 24:16]. The Lord Jesus says, *Let your loins* (waist) *be girded about, and your lights burning* [Luke 12:35]. He is telling His disciples to be alert.

What happens when the saints and faithful do not use the armor, neglect it, or become weary? Think of Christ in the wilderness for forty days. Satan thought Him to be tired, weary, and hungry, so what did he do? He tempted Him. If he did that to Christ, how much more will he tempt us when we are weary, tired, hungry, and at other difficult times, especially when we believe we have been doing our duty and serving the Lord.

Some may say that it is burdensome to have *the whole armor* on all the time and to use it continually. However, they do not think it a burden to eat, drink, and many other things. Using *the whole armor of God* is like exercising faith in the Lord Jesus Christ. It is burdensome only to those using it infrequently or practicing with it occasionally. Certainly, the clothes we are accustomed to wearing are not burdensome.

What are the saints to do when they have put on *the whole armor of God*? They are to exercise grace each day. When they do, the amount of grace bestowed on them will increase. As the psalmist says,

> *O how love I thy law! It is my meditation all the day.*
> *Thou through thy commandments hast made me wiser than mine enemies: for they are ever with me.*
> *I have more understanding than all my teachers, for thy testimonies are my meditation.*
> *I understand more than the ancients (aged), because I keep thy precepts.*
> *I have refrained (restrained) my feet from every evil way, that I might keep thy word.*
> *I have not departed from thy judgments: for thou hast taught me.*
> *How sweet are Thy words unto my taste! yea, sweeter than honey to my mouth.*
> *Through thy precepts I get understanding: therefore I hate every false way* [Ps. 119:97–104].

We are to *put on the whole armor of God*. Once we have put it on we are to keep it on. We are to use it, we are to exercise it, we are to serve the Master, and we are to witness to others. As Paul says, *I THEREFORE, . . . beseech you that ye walk worthy of the vocation* (calling) *wherewith ye are called* [Eph. 4:1]. When we do, we will stand, not fall, in all our relationships as we journey through life as the Master's disciples.

Amen!

11

Prepare to Wrestle

Finally, my brethren, be strong in the Lord, and in the power of his might.
Put on the whole armor of God, that ye may be able to stand against the wiles (schemes) *of the devil.*
For we wrestle not against flesh and blood, but against principalities, against powers, against the rulers of the darkness of this world (age), *against spiritual* (hosts of) *wickedness in high places* [Eph. 6:10–12].

The Apostle Paul has definite reasons for saying, . . . *be strong in the Lord and in the power of his might. Put on the whole armor of God.*

Why does he say this? So we can be happy, enjoy life, have all our prayers answered, receive rewards, and live a long life? No, not for any of those reasons. The real reason is *that ye may be able to stand against the wiles* (schemes) *of the devil* [Eph. 6:11]. That is not what we would expect. Yet that is what the Apostle says under the influence of the Holy Spirit. We would not expect Scripture to say that we are to put on this power and might *to stand against the wiles* (schemes) *of the devil.* But that is what it says.

Some will say, this is the twenty-first century. We are more enlightened and better educated than the people in the first century. Therefore, what is this talk about *the wiles* (schemes) *of the devil*? Or, who even says there is a devil?

The portion of Scripture we are now considering (Eph. 6:10–18) "Reveals a battlefield where the empowered, energized hosts of the Lord are pitted against the demonized, mobilized hosts of the devil. It is a mass organization of the supernatural forces of heaven against the subtle fiends of hell. One necessity in victorious warfare is to know the enemy.

"Scripture everywhere shows Satan as the bitterest enemy of God and His people; the implacable foe of Christ and the Christian. It distinctly warns us against him as a cruel adversary seeking whom he may devour.

"The Names given him indicate personality; Satan, spelled with a capital S, deceiver, liar, murderer, accuser, tempter, prince, Apollyon (destroyer), the evil one, Beelzebub. Every name is repulsive and repellent and discloses his nature. God speaks also of "the working of Satan," and every one of his works, which are defined as "wiles, "devices," "snares," reveal personality. He beguiles, seduces, opposes, resists, deceives, sows tares, hinders, buffets, tempts, persecutes, blasphemes. Every work of Satan is diabolical and destructive. Our Lord spoke of Satan many times and every time in a way and by a name that confirms his personality. Our adversary, then, is personal, aggressive, intelligent, cunning and destructive, who is to be reckoned with seriously, vigilantly and intelligently.

"He occupies a very superior position which is twofold. In governmental authority he is a "prince" in two localities—in the earth and in the air; and rules over both evil men and evil spirits. Christ never acknowledged Satan asking, but three times he calls him "the prince of this world," thereby acknowledging his governmental authority. Ephesians teaches that he is the ruling spirit over "the children of disobedience," which includes all unregenerate mankind," as astutely described by Ruth Paxson.

Others will say, let's skip over that part, let's pick and choose what we are going to study. Our responsibility to Christ and ourselves runs much deeper than exhibiting a selective or superficial interest in the Word of God. It is His Word! Therefore, we are to consider all of it, not just bits and pieces.

One of the fascinating aspects of being a member of Christ's body is that you do not reason yourself into it, you do not learn a table of contents or solve problems, nor do you memorize material. You are called. You respond in faith.

When your heart and mind are triggered, you find that Scripture contains logical explanations, understandable reasons, and knowledge that you can apply to yourself and the world about you. It is important not only to examine everything the Apostle says, but to understand it.

There is a prevalent practice in this country and in most congregations to take the things of the world and apply them to the church and to the practice of the Christian faith. What is really needed is to know the truth as it is found in the Lord Jesus Christ, then apply it to ourselves and practice it in every aspect of our daily living. Unfortunately, too many things have become reversed.

What is the greatest need in the world today? There may be several answers suggested for that question, such as peace, disarmament, disease, famine, hunger, race relations. However, I submit to you that these things are merely symptoms; they are not the real cause. The real cause goes much deeper. If someone has chills and a fever, and you treat either one with an aspirin, you may not cure either one. Especially if he or she has pneumonia or requires surgery.

The Apostle is getting at the root cause in these final verses of Ephesians. He wants us *to stand against the wiles* (schemes) *of the devil*. He adds considerable emphasis to his exhortation, saying, *For we wrestle not against flesh and blood, but against principalities, against powers, against the rulers of the darkness of this world* (age), *against spiritual* (hosts of) *wickedness in high places* [Eph. 6:12]. The enemy is formidable and powerful. The Holy Spirit does not want us to be ill-prepared, nor does He want us to succumb.

Scripture tells us the root cause is the devil. The ongoing battle is the devil and his forces against God, the Lord Jesus Christ, you and me, and the other members of Christ's body. It is important to consider this teaching in detail. Therefore, several words and their meanings should be examined before proceeding. They are *stand, wrestle, devil,* and *wiles*.

The word *stand* means "to cause to stand," not just to stand. It is to stand in the face of severe, intense, and difficult struggles. When you took examinations or received difficult assignments you knew you had to prepare yourself if you wanted to stand victoriously. The same is true of the life in Christ. We have to prepare ourselves in order to stand victoriously in life. The Holy Spirit wants us to have the strength, power, might, and *the whole armor of God* because the conflicts of life can be fierce and tough. They also continue throughout the days God gives us. Ecclesiastes says, *There is no man that hath power over the spirit to retain the spirit; neither hath he power in the day of death; and there is no discharge in that war; neither shall wickedness deliver those that are given to it* [Eccl. 8:8]. This truth should be emphasized and understood. When it is, hopefully we will do something about it. When people understand the magnitude of the situation, they should make the proper preparations.

To whom is the Apostle addressing his teachings? To the saints and faithful. Who are these people? They are the ones who have been called and are being prepared. But once prepared, they must continually practice. They must exercise their capabilities and be ready to use them at a moment's notice.

We are exposed to a heavy dosage of bowl games, the pro playoffs and the Super Bowl. When a football player makes it to "the Pros," he does not stop learning, nor does he stop practicing. When a person becomes a member of Christ's body, he or she needs to recognize that they are to continue learning and practicing for the remainder of their days.

Football players have their playbooks and coaches. Musicians have their scores of music and their conductors. Members of Christ's body have the Bible and the Holy Spirit. The Bible is the most unique of all books: it is special, it has insight, it has understanding, and it gets to the root cause of things.

The saints and faithful are not "professionals" unless they prepare and practice, and get to the root of it. "The saints are able bodied men, not by nature, nor by one act of ordination, (e.g. by their baptism), but only in as much as again and again they take up the special armor given to them. Whoever renders service, (shall do it) as one who renders it by the strength which God supplies . . . the armor, or strength, that is *put on* is equated with the 'New Man' who is identified with Christ," as described by Markus Barth.

"If the Lord aids us by His extraordinary power, we have no reason to be irresolute in battle. But someone will say, 'What purpose did it serve to bid the Ephesians to be strong in the Lord's power, which was certainly not at their command?' I answer, there are two clauses here which must be considered. He exhorts them to courage, but then reminds them to ask from God a supply of what in themselves they lack; and at the same time promises that, if they ask for it, the power of God will be displayed," as revealed by the Holy Spirit unto John Calvin.

The more we study and the further we proceed, the clearer it becomes. As the Greeks said to Philip, *Sir, we would see Jesus* [John 12:21]. We are to see Christ. For it is in Him that we stand. It is in Him that we stand firm and stand victoriously.

The second word on which to focus our attention is *wrestle*. It is used only once in the New Testament. It is used figuratively, in this twelfth verse, to describe the spiritual conflict engaged in by the believers. As Jimmy Millard asked, "How can you wrestle, if you put on all that armor?" The Apostle says, *We wrestle*, but he also says, *put on the whole armor of God*. How do we reason with these terms and gain an understanding of this teaching?

There are those who believe that when the Apostle talks about being strong in the power of His might and *putting on the whole armor of God* that he is talking about two armies that have taken the field and are about to enter into an all out battle. In some respects that is true, but there is more to it. Yes, there are opposing forces, but the participants are individuals. Paul says, *For we wrestle*. That means you and me.

The Apostle begins his letter to the Ephesians saying, *PAUL, an Apostle of Jesus Christ . . . to the saints . . . and to the faithful . . . In whom we have redemption through his blood* [Eph. 1:1, 7]. Throughout this magnificent letter, Paul uses the personal plural pronoun "we" to describe our relationship with Christ. Consider the following:

> *We were dead* [Eph. 2:5];
> *We were quickened (made alive) together with Christ* [Eph. 2:5];
> *We were raised* [Eph. 2:6];
> *We sit together in heavenly places* [Eph. 2:6];
> *We are his workmanship (creation)* [Eph. 2:10];
> *We both have access . . . unto the Father* [Eph. 2:18];
> *We are members one of another* [Eph. 4:25]; *and*
> *We are members of his body, of his flesh, and of his bones* [Eph. 5:30].

He continues this line of reasoning saying, *We wrestle*.

What thoughts come to mind when considering these two words? First, it is *one-to-one* combat. Wrestling involves two opponents, who are enemies. Each one exerts all his strength and force to defeat or overcome the other. Each one is engaged in the battle. Neither one can rest until the battle is over or one is defeated. When considering this we should bear in mind that Satan not only hates the body of Christ in general, but has an intense malice toward the individual members of that body. Each of us should realize that God enjoys and cherishes having communion with each saint. Since this is true, we should recognize that Satan wants to engage each person individually.

Second, wrestlers engage in combat on a hand-to-hand basis. They do not shout at each other from long distances. Satan wants to grab hold of us, he wants to subdue us individually. He hates to encounter a young person, an old person, or one in between, who will not fall but who stands and serves as a witness to others.

There is a third significant point. Though it involves individuals and is personal in nature, it is universal in practice. Each and every member of Christ's body is attacked and must defend him or herself. This is true no matter what their position or responsibility may be.

There is a fourth point regarding this verb "wrestle." It is in the present tense. It is a continuous situation. We do not wrestle just before or after our conversion. Nor do we wrestle only in our early years or during our initial stages. Paul wrote to the Ephesians a number of years after his conversion and said, *We wrestle*. He had wrestled with Satan, he was wrestling with him, and knew he would continue to wrestle with him the rest of his earthly days.

There are two ways a person can wrestle with God: by wrestling with His Spirit; and by wrestling against His providence. When considering this term, we are to exercise great care not to wrestle against God. There are those, who through ignorance or self-centeredness wrestle with God. Isaiah says,

> *Woe unto him that striveth with his Maker* [Isa. 45:9]!

God said,

> *My Spirit shall not always strive* (abide) *with man* [Gen. 6:3].

The striving is not always in anger and wrath, but it is out of God's loving, merciful wrath that man may see and accept His way, and turn from his lusts, greed, and covetousness.

> *Ye stiffnecked* (stubborn) *and uncircumcised* (unrepentant) *in heart and ears, ye do always resist the Holy Ghost; as your fathers did, so do ye* [Acts 7:51].

Men soon forget what they hear, or they do not pay attention in the first place. They do not listen to the prophets or the apostles or the evangels. As Jesus says, *They have Moses and the prophets; let them hear them* [Luke 16:29].

People wrestle by wanting to pick and choose what God has to say. They want to resist the truths of God which bless them. They wrestle against God. What happens when people wrestle with God and resist His Word? The prophet Zechariah vividly describes what happens when a people wrestle with God, saying,

> *IN the eighth month, . . . came the word of the Lord unto Zechariah . . . saying,*
>
> *The Lord hath been sore displeased (very angry) with your fathers.*
>
> *Therefore say thou unto them, . . . Turn (return) ye unto me, . . . and I will turn (return) unto you, saith the Lord of hosts.*
>
> *Be ye not as your fathers, . . . Turn ye now from your evil ways, and from your evil doings (deeds): but they did not hear, nor hearken (heed) unto me, saith the Lord* [Zech. 1:1–4].
>
> *But my words and my statutes, which I commanded my servants the prophets, did they not take hold of* (overtake) *your fathers? and they returned and said, Like* (Just as) *the Lord of hosts thought* (determined) *to do unto us, according to our ways, and according to our doings* (deeds), *so hath he dealt with us* [Zech. 1:6].

These are strong words of the Lord. They are to be heard, they are to be hearkened unto, and they are to be obeyed. We do not want the Lord to deal with us according to our ways and our doings, as he did with our fathers. Therefore, when hearing the Holy Spirit knocking at your heart and mind, welcome Him, do not reject Him.

In addition, we wrestle with God when we wrestle against His providence. We do this by becoming discontented with His dealings toward us or by objecting to what He has done or is doing. God says to Job, *Shall he that contendeth with the Almighty instruct him? He that reproveth* (rebukes) *God, let him answer it* [Job 40:2].

It is either a bold or foolish man that finds fault with the Almighty. We wrestle against the providences of God when we remain incorrigible or unmoved in light of God's dispensations toward us.

There are those who wrestle against sin, but not according to Christ's commands. They must wrestle according to Christ's teachings. They are to be obedient. They are to do as they have been commanded.

There are some who wrestle against one sin for a moment or a season, then they embrace another one. They wrestle against some lusts but are covetous in other areas. They conceal their wrath but plot revenge.

There are others who wrestle with sin, but they do not hate it. Actually, they are favorably disposed to it. They do not consider the life of sin to be their enemy. "These wrestle in jest, and not in earnest; the wounds they give sin one day, are healed by the next," as aptly described by William Gurnall. The only way the love of sin can be quenched is to replace it with another love: the love of Christ.

How are we to wrestle? When realizing we are going to wrestle, it is best to make preparations. Undoubtedly, each person professes to want to win wrestling matches. Therefore, there are things to do.

First, we are to "Engage God by prayer to stand at thy back," as wisely encouraged by William Gurnall. Before we enter into prayer, we are to turn to God and beseech Him to go with us and protect us. Though He is ready and willing, we are still to call upon Him. If He is engaged, then the enemy cannot attack you from the rear. Certainly, there are examples of this in the Old Testament with Moses, Jacob, and David.

Second, do not give the opponent anything to grab that will allow Him to pull or throw you down. Take care to lay aside those things that are part of you that are weaknesses to temptations. In other words, *put off* the old. At the same time, anoint yourself with preparations and exercises that will repel the attacks of Satan and his followers. When and where Christ is present in your heart and mind, the opponent will find little to grab. Therefore, *put on* the new.

Third, when you have the advantage, when you can crush the opposition—do it! Exercise both your strength and wisdom to overcome the temptations besetting you and the weaknesses within. Some may ask, why do we have these inward conflicts, temptations, and difficulties? Gideon stated it for all of us: *Oh my Lord, if the Lord be with us, why then is all this befallen* (happened to) *us* [Judg. 6:13]? How many of us have thought and said the same thing?

Why do we have struggles? Have you ever thought the reason we have struggles is that we are wrestlers, not conquerors, not spectators, not announcers, not officials? We are combatants! When we are called by God's grace we are called to *put off* the old and to *put on* the new.

My wife and I have noticed that our young grandson struggles to put off old, comfortable clothing and to put on new, clean, attractive garments. The wrestling that takes place is between the old, earthly, worldly nature within us and the new nature as found in Christ and available from Him. We have a choice as to what we will put on.

Fourth, why do we wrestle? Why does it go on continuously? Have you ever thought that the answer lies in the Lord Jesus Christ and His redemptive ministry? God, in order to reconcile man to Himself, sent His Son in a human body to accomplish this task. After His death and resurrection another body was needed to continue the work and to make Christ available to all people. Therefore, on Pentecost "the Holy Spirit descended to form the Body of Christ," as Ruth Paxson lovingly declares. Since that time, everyone who has been redeemed by the shed blood of Christ has been baptized into His body. Therefore, we have the mystical union between Christ and ourselves.

Satan tempted and attacked Christ during His earthly ministry. Therefore, he continues to tempt and attack those who are members of His body. Satan uses many different people to attack the living church, the saints, and the faithful. Recall Saul of Tarsus

Consenting unto his (Stephen's) *death* [Acts 8:1].

Breathing out threatenings and slaughter (murder) *against the disciples of the Lord* [Acts 9:1].

Saul was then confronted by Christ who said to him,

I am Jesus whom thou persecutest [Acts 9:5].

Saul was persecuting the members of Christ's body; therefore, he was persecuting Jesus Himself. What a defeat Satan suffered when Christ redeemed Paul! However, this reveals that there will be other attacks on the saints and the faithful.

Why does Satan wrestle with us? Yes, we wrestle with Satan, but he initiates the combat. Why does he? Because he is concerned *That Christ may dwell in your hearts by faith* [Eph. 3:17]; that you *may grow up into him in all things, which is the head, even Christ* [Eph. 4:15]; and that you will *be filled with the Spirit* [Eph. 5:18]. Satan opposes these things happening because when they do he suffers setbacks and loses wrestling matches.

When *ye walk worthy of the vocation* (calling) *wherewith ye are called* you are walking in unity with Christ and putting on the new creature. This exhibits the blessings and strength of life in the Spirit as opposed to life in the flesh. Satan does not want these things to happen, nor does he want them to continue; therefore, he engages us and wrestles with us.

Fifth, have you ever considered that your wrestling is part of God's great plan so that prophesy might be fulfilled?

> *That in . . . the fullness of times he might gather together in one all things in Christ* [Eph. 1:10].

> *To him that overcometh will I grant to sit with me in* (on) *my throne, even as I also overcame, and am set down with my Father in* (on) *his throne* [Rev. 3:21].

> *And hast made us unto our God kings and priests: and we shall reign on the earth* [Rev. 5:10].

> *Do ye not know that the saints shall judge the world* [1 Cor. 6:2]?

> *Know ye not that we shall judge angels* [1 Cor. 6:3]?

What does this have to do with our wrestling? Probably, it intensifies the attacks and temptations hurled at the members of Christ's body. Therefore, the saints and faithful are to be trained, and prepared. We are to know the Word of God. We are to see Jesus. We are to *walk worthy of the vocation* (calling) *wherewith ye are called* [Eph. 4:1].

In closing, consider two verses from 1 John:

> *For whatsoever is born of God overcometh the world: and this is the victory that overcometh the world, even our faith* [1 John 5:4].

> *I have written unto you, young men, because ye are strong, and the word of God abideth in you, and ye have overcome the wicked one* [1 John 2:14].

Yes, we wrestle, our strength will be tested, and there will be severe trials, but the outcome is assured . . . *because ye are strong, and the word of God abideth in you* [1 John 2:14]. Therefore, we wrestle and we triumph by God's strength, power, and might.

Amen!

12

Satan

> *Put on the whole armor of God, that ye may be able to stand against the wiles* (schemes) *of the devil.*
> *For we wrestle not against flesh and blood, but against principalities, against powers, against the rulers of the darkness of the world* (age), *against spiritual* (hosts of) *wickedness in high places* [Eph. 6:11–12].

The twentieth century was noted for two factors having an impact upon the thinking and attitudes of many people. First is the evolutionary theory and its acceptance by many elements in society that man is improving and that the world is becoming a better place. Second is the belief that increasing the spread of knowledge and education throughout the world will improve living conditions and relationships between governments and people.

It is amazing that anyone staying abreast of current events during the past one hundred years can accept these pronouncements. These suppositions are saying that the problem is not with man, but that he has simply neither had the time to develop nor received his full portion of knowledge, culture, and education. These ideas are not in accord with the teachings in Scripture.

The problem with man is man. Man's sinfulness, his alienation from God, is the root cause. Man's self-centeredness, man's covetousness, and man's desires do not go away of their own accord. There is not any amount of evolution, knowledge, culture, or education that will change man or make him into something else.

The Gospel of the Lord Jesus Christ and that alone changes a person. The Holy Spirit working within someone and the power and might of God change and strengthen him or her. It is the spirit that needs to be reached, which only God through the Holy Spirit can do.

Paul states concisely that man's problem is not just flesh and blood, but it is: principalities, powers, rulers of the darkness, and spiritual wickedness. What does this have to do with the devil and his wiles? Plenty! As we study this fountain of living waters, you will realize it has more to do with us than you may have originally conjectured. Unfortunately, people focus on political developments or events, certain symptoms, particular sins, or personal happiness, yet ignore or omit the root of the problem.

Before focusing on the devil and his wiles, there is a question to ask. Do you believe there is a spiritual realm? There are people who do not. There are professing Christians who do not. Some church members think that Christianity consists only of moral and ethical teachings, or that if you do a certain amount of good works, you will earn your way into a right relationship with God, or that since there is a clergy and a laity, the clergy will handle religious matters.

The person not believing in God and the powers of the Spirit or in the devil is at least consistent in his or her outlook and belief. But the person saying he or she believes in God, yet says they do not believe in the Holy Spirit, the power of the Spirit, or the devil, is quite inconsistent. Some people want to believe in part but not in the whole. Some want to pick and choose.

This leads to other deductions or qualifications about Scripture and one's relationship to God and the Lord Jesus Christ. What they are doing, in reality, is questioning the authority of Scripture. They are limiting their exposure to the teachings contained in the Word of God. They are picking and choosing. They will not let the Spirit work within them. Consequently, they may not believe in the: virgin birth, miracles, substitutionary atonement, the Holy Spirit, or *the wiles* (schemes) *of the devil*.

Others will say the Bible is an old book, written by men, with errors in it that was fine for people two thousand years ago; but we are more enlightened, better educated, and more advanced culturally today. You know what these people are really saying? "I am an authority on Scripture, I am an authority on God, and I want God to conform to my ideas and thoughts."

The truth is, the Bible is the authority. The Holy Spirit working within our hearts and our minds interprets Scripture correctly. This is awesome! It is ineffable! Think of it: Jesus says, *I am the way, the truth, and the life* [John 14:6]. Everyone likes that, but the last half of the same sentence says, *No man cometh unto the Father, but by me* [John 14:6].

We want to go to the Father. We want to be in a right relationship with God. Jesus wanted to go to His Father. The apostles wanted to go to the Father. The saints and faithful through the ages have wanted to go to the Father. The way to the Father is through the Lord Jesus. If He is not our road map and our guide, we cannot get there.

The truth is in Christ and in Scripture. The truth is revealed in Him and through the Word. The power and might is in the Lord and made available through the Holy Spirit.

Why emphasize these points? A belief in the authority of Scripture is of primary importance, if we are to grow in the Lord and *walk worthy of the vocation* (calling) *wherewith ye have been called*. A belief in the devil and his wiles is necessary in order to understand the Doctrine of Salvation. Paul sheds additional light on salvation through Christ when he says,

> *And you, being dead in your sins and the uncircumcision of your flesh, hath he quickened* (made alive) *together with him, having forgiven you all trespasses;*
> *Blotting out the handwriting* (certificate of debt) *of ordinances that was against us, which was contrary to us, and took it out of the way, nailing it to his cross;*
> *And having spoiled* (disarmed) *principalities and powers, he made a show* (spectacle) *of them openly, triumphing over them in it* [Col. 2:13–15].

What does it say Christ did on the Cross? He blotted out all the handwritten debts that had been recorded against each of us individually or ever would be written down. "For as He (Christ) fastened to the Cross our curse, our sins, and the punishment due to us, so also that bondage of the law and everything that tends to bind consciences," as John Calvin provides additional illumination on this supreme sacrifice offered by God through His Son, our Lord and Saviour. By going to the Cross, Christ "spoiled (the) principalities and powers, . . . triumphing over them in it," as John Calvin further stated.

According to Calvin, there is no doubt that Scripture is referring to the devil and his subordinates. Anyone who claims differently is espousing the devil or false prophets. The Cross signifies Christ's triumph over Satan.

Why bring these things to your attention? Because you cannot understand the teaching and authority of the Bible, you cannot understand the history of man, current situations, or people (family, friend, members of this group or congregation) unless you comprehend the truth as it is found in the Lord Jesus Christ and revealed to us by the Holy Ghost.

We need to obtain "A clear understanding of what the Apostle teaches here about the devil and the principalities and powers, the world rulers of this darkness, the wicked spirits in the heavenlies," according to Martyn Lloyd-Jones. We are to *be strong in the Lord, and in the power of his might* and we are to *stand against the wiles* (schemes) *of the devil* [Eph. 6:10–11].

What does Scripture say about Satan? Satan is mentioned thirty-five times in the New Testament and fifteen times in the Old Testament. He is identified by our Lord in each of the four Gospels. He is spoken of as a person. In addition, he is referred to by his name Beelzebub seven times in the Gospels.

Scripture reveals that the devil is the bitterest and most formidable enemy of God and God's people. He is a cruel, ingenious, deceptive, and persistent adversary. "The devil" is one of the names given to Satan. It appears thirty-five times in the New Testament, the same number of times as Satan.

"Devil" is the translation for the Greek word *diablos*. This is not to be confused with the Greek word *daimon*, which means "demon" or "demons." There is only one devil, but there are many demons.

What about the devil? Peter provides valuable insight, saying, *Be sober, be vigilant; because your adversary the devil, as a roaring lion, walketh about, seeking whom he may devour* [1 Pet. 5:8]. Peter tells us that we are not doing battle with a common or weak enemy, but with one ready to devour us. Therefore, *Be sober, be vigilant.*

The names given to Satan tell us a great deal about him. "He is called, among other things, a deceiver, liar, murderer, accuser, tempter, destroyer, and an evil one. Also, his workings are referred to as wiles, snares, and devices.

"In addition, we are told that he beguiles, seduces, opposes, resists, deceives, hinders, tempts, sows tares, persecutes, blasphemes, and buffets the saints and the faithful. He is also cunning, destructive, and a relentless adversary" to paraphrase Ruth Paxson. Yet there are people who deny that he exists or that he influences professing Christians, let alone those outside Christ's body.

What is the devil's position? Basically, he controls evil men and evil spirits. He continually attacks the saints and faithful. The Lord Jesus Christ refers to him as the *prince of this world* three times [John 12:31, 14:30, 16:11].

What does Paul say to the Ephesians about him? He calls him, . . . *the prince of the power of the air, the spirit that now worketh in the children of disobedience* [Eph. 2:2]. Satan exercises great control and power. He is known for his power, greed, ambition, intrigue, hatred, lies, aggression, and brutality. He offered Christ the kingdom of this world. What does he offer us?

Jesus says that there is a Kingdom of Satan when saying,

> *And if Satan cast out Satan, he is divided against himself; how shall then his kingdom stand* [Matt.12:26]?

Jesus informs us that the devil has his angels when He says,

> *Depart from me, ye cursed, into everlasting fire, prepared for the devil and his angels* [Matt. 25:41].

Paul reveals this about the devil, saying,

> *In whom the god of this world hath blinded the minds of them which believe not, lest the light of the glorious gospel of Christ* (the Gospel of the glory of Christ), *who is the image of God, should shine unto them* [2 Cor. 4:4].

Satan uses his position to exercise control over people, especially those who have professed faith in the Lord Jesus Christ. The parable of the sower as told by the Lord Jesus sheds additional light on Satan's methods and workings when He says,

> *The sower soweth the word.*
> *And these are they by the wayside, where the word is sown; but when they have heard, Satan cometh immediately, and taketh away the word that was sown in their hearts.*

> *And these are they likewise which are sown on stony ground; who, when they have heard the word, immediately receive it with gladness;*
>
> *And have no root in themselves, and so endure but for a time: . . . when affliction (tribulation) or persecution ariseth for the word's sake, immediately they are offended (caused to stumble).*
>
> *And these are they which are sown among thorns; such as hear the word,*
>
> *And the cares of this world, and the deceitfulness of riches, and the lusts (desires) of other things entering in, choke the word, and it becometh unfruitful.*
>
> *And these are they which are sown on good ground; such as hear the word, and receive it, and bring forth fruit, some thirtyfold, some sixty, and some an hundred* [Mark 4:14–20].

The Lord Jesus accurately describes what happens when the Word is sown on different types of ground: Satan watches like a hawk and springs into action. He does not want the seed to germinate and produce abundant fruit.

Satan will prey upon those who have recently received the Word and accepted the Lord Jesus Christ, but have not allowed it to take root. In addition, he will prey on those who have suffered affliction or persecution, those who have properly interpreted the Word, and those who are pressured and pursued by the world and are not able to stand. Then there are those who hear the Word, receive it, and bring forth much fruit. However, they are able to bring forth fruit only by hearing the Word and receiving it, otherwise Satan overcomes them.

"The power of the devil is very definitely acknowledged in Scripture, so, for us to deny it when God admits it, is sheer folly. In fact, men are held captive by the power of Satan until delivered from it by the power of the Saviour.

"Our adversary is a supernatural person occupying a superior position and exercising supernatural power. He is supreme dictator over the kingdom of evil; a pastmaster in every phase of diabolical deception and deviltry to be used in the seduction and destruction of human souls, and the instigator of all hatred and rebellion toward God and His Son," as vividly described by Ruth Paxson.

What does Scripture say about the power of Satan? Certainly, his power is acknowledged! The Lord Jesus says,

> *Delivering thee from the people, and from the Gentiles, unto whom now I send thee,*
> *To open their eyes, and to turn them from darkness to light, and from the power of Satan unto God* [Acts 26:17–18].

Note that Jesus says to deliver the people from the power of Satan. Paul talks about the power of Satan saying, *Satan with all power and signs and lying wonders, And with all deceivableness of unrighteousness in* (unrighteous deception among) *them that perish; because they received not the love of the truth, that they might be saved* [2 Thess. 2:9–10]. We have seen that Satan has a position and power. Therefore, it is well to ask, what is his purpose?

Isaiah reveals much about Satan saying,

> *How art thou fallen from heaven, O Lucifer* (Day Star)*, son of the morning! how art thou cut down to the ground, which didst weaken the nations!*
> *For thou hast said in thine heart, I will ascend into heaven, I will exalt my throne above the stars of God: I will sit also upon the mount of the congregation, in the (farthest) sides of the north:*
> *I will ascend above the heights of the clouds: I will be like the most High* [Isa. 14:12–14].

"From Genesis through Revelation Satan is revealed as an arch-traitor in open revolt against God. Was he always thus? . . . As Lucifer, son of the morning, he was God's noblest and most beautiful angelic creation. 'Perfect in beauty and in all his ways' and 'full of wisdom,' he was a being gifted with marvelous intelligence and glorious in holiness. In position . . . , being nearer to God Himself and in closer relationship to His throne . . . Such a position gave him power second to that of God alone.

"But, incredible as it seems, his heart was lifted up with pride, which led to self-exaltation, ending in rebellion. Open revolt against God followed, and Lucifer, son of the morning, became Satan, father of the night, and king over the kingdom of darkness, Satan would no longer be second in position and power, but first. So he purposed to dethrone God . . . and to displace Him in the worship of angels and men by becoming their god.

"When Lucifer said 'I will,' sin began in God's universe. How awful was the fall of heaven's greatest and most glorious archangel! Satan's sin was high treason, and brought down upon him the immediate condemnation and punishment of God. He was cast out of heaven and [from] the immediate presence of God and deprived of his position," as related by Ruth Paxson under the influence of the Holy Spirit.

Satan's objective is to be like God. When he committed treason, he was cast from heaven and will never be allowed to return unless he asks for forgiveness, and he will not do that! Though Satan has been cast from heaven he continues to attack and to fight God and the people of God.

What then can we say about the devil? He is a person with power, a purpose, and a position. He is an adversary who is completely and totally against us. Two verses aptly describe him. First,

> *And the dragon* (the devil) *was wroth with the woman, and went to make war with the remnant of her seed, which keep the commandments of God, and have the testimony of Jesus Christ* [Rev. 12:17].

Second, Jesus says,

> *Ye are of your father the devil, and the lusts* (desires) *of your father ye will do. He was a murderer from the beginning, and abode* (stands) *not in the truth, because there is no truth in him. When he speaketh a lie, he speaketh of his own* (nature): *for he is a liar, and the father of it* [John 8:44].

Further, Jesus says,

> *If Satan also be divided against himself, how shall his kingdom stand? because ye say that I cast out devils* (demons) *through Beelzebub.*
> *And if I by Beelzebub cast out devils* (demons), *by whom do your sons cast them out* [Luke 11:18–19]?

When considering these teachings is it any wonder that Paul says,

> *For we wrestle . . . against principalities, . . . powers, spiritual wickedness in high places* [Eph. 6:12].

What is Satan's plan? What did he do to Adam and Eve? He tempted them into self-will and disobedience to God, and he succeeded. He does not want us to be in a right relationship with God. He does not want us to obey God and to worship Him. Further, as stated in Isaiah, the devil wants to be like the most high. What does the devil plan to do? The Apostle Paul says,

> *Let no man deceive you by any means: for that day shall not come, except there come a falling away first, and that man of sin be revealed, the son of perdition;*
>
> *Who opposeth and exalteth himself above all that is called God, or that is worshipped; so that he as God sitteth in the temple of God, showing himself that he is God* [2 Thess. 2:3–4].

Satan gladly gives his power and authority to any man. He will support those who have revolted against God and are outside His kingdom.

The activities of Satan are apparent throughout the world. They are seen in the developments between nations, in the apostasy among professing Christians, in the false religions, and in local affairs.

What is the result of Satan's revolt and his activities? There has to be just retribution for Satan, his followers, and all those who rebel against God. A place had to be prepared for them. Jesus is explicit about this, saying, *Depart from me, ye cursed, into everlasting fire, prepared for the devil and his angels* [Matt. 25:41]. Most importantly, God prepared and provided a way to redeem sinners from serving Satan. This redemption is accomplished through His Son, the Lord Jesus Christ.

The Apostle Paul makes this very clear, saying, *Then cometh the end, when he shall have delivered up the kingdom to God, even the Father; when he shall have put down all rule and all authority and power* [1 Cor. 15:24]. No wonder Paul says,

> *Finally, my brethren, be strong in the Lord, and in the power of his might.*
>
> *Put on the whole armor of God, that ye may be able to stand against the wiles* (schemes) *of the devil* [Eph. 6:10–11].

Paul knew the devil and what he was like. However, much more importantly, he knew the Lord Jesus Christ and what he was like. He knew the power and strength available from His Lord would overcome the devil and his legions. It is the things of the Spirit that change us, strengthen us, and provide for our every need. Remember: Jesus said, *I am the way, the truth, and the life: no man cometh unto the Father, but by me* [John 14:6]. Amen!

13

The Combatants

> *For we wrestle not against flesh and blood, but against principalities, against powers, against the rulers of the darkness of this world* (age)*, against spiritual* (hosts of) *wickedness in high places* [Eph. 6:12].

The wiles (schemes) *of the devil.* Doesn't that have an interesting ring? It has a certain attractiveness. At first glance, it appears to be a rather innocuous phrase referring to something that can be handled rather easily. Certainly something that cannot be controlled or cast off without too much difficulty.

What about *the wiles* (schemes) *of the devil*? What does it mean? What does it involve?

The more I study Scripture and seek to understand the teachings contained in the Old and New Testaments, the more amazed I am at the breadth and depth of knowledge contained in the Word of God. You will recall that Paul spent three years among the Ephesians teaching them from house to house. His letter is a synopsis of those teachings. Therefore, it is our responsibility to probe the verses, the phrases, and the words in order to acquire the proper understanding.

The words *wile* or *wiles* appear only in the New Testament and only in Ephesians. It must have had significance to Paul. Look how he uses the word, where it is located, what precedes it, and what follows. He has told us to . . . *be strong in the Lord, and in the power of his might.* And to *Put on the whole armor of God, that ye may be able to stand against the wiles* (schemes) *of the devil* [Eph. 6:10–11]. To stand against what? *The wiles* (schemes) *of the devil*!

It does not take a lot of imagination to realize that the Apostle is exhorting us to be strong, to use the full power and might of the Lord, and to *put on the whole armor of God*. He is not going to counsel us to do those things and to take appropriate precautions against a foe that is not formidable and aggressive. Certainly, he would not use the same language if he were talking about a weak, passive enemy.

One night after the Boston Celtics beat a weak team by a large margin, Kevin McHale said by way of explanation, "A team you are supposed to beat badly, you are supposed to go out and beat them badly." Paul tells the saints and faithful, if you want to stand against this formidable foe, then you had better prepare yourself by becoming dependent not upon yourself but upon God Almighty.

Paul "puts before us a formidable enemy, not to overwhelm us with fear, but to sharpen our diligence and earnestness. For there is a middle course to be observed. When the enemy is neglected, he does his utmost to oppress us with sloth, and afterwards discourages us by terror; so that, before we have been touched, we are vanquished. By speaking of the power of the enemy, Paul labours to keep us more zealous.

"He names *principalities and powers*, to strike us with alarm, yet not to fill us with dismay, . . . but to arouse caution. He then calls them . . . princes of the world; and in explanation he adds *of the darkness of the age*. He means that the devil reigns in the world, because the world is nothing but darkness, hence it follows that the corruption of the world gives place to the kingdom of the devil. For he could not reside in a pure and sound creature of God. It all arises from the sinfulness of men. By 'darkness,' . . . he means unbelief and ignorance of God, with their consequences," according to John Calvin.

After warning us to take the utmost precautions, he tells us how vast, far flung, and extensive are the adversaries loyal to the devil. They include principalities, powers, *the rulers of the darkness of this world* (age)*, and spiritual* (hosts of) *wickedness in high places*. Paul is not talking about a friendly game of bridge, backgammon, golf, or numerous other contests. He is talking about the game of life, about your relationship to the Lord Jesus Christ, and about being obedient to God's will. The Apostle knows what is required to stand and knows that the devil will use everything he possibly can to cause one of the faithful saints to fall.

Second, what does *wiles* mean? It denotes dexterity and skill, especially as it relates to deceit or cunning devices. It is getting people to succumb to errors, to do the wrong things. It is used to denote not only lying in wait to deceive, but actively seeking to deceive.

The wiles (schemes) *of the devil* are not gentle drops of spring rain that nourish the flowers, plants, and crops that bring forth abundant fruit. They are snares, traps, and evil forces causing a person to stumble and fall, thereby becoming subject to Satan.

The third point is: who is involved in *the wiles* (schemes) *of the devil*? You and me. We are both involved. Remember, the Apostle starts this section saying, *Finally, my brethren.* Next it involves the Lord, His strength, power, and might, and His whole armor. Last, it involves the devil, his wiles, and his evil forces.

There are certain things to bear in the forefront of our minds when studying these last verses of Ephesians. First, we are to understand that we are intimately involved in this whole process. Either we are in the body of Christ and obedient to Him, or we are subject to the dictates of the devil. We cannot extricate ourselves from this struggle. We are part and parcel of it.

We are to realize that in this struggle we are to focus on the Lord Jesus. We are to look for Him. We are to see Him as we consider these truths. We are to be like the Greeks who said, *Sir, we would see Jesus.*

Pray God that we will see Jesus at close hand when studying these truths. We are not, and I repeat not, studying about Jesus or about the Scripture. We are studying with Jesus, we are walking with Him. He is not afar off, He is nigh. He is in the midst of us if we but let Him.

By the same token the devil is not a figment of our imagination. Peter accurately describes him, saying, *Your adversary, the devil, as a roaring lion, walketh about, seeking whom he may devour* [1 Pet. 5:8]. Suffice it to say, there is a struggle. And like it or not we are involved, we support one side or the other. Therefore, it is important to know more about this great conflict and our role in it.

What is this conflict between God and the Lord Jesus Christ on one side and the devil and his evil forces on the other side that involves us? Today there is not much written about the devil, nor is there much preaching or teaching about him and his legions. However, as noted previously, the devil is identified many times in both the Old and New Testaments.

Ezekiel, Isaiah, and Job tell us about the devil and his conflict with God. It involves them, and it involves us. Job says, *Now there was a day when the sons of God came to present themselves before the Lord, and Satan* (the adversary) *came also among them* [Job 1:6]. Isaiah and Ezekiel tell us that Lucifer, the son of the morning, was cast out of heaven. Job tells us that Satan was . . . *going to and fro in the earth, and from walking up and down in it* [Job 1:7]. Ezekiel tells us that Satan wants to be as God, to sit in the seat of God, and to set his *heart as the heart of God* [Ezek. 28:6].

Satan opposes God. Jude says,

> *Likewise also these filthy dreamers defile the flesh, despise dominion* (reject authority), *and speak evil of dignities* (glorious ones).
>
> *Yet Michael the archangel, when contending* (disputing) *with the devil he disputed* (discussed) *about the body of Moses, durst* (dared) *not bring against him a railing* (reviling) *accusation, but said, The Lord rebuke thee.*
>
> *But these speak evil of those things which they know not: but what they know naturally, as brute beasts, in those things they corrupt themselves* [Jude 8–10].

Note what Michael said when encountering Satan, *The Lord rebuke thee*. Nothing more, nothing less, nothing else. Both the Old and New Testaments are definite about the existence of the devil.

Another fine example is given in Paul's letter to Timothy. *Not a novice* (new convert), *lest being lifted up with pride he fall into the condemnation of the devil* [1 Tim. 3:6]. Calvin and Chrysostom believed that the condemnation of Satan in this instance is passive, not active, but it is still real, not hypothetical. Paul urges Timothy not to let the elders *fall into reproach and the snare of the devil* [1 Tim. 3:7]. Calvin interprets this lest the person "begin(s) to harden his heart and abandon himself more freely to all kinds of wickedness, which is indeed to entangle himself in the devil's snares."

Why did Satan rebel? Why was he cast out? Why is he at enmity with God? Why did God allow this to happen? Why are we involved? Certainly, these are questions to ponder.

Satan was one of the most able, gifted, and powerful angels. However, he did not want to remain in a position of subservience to God. So what did he do? He rebelled against God. What happened? He was cast out. He was punished. He was degraded.

Think of that for a moment. Here was an angel created by God, and what happened to him? If God will cast out one of his angels, what about us? What about those who deny Him or disobey Him? It gets pretty tough! It is something to think about! Of course, the question is bound to be asked, "Why would God allow this to happen?"

We will not know the answer in this life. However, it may be that the answer is closely akin to this: God created the angels and He created them perfectly. This means that they probably were endowed with free will, since they were created by God. Therefore, Satan used his free will to disobey God and to try to be like Him. Satan exercised his free will in the wrong way; He became opposed to God. Therefore, he was cast out. Since then he has been at enmity with God.

What about Adam? He was created perfect and free. He was in the garden. He had everything he needed. However, God commanded Adam not to eat . . . *of the tree of the knowledge of good and evil, . . . for in the day that thou eatest thereof thou shalt surely die* [Gen. 2:17]. So what did Adam do? He disobeyed God and succumbed to the wiles of the serpent. Adam exercised his free will, and as a result he fell, he was not able to stand. He was neither strong in the Lord nor in the power of his might.

Certainly, we need to be aware of these truths concerning God, Satan, and Adam. Fortunately, more knowledge is available to enlighten us. The Book of Revelation [Rev. 12:4] reveals that when Satan was cast down he took other angelic beings with him. He did not go by himself. The Apostle Peter says, *For if God spared not the angels that sinned, but cast them down to hell, and delivered them into chains of darkness, to be reserved unto judgment* [2 Pet. 2:4]. Jude says, *And the angels which kept not their first estate* (proper domain), *but left their own habitation, he hath reserved in everlasting chains under darkness unto the judgment of the great day* [Jude 6]. The devil and others were cast out because of disobedience and enmity against God. Adam was cast out of the garden because of disobedience and going against the will of God.

What impact does this have upon us? Hopefully, we understand that Almighty God is a God of order interested in us and our welfare, whereas the devil is opposed to God, wants to produce chaos, and wants us to be disobedient to Him. The devil wants the world in darkness, while God wants it in light.

In order to understand conditions in the world, we need to realize what causes the chaos. It is opposition to the will of God. It is enmity to God. It is disobedience to God. It is self-centeredness. It is succumbing to *the wiles* (schemes) *of the devil*. This condition existed prior to Adam and Eve.

It goes back to Lucifer, son of the morning. God created the world and Adam and all that was on the earth. And God saw that it was good. *And God saw that everything that he had made, and, behold, it was very good* [Gen. 1:31].

How and when evil came into the world remains a mystery. However, we know Satan came into the world and beguiled the woman. As a result Adam and Eve disobeyed God and became slaves to the devil. This should help us understand why Satan is referred to as *the god of this world* or as *the prince of the power of the air, the spirit that now worketh in the children of disobedience* [Eph. 2:2]. Also, it should help us to understand our Master's words to Paul, *To open their eyes, and to turn them from darkness to light, and from the power of Satan unto God* [Acts 26:18].

Paul's words to the Colossians support Peter's words. *Who hath delivered us from the power of darkness, and hath translated* (transferred) *us into the kingdom of his dear Son* (the Son of his love) [Col. 1:13]. Paul says to the Romans, *For sin shall not have dominion over you* [Rom. 6:14]. The "implication is that it (sin) had dominion over them before they became Christians," as clarified by Martyn Lloyd-Jones.

Scripture enlightens us regarding the difference between those who are of God and those who are of Satan. *And we know that we are of God, and the whole world lieth in wickedness* [1 John 5:19]. The Apostle John wants us to know that sin is evident and that it takes its toll in the community. He wants the faithful believers in Christ "To beware of sin and to encourage them to repel the assaults of Satan," as John Calvin admonishes and encourages us.

The saints and faithful are exposed to sin and encounter it in their daily activities and duties. Therefore, they are to be strengthened in the power of His might. Why? Because wherever they go, wherever they look, whatever they do, they will find Satan with all his allurements and enticements.

The Apostle reminds us that God has called us and He strengthens us. On the other hand, there is wickedness in the world which separates us from God. One thing we need to understand is that man's history has been greatly influenced by God, Satan, and Adam. This disobedience, rebellion, and self-centeredness of Satan and Adam affects each and every one of us.

Man is subject to *the wiles* (schemes) *of the devil* unless he becomes *strong in the Lord, and in the power of his might*. If this does not happen then a person becomes Satan's slave. Hopefully, understanding the origin of evil enables us to understand the condition of the world and the actions of different people. Also, it enable us to understand the wiles of the evil one, and to change our ways, attitudes, thoughts, and conduct. Then by God's grace and the power of His might we will be able to stand against *the wiles* (schemes) *of the devil.*

What is required to do that? What must we *put on*? What must we know? What must we do? The answer to each of these questions is exactly the same: the Lord Jesus Christ. Who is Satan's adversary that is able to defeat him? It is none other than Christ Himself. He is the one who can stand against him by Himself, and He is the only one who can.

You can search the scriptures, you can search recorded history, and you can look far and wide, but there is only One who can stand against the devil and his wiles. That is why Paul exhorts us to . . . *be strong in the Lord, and in the power of his might.* We are to be involved with Him; we are to be in Him. It is more than knowing Him. It is more than knowing about Him.

Martin Luther forcefully and revealingly captures the essence of these truths in his great hymn, "A Mighty Fortress Is Our God."

> *A mighty fortress is our God, a bulwark work never failing;*
> *Our helper He amid the flood of mortal ills prevailing;*
> *For still our ancient foe doth seek to work us woe;*
> *His craft and power are great, and, armed with cruel hate,*
> *On earth is not his equal.*
>
> *Did we in our own strength confide, our striving would be losing;*
> *Were not the right Man on our side,*
> *The man of God's own choosing.*
> *Dost ask who that may be?*
> *Christ Jesus, it is He, Lord Sabaoth His name,*
> *From age to age the same, and He must win the battle.*
>
> *And though this world, with devils filled,*
> *should threaten to undo us,*
> *We will not fear, for God hath willed His truth*
> *to triumph through us.*
> *The prince of darkness grim, We tremble not for him;*
> *His rage we can endure,*
> *For lo! His doom is sure, One little word shall fell him.*

> *That word above all earthly powers, No thanks to them, abideth;*
> *The Spirit and the gifts are ours through Him who with us sideth;*
> *Let goods and kindred go, This mortal life also;*
> *The body they may kill:*
> *God's truth abideth still, His kingdom is forever.*

Naturally, we love to read, especially at Christmas, those beautiful verses from Isaiah,

> *For unto us a child is born, unto us a son is given: and the government shall be upon his shoulder: and his name shall be called Wonderful, Counselor, The mighty God, The everlasting Father, The Prince of Peace.*
> *Of the increase of His government and peace there shall be no end* [Isa. 9:6–7].

We also love the opening chapters of Matthew and Luke, which beautifully describe the coming of the Christ child. But we are to grow beyond that. We are to move from being observers to being combatants. That is what we are called to be.

Why was the Christ child born? Why did He go to the Cross? To defeat His antagonist, Satan; to call us unto Himself; to enable us *to stand against the wiles* (schemes) *of the devil*; to strengthen us so that we may be obedient to God the Father; and to enlighten us regarding *the way, the truth, and the life.*

It is quite apparent that Satan did not want Christ to come into the world. He did not want Him to embark upon His ministry. He did not want Him to go to the Cross. And, he did not want Him to rise again. These events assured Satan's defeat, even though the struggle against him continues.

> *Forasmuch then as the children are partakers of flesh and blood, he also himself likewise took* (shared) *part of the same; that through death he might destroy him that had the power of death, that is, the devil;*
> *And deliver them who through fear of death were all their lifetime subject to bondage* (slavery) [Heb. 2:14–15].

The devil cannot have power against us when we are in Christ. It is when we seek to go it alone that Satan causes us to fall. *He that committeth* (practices) *sin is of the devil; for the devil sinneth from the beginning. For this purpose the Son of God was manifested, that he might destroy the works of the devil* [1 John 3:8]. Colossians, according to Weymouth's translation, says, *And the hostile princes and rulers He stripped off from Himself, and boldly displayed them as His conquests, when by the cross He triumphed over them* [Col. 2:15]. It is Christ who has triumphed, not us. But as members of His body we are victorious.

Have you ever noticed how people like to be part of the winning team or party? Paul knew he was part of the winning team. He knew the Captain. He mentions the Lord Jesus no less than sixty-six times in this letter to the Ephesians. He wants us to know that wherever we walk on earth, or whatever we do, the Master is nigh, He is available. He will enable us to stand. We can have communion with Him.

Make no mistake, Satan is still a formidable foe, but he is no match for the Lord Jesus Christ, who has all authority. *All power* (privilege and authority) *is given unto me in heaven and in earth* [Matt. 28:18]. Satan's power falls into several categories. It is permitted of God. *For there is no power but of God* [Rom. 13:1].

Satan offered Christ the kingdom of the world saying when making the offer, *All these things will I give thee, if thou wilt fall down and worship me* [Matt. 4:9]. Satan's power is limited. This is confirmed in Job, when God told Satan not to put forth his hand on Job, and He saved his life.

Satan could do certain things, but not others. Satan's power is resisted by and through prayer. The Lord Jesus tells Peter on the night He was betrayed, *Simon, Simon, behold, Satan hath desired to have you, that he may sift you as wheat: But I have prayed for thee, that thy faith fail not* [Luke 22:31–32]. The author of Hebrews says, *Wherefore he is able to save them to the uttermost that come unto God by him, seeing he ever liveth to make intercession for them* [Heb. 7:25]. Satan's power has been broken. This occurred on Calvary's Hill on the Cross where Jesus shed His blood for you and me.

Satan's power is doomed. The Apostle John is very explicit:

> *And he laid hold on the dragon, that old serpent, which is the Devil, and Satan, and bound him a thousand years,*
> *And cast him into the bottomless pit, and shut him up, and set a seal upon him, that he should deceive the nations no more, till the thousand years should be fulfilled* [Rev. 20:2–3].

Yes, Satan is a formidable foe, but we are members of Christ's body, and He is with us.

Remember, Paul said, *Finally, my brethren, be strong in the Lord, and in the power of his might. Put on the whole armor of God, that ye may be able to stand against the wiles* (schemes) *of the devil* [Eph. 6:10–11]. We are facing a formidable foe. However, we have the whole armor of God, and the strength of the Lord Jesus Christ on our side, enabling us to defend ourselves against *the wiles* (schemes) *of the devil* and to repel him.

May we remember these truths and act accordingly all the days that God gives us.

Amen!

14

The Devil and His Forces

Put on the whole armor of God, that ye may be able to stand against the wiles (schemes) *of the devil* [Eph. 6:11].

We previously considered "The Combatants" in the epic struggle between God and Satan. Whether we like it or not, we are participants in this struggle. Therefore, it is important to acquire knowledge about the adversaries to understand the antagonists, the conflict, and the impact it has upon our daily lives, as well as our relationships to God, the Lord Jesus Christ, our families, and members of the community of believers.

Daily living, contacts, and responsibilities guide us in shaping our thoughts and actions. Therefore, it is important to consider daily situations as well as the more monumental ones occurring at different intervals in our lives. Yes, we are to prepare ourselves not only for the more significant situations or developments, but also for the routine encounters and relationships contributing to our pleasure or displeasure.

As we continue studying Ephesians, remember we are studying with Jesus, and we are walking with Him. We are not just studying about Him, nor about the Word of God, nor about the Apostle Paul. We are proceeding to become intimately involved with Jesus: rejoicing with Him, suffering with Him, seeking to do His will, obeying His commands, and striving to do as He would have us to do.

Our focal point is the Lord Jesus Christ. This is not easy. Why? Because old self has a habit of getting in the way. If our focal point is the Lord Jesus Christ, then we should be interested in those things in which

He was interested. Further, we are to learn from His vast teachings, His conduct, and apply them to our lives.

Certainly, the Lord Jesus acknowledged the existence and the presence of the devil. Can we do less? Christ encountered the devil at the beginning of His ministry, at the close of it, and during it. It was a continuing encounter.

The apostles were well aware of the devil and his forces. They wrote about him, and they counseled the saints and the faithful regarding his power and cunning deceitfulness. The Apostle Paul wrote his letters prior to the four Gospels being written. They stress the importance of being in a right relationship with God when combating Satan and his power.

Under the influence of the Holy Spirit, Paul was concerned with the basic relationships a person has during his lifetime. First, our relationships with God, the Lord Jesus Christ, and the Gospel; second, with other people, those who are members of Christ's body and those who are not; and third, with ourselves. The Apostle was interested in people, their challenges, and spiritual growth. He was interested in relationships, as well as the devil and his malignant, negative impact on people, especially the saints and faithful.

Paul tells the Corinthians, in his Second Letter that it is the Gospel of the Lord Jesus Christ, not his Gospel nor his ministry, that is so wonderful. He stresses the fact it was God's mercy that revealed the Gospel to him. Further, he was trying to make manifest the Gospel so that the followers would receive *the light of the knowledge of the glory of God in the face of Jesus Christ* [2 Cor. 4:6].

Calvin amplifies upon the phrase, *in the face of Jesus Christ* saying that "Christ is the image of the Father and when he says here that in His face God's glory is revealed to us his meaning is the same. This is an important passage from which *we may learn that God is* not to be sought after in His inscrutable majesty . . . but is to be known so far as He reveals Himself in Christ. Thus the attempts of men to know God apart from Christ are ephemeral for they wander from the right way. It is true that at first sight God in Christ seems to be low and abject, but His glory appears to those who have the patience to pass on from the Cross to the resurrection. Again we see that in the word *persona*—here rendered 'face'—there is reference to us, because it is more profitable for us to behold God as He appears in his only begotten Son than to investigate His secret essence."

Paul knew the Corinthians and many others through the ages within the community of believers would be exposed to *hidden things of dishonesty, not walking in craftiness*, and *handling the word of God deceitfully* [2 Cor. 4:2]. He knew that these things were happening and would continue to happen. Then he inserts that little, big word "but" and says, *But if our gospel be hid, it is hid to them that are lost* [2 Cor. 4:2]. Why are they lost? Why don't they receive the Gospel? Why don't they know the Lord Jesus Christ?

He provides the answer, saying, . . . *the god of this world hath blinded the minds of them which believe not, lest the light of the glorious gospel* (the glory) *of Christ, who is the image of God, should shine unto them* [2 Cor. 4:4]. Paul is saying, " . . . those who find his message difficult to accept . . . (and are) criticizing his ministry (are) lost, unbelieving, and . . . blinded by Satan," (King James Study Bible). There is no question that the Apostle is speaking of the devil. This raises an interesting point. The devil is called a god. *For though there be that are called gods, . . . (as there be gods many, and lords many,)* [1 Cor. 8:5]. Baal was called a god by those who worshipped him.

The devil is said to blind people and to have dominion over them. According to Calvin's exposition, Satan does have power and dominion. Scripture speaks of the devils as ministers of God. Satan is referred to as the prince of the world. However, his power is limited.

Yet when his power is exercised over people, they do not see the light of the Gospel, nor do they see and know the Lord Jesus. Paul says to the Corinthians that if anyone rejects our Gospel it is because their blindness keeps them from accepting it. It is Christ who is the image of God and allows the Gospel to shine. If we are to know the Father, we must see and know the Son first. Jesus Himself says, *If ye had known me, ye should have known my Father, also* [John 14:7]. Paul wants the light of the Gospel to shine, nothing else, and certainly not himself.

In writing to the Corinthians, Paul wanted to bring out into the open a sin committed by one of the members. He knew this act would have a negative impact upon the local congregation and their relationships with God and each other. Therefore, he condemned the sin, but he strongly urged forgiveness. Paul realized that sin should be dealt with severely, but he believed the sinner should be forgiven when he truly repented. The people needed to know that the sin was not acceptable, but the person who sincerely repented and changed his or her ways was to be forgiven and accepted.

Paul's words in 2 Corinthians are so meaningful, so vitally important to the life of a family, to the life of a class, to a congregation, and to any group. Therefore, give heed to his words, *To whom ye forgive any thing, I forgive also: for if I forgave anything, to whom I forgave it, for your sakes forgave I it in the person* (presence) *of Christ; Lest Satan should get an advantage of us: for we are not ignorant of his devices* [2 Cor. 2:10–11]. Paul emphasizes that it is not himself who is forgiving them, nor are they themselves forgiving a member, but it is in Christ that they are forgiving another person. The act of forgiveness occurs because of and in the name of Christ. Without Him, there is not forgiveness. Then he adds a reason for forgiving when he says, *Lest Satan should get an advantage of us; for we are not ignorant of his devices.*

What does Scripture teach? If we do not forgive others, then Satan will take advantage of us. People are willing to forgive the preacher at certain times or to forgive certain people. However, our Lord never put any limits on forgiveness. We are to forgive and to accept the repentant sinner. People can talk about love, about God, about Christ, but if they do not truly and sincerely bestow forgiveness upon all repentant sinners without limitation, then they are not doing the will of the Father, nor are they obeying the commands of the Lord Jesus Christ.

Like his Master, Paul was concerned with the attitude and disposition of the Pharisees. They wanted to cast the sinner down and stomp on him, berate him, and castigate him, but they did not want to heal him and forgive him. Scripture teaches we are to be hard on the sin, but not on the sinner.

Paul makes a succinct and revealing statement regarding Satan saying, *for we are not ignorant of his devices.* He is saying we have knowledge of his devices. The Greek word for *devices* in this verse is *noēma* which denotes "having thought" or "thought out" what he is doing. He understands the purposes, mind, and thoughts of the devil. These verses reveal that Paul, as well as the Holy Ghost and the Lord Jesus, knew the devil. They knew him as an individual entity; they could identify him and relate to him.

The members of Christ's body are to be aware of the fact that the devil uses direct and indirect attacks in an effort to catch us off guard and subdue us. We need to know that Satan will do everything possible to find a chink in our armor and exploit it to weaken and subdue us. In addition, we have the teachings in Ephesians, which are directed toward the individual and enable him or her *to stand against the wiles* (schemes) *of the devil.*

What must we do to stand? We must know how the devil operates. Satan will do anything and everything to draw us into sin and to get us to disobey God's commandments. He will attack us actively, directly or indirectly, in any conceivable way to get us to disobey God, or to keep us from knowing the Lord Jesus. He is subtle beyond imagination. He will use any conceivable advantage or ploy.

The devil is after the mind of each person. He does not want anyone to glorify God or to enjoy Him forever. How does he do this? There are many, many ways. Consider a few of his ploys.

He will do it by insinuation. In Genesis the devil said unto Eve, *Yea, hath God said* [Gen. 3:1]. Prior to that time neither Adam nor Eve ever questioned God.

Satan will deny Scripture. He will belittle repentance. He will extol virtues such as good works. He will prod people to think of their rights. He will poke fun at the scriptures. "O, what need have we to study the Scriptures, our hearts, and Satan's wiles, that we may not bid this enemy welcome and all the while think it is Christ that is our guest," as William Gurnall states with incisive wisdom.

Satan seeks to have us succumb to his invitations and to travel with him, on the pretense that it does not make any difference, or everyone is doing it, or who will know, or for any other seemingly plausible reason. Satan plays upon emotions, not the mind.

We need to realize that any number of people have said they would only go a short distance with Satan, then they go a mile, and before they know it, they go two or three. Remember, these teachings are directed toward the saints and faithful. They are not directed toward those who are outside the body of Christ.

Satan will instigate false teachings. *NOW the Spirit speaketh expressly, that in the latter times some shall depart from the faith, giving heed to seducing* (deceiving) *spirits, and doctrines of devils* [1 Tim. 4:1]. Some teachings will turn away from the *doctrines of devils* or *Satan* or *seducing spirits*, or *the antichrist*, or John's First Letter, or the Book of Revelation. There are also teachings or expressions questioning the virgin birth, God incarnate, the resurrection, or the presence and power of the Holy Spirit.

The devil with his wiles will use a two-pronged approach. He will instigate false teachings, and he will get preachers and teachers to concentrate on certain subjects or portions of Scripture, while completely ignoring other parts, especially the grief, misery, allurements, and enticements of the devil. There needs to be a balance, but Satan does not want that.

Satan loves to tempt the saints and faithful. He loves to attack the members of Christ's body. That is why we are to know about him and what he does, how he operates, and how he uses people.

It makes a great difference in our attitude toward others when we understand that it is the devil that causes them to do certain things. When we understand that Satan tempts us and attacks us directly and indirectly, we will have a different attitude toward ourselves and others.

Therefore, we are to take refuge in the Word of God. It is stated appropriately by the psalmist.

> *The law of the Lord is perfect, converting* (restoring) *the soul: the testimony of the Lord is sure, making wise the simple.*
> *The statutes of the Lord are right, rejoicing the heart: the commandment of the Lord is pure, enlightening the eyes.*
> *The fear of the Lord is clean, enduring forever: The judgments of the Lord are true and righteous altogether.*
> *More to be desired are they than gold: yea, than much fine gold: sweeter also than honey and the honeycomb* (drippings of the honeycomb) [Ps. 19:7–10].

There is another area in which the devil is very active. That is in scholarship, in modern knowledge, and in man's pride of his intellect. Yes, thanks to God there have been developments during the centuries, and more knowledge is available for man to use. But what is new when it comes to God's revealed truth and our relationship to Him? What is new regarding the earthly ministry and teachings of Christ, or man's relationship with man, or man's relationship with himself?

The Apostle wrote about these questions and issues. It is the same old thing; people want to put themselves first and God second, third, or fourth. Therefore, they are "ripe pickings" for the devil, who will tempt and seduce them. He loves to create confusion, to be a troubler, an accuser, a molester, and a disquieting influence.

Another one of the devil's wiles is to aggravate the sins of the saints and faithful. He does this in various ways. He will try to create doubt that you are a child of God or a member of Christ's body. He is not above accusing you of something in God's name. He will twist information. He will want you to think that he, Satan, would never attack you. He will strive to keep you from acquiring knowledge about God, from learning the truths of Christ, from walking with the Master. If he can do those things then he will be able to keep you from knowing the full grace, mercy, and love of God in the Lord Jesus Christ. He wants people to think that their sins exceed God's mercy, grace, and love, but they cannot.

The devil will attack us with evil thoughts and try to create the idea that since we have evil thoughts, we must not be members of Christ's body, or we are not members in good standing. Consequently, we will believe there is something wrong with us.

The real question is: do we encourage these thoughts or do we reject them, dislike them, and turn from them to God? The rain falls on the just and unjust. So do temptations and evil thoughts. They are so personal and have a real allurement. Therefore, we must address them and deal with them.

This leads to two old bugaboos that plague the saints and faithful from time to time or for extended periods. They are depression and discouragement. How does Satan do this? How does he attack us? Satan employs the following against us in his ongoing war with God: appealing to one's ego or guilty conscience through guile and subtlety; deceiving one to turn his/her eyes inwardly, instead of focusing upon God the Father; and having someone dwell inordinately on life's negatives and sins committed, rather than on God's mercy, love, grace, and forgiveness.

Satan will try to make us miserable and unhappy. He will taunt us, saying, "So you thought you were a Christian," "You thought God cared for you," "Why would God let this or that happen to you?" Satan keeps up this barrage. Why? Because he does not want us to turn to God, confess our sins, and claim His promises. The Apostle John reveals that *If we confess our sins, he is faithful and just to forgive us our sins, and to cleanse us from all unrighteousness* [1 John 1:9]. Difficult as it may be, our attention is to be focused upon God and His Son, not upon ourselves.

Satan will raise trivial objections to our duties and responsibilities as members of Christ's body. How can we deal with these things? By becoming familiar and knowledgeable about Scripture and the Lord Jesus Christ. William Gurnall tells us with sage understanding that we are to "Observe the fallacy of Satan's argument, which discovered, will help thee to answer his cavil."

Last, there is that one nemesis that causes us to fall and not stand. It is called pride. We see it at the beginning in Genesis, where Satan says, *Yea, hath God said*. We see it in the Old Testament. *AND Satan stood up against Israel, and provoked* (moved) *David to number* (take a census of) *Israel* [1 Chr. 21:1]. Satan attacked David by tempting his pride. What happened? Dire consequences followed for David and Israel.

In addition, we see pride throughout the New Testament. Paul advises Timothy not to appoint a novice or a person young in the faith to be an elder or bishop. The failure to heed this instruction has resulted in people being elected to office who should not have been and in errors being perpetrated within the church. The Apostle cautioned against appointing novices because the devil is almost certain to trap them. How true this is!

Pride exhibits itself in many ways. We can be oversensitive or insensitive. Pride leads to envy, jealousy, and carrying grudges. Pride is no respecter of persons. One thing is certain, pride spoils God's handiwork.

There are many *wiles* (schemes) *of the devil*. He will use them to attack us from different directions. The only way to deal with Satan and his wiles is to send them to Christ. That is one strong reason for Walking With Jesus. Another is *to be strong in the Lord, and in the power of his might* [Eph. 6:10].

It is comforting, stimulating, and strengthening to grasp and digest the meaningful truths of that great hymn "A Mighty Fortress Is Our God" by the renowned Martin Luther:

> *A mighty fortress is our God, a bulwark work never failing;*
> *Our helper He amid the flood of mortal ills prevailing;*
> *For still our ancient foe doth seek to work us woe;*
> *His craft and power are great, and, armed with cruel hate,*
> *On earth is not his equal.*
>
> *Did we in our own strength confide, our striving would be losing;*
> *Were not the right Man on our side,*
> *The man of God's own choosing.*
> *Dost ask who that may be? Christ Jesus, it is He,*
> *Lord Sabaoth His name,*
> *From age to age the same, and He must win the battle.*

And though this world, with devils filled,
should threaten to undo us,
We will not fear, for God hath willed His truth
to triumph through us.
The prince of darkness grim, We tremble not for him;
His rage we can endure,
For lo! His doom is sure, One little word shall fell him.

That word above all earthly powers, No thanks to them, abideth;
The Spirit and the gifts are ours through Him who with us sideth;
Let goods and kindred go, This mortal life also;
The body they may kill:
God's truth abideth still, His kingdom is forever.

Amen!

15

The Devil's Disguises

> *Put on the whole armor of God, that ye may be able to stand against the wiles* (schemes) *of the devil.*
> *For we wrestle not against flesh and blood, but against principalities, against the rulers of the darkness of this world* (age), *against spiritual* (hosts of) *wickedness in high places* [Eph. 6:11–12].

Why should we be concerned about *the wiles* (schemes) *of the devil,* and his followers?

The devil is opposed to God. He wants to attack, injure, defeat, neutralize, and overcome the members of Christ's body who are trying to obey God's commandments. The devil does not want us to be in a right relationship with God. Why? The more people in a right relationship with God and obeying His commandments, the stronger is Christ's impact on the members of His body. When more people accept Christ, the impact is seen in society, families, classes, businesses, education, and all other activities.

We are cognizant of the impact on non-church members and the occasional attendee or backslider when an active member of Christ's body succumbs to *the wiles* (schemes) *of the devil.* Therefore, the saints and faithful are prime targets for the devil and his forces. Paul knew that the devil would attack, attack, and attack the followers. He knew that the devil was an insidious and subtle foe who would use every conceivable tactic in order to gain an advantage. When considering the devil as being subtle it should alert our hearts and minds to the formidableness of this deceitful and devious opponent.

Subtle means all of the following: being delicate and refined; being mentally acute; exhibiting quick and ardent responsiveness; being highly skillful; being cunning, contriving, and ingenious; and being crafty, deceitful, and devious. It is important to know this subtle foe, if we are to serve the Lord Jesus and obey His commands.

It is likely that the Apostle placed this exhortation where he did because it follows immediately after the practical applications to guide us along life's pathway. The Apostle knew that people were susceptible to *the wiles of the devil* in their daily living and in their relationships with others, Almighty God, and to the Lord Jesus Christ. He wanted them to be prepared and conduct themselves as members of Christ's body.

He warned them because he wanted them to enjoy the wealth available from Christ, to walk with Christ, and to be capable of defending themselves.

Paul was intimately aware of these things. At one time, he had been the tool of the devil. He had been *breathing out threatenings and slaughter* (murder) against Christ's disciples. He had been persecuting the followers of the Lord. Then, he had seen in a most marvelous way the overwhelming power of God through the Lord Jesus on the road to Damascus. He had realized the strength of the Lord to prepare him for his life and ministry as an apostle. He realized the power of that strength through all his persecutions, beatings, failings, and rejections. Despite all these things, he was able to discuss the conflict between God and the devil, to place his trust in Christ, and to exert every effort to obey the Lord's commands.

As previously noted, the teaching and preaching of the twentieth century and of the early twenty-first century basically ignored the devil and his wiles. This is in direct contrast to the New Testament writers, who gave significant time and emphasis to the devil and how he operates.

Why did the New Testament authors write as they did? They could see what was happening among the saints and faithful. They knew Satan had tempted the Lord. They could see how people were being misled. They noticed that the followers were not always focusing on the Lord. They realized the people needed to know what Christ said and did in different situations. They were convinced the people of God needed to be forewarned and forearmed. They knew that it was anything but easy to follow the Master. The New Testament writers focused attention on

Satan. It is our responsibility to expound the scriptures and to know the teachings of our Master and the apostles concerning this relentless foe.

The apostles agreed with the teachings of the Lord Jesus. They agreed that the process of sanctification was difficult. That is why the teachings in the various Epistles are so direct and explicit. It is our responsibility to expose ourselves to them and to acquire knowledge so that we will not succumb to Satan and his subtle ploys.

How does the devil attack us? There are many, many ways. He attacks us from within and from without. First, the devil brings up old sins, mistakes, or errors in order to grieve us and to weaken us. Even though God has forgiven us and cleansed us, the devil will dredge up the past. He will try to get us to question God's pardoning mercy. When Moses was leading the Israelites they blamed their grief and miseries on him.

There are those who will sin in a saint's presence or tell him or her about it in order to taunt them. There are those who become smug because the devil makes them believe that their sins are not as grievous as someone else's. These people neither recognize the grace of God in bestowing His favor upon them nor realize it when God favors them. Why? Their attention is focused inwardly.

Of course, there are outside factors used by Satan to assail a person.

> BUT *there were false prophets also among the people, even as there shall be false teachers among you, who privily* (secretly) *shall bring in damnable* (destructive) *heresies, even denying the Lord that bought them, and bring upon themselves swift destruction.*
> *And many shall follow their pernicious* (destructive) *ways; by reason of whom the way of truth shall be evil* (blasphemed) *spoken of.*
> *And through covetousness shall they with feigned* (deceptive) *words make merchandise* (exploit) *of you: whose judgment now of a long time lingereth not* (has not been idle), *and their damnation* (destruction) *slumbereth not* [2 Pet. 2:1–3].

Calvin stressed during his ministry the importance of worshipping God and acquiring knowledge. Knowledge was second to worshipping God and the Lord Jesus Christ.

The people in the first century were plagued with false teachings. It has not been any different in every century since then, including this one. The false prophets and teachers disturbed the Israelites. After Christ's earthly ministry the converts to the Way thought that anyone who came in the name of Christ was preaching and teaching the truth. As Calvin notes, they "thought that the state of the church under the reign of Christ would be peaceful." People think the same today. Why?

Why did they think this? The prophets had promised that there would be lasting peace, that heavenly wisdom would provide a light to the world, and that all things would be restored. The early followers also thought that there would not be any conflicts within the church or among the called out.

Does any of that sound familiar? Pray God that we may be taught the truths of Christ. Pray God that He will meet the ever- present needs of churches and send preachers who will present the whole truth of God as it is revealed in Christ Jesus. Pray God that He will enlighten our hearts and minds so that we can distinguish between the truth as it is found in Christ and false teachings. We must progress to the point where we search the scriptures and hear what Christ is saying, not what I say or the preacher says, but what Scripture says.

Ruth Paxson points it out clearly and concisely, saying, "There is no length to which Satan will not go to dislodge the saint from his faith position in Christ." Satan will use teachers, preachers, and things of the world to lead people into wrong ways or provide them with false interpretations. Sometimes there are half-truths, a mixture of truths and errors.

Though it is distasteful, it is important to recognize that the devil works within the organized church. He preys upon officers, teachers, and preachers. One thing is certain, he does not establish the church of Satan. In many respects, he does not have to do so. Peter warns us about false teachers *who privily* (secretly) *shall bring in damnable* (destruction) *heresies*. That is strong language. The word *privily* means "to bring in secretly" or "unaware," as bringing in spies or traitors. They come clothed as sheep, but they are ravenous wolves. Knowingly or unknowingly, they distort and pervert the truths of Christ.

Those *damnable heresies* mean "leading one to division and ruin." They do so by being part of a respected church, organization, or institution; stating that this is what a certain seminary or group has to say; and denying the words of our Master indirectly, or by innuendo, or by saying people are different in this day and time.

The true members of Christ's body must be: knowledgeable about the teachings in Scripture; and on guard against Satan's subtle innuendos. If they are not, then they are subject to following and expounding the pernicious, destructive ways of Satan.

Unfortunately, people write for publications that are sponsored by organized churches that do not know or do not present the truth as contained in Scripture. They have their own axes to grind.

An illustration of this is a young person presenting a message from material prepared by a church organization or publication. When challenged, the person responded, "Why, I got the information from such-and-such periodical." The real source, the only source, must be in checking what Scripture says and what it says in the original.

Note Peter's statement, *And through covetousness shall they with feigned* (fabricated) *words make merchandise* (exploit) *of you* [2 Pet. 2:3]. This is a graphic statement. It tells an important truth. The Apostle wants us to be aware of it, and so does Christ.

Peter wants the followers in the Way to beware of false teachers and their teachings. He realizes that the fabricated words are designed to deceive people, not to enlighten them. Other portions of Scripture warn us of false teachers and prophets:

> *For there shall arise false Christs, and false prophets, and shall show great signs and wonders; insomuch that, if it were possible, they shall deceive the very elect* [Matt. 24:24].

> *And many false prophets shall arise, and shall deceive many* [Matt. 24:11].

> *That we henceforth be no more children, tossed to and fro, and carried about with every wind of doctrine, by the sleight* (trickery) *of men, and cunning craftiness, whereby they lie in wait to deceive* [Eph. 4:14].

These truths are forcibly brought to our attention by Paul writing to the Thessalonians and saying,

> *Even him, whose coming is after the working of Satan with all power and signs and lying wonders,*
> *And with all deceivableness of unrighteousness* (unrighteous deception among) *in them that perish; because they received not the love of the truth, that they might be saved.*
> *And for this cause God shall send them strong delusion, that they should believe a (the) lie:*

> *That they all might be damned* (condemned) *who believe not the truth, but had pleasure in unrighteousness* [2 Thess. 2:9-12].

John Calvin adds significant emphasis to Paul's words that should send tremors through many professing Christians when he says, "They will receive punishment appropriate for their ungodliness."

Satan uses other ways to assault people. First, he tries to create doubt in their minds, just as he did with Adam and Eve asking, *Hath God said*? He will raise questions concerning God's Word and God's authority. Second, he tries to get us to disobey God's Word and His commandments.

The Bible states unequivocally that we have all sinned and come short of the glory of God. However, some teach there is no such thing as sin, or that sin is really not grievous in the sight of God, or that we do not have to be saved from our sins, or that everyone is going to heaven. Such rationalizations are asking people to disobey God.

Satan will try to deceive and delude us. What methods does he use? Paul says to the Corinthians, *For Satan himself is transformed* (transforms himself) *into an angel of light. Therefore it is no great thing if his ministers also be transformed as the ministers of righteousness* [2 Cor. 11:14-15]. When Satan tempts us to do evil against the will of God, he does not tell us what he is really doing. He changes colors, or he camouflages his real intentions. He masquerades as an apostle, preacher, or teacher. Therefore, it is important to be knowledgeable and discerning.

If that does not work then he will try other methods, beguiling or enticing the saint, or making insinuations. You will recall the tactic he used in the wilderness with our Lord when he said, *If thou be the Son of God* [Matt. 4:6]. What does he say to us? If thou be a Christian? If thou be a follower of Christ? If thou be strong in the faith? Of course, if these approaches do not work, he has other means he will employ. He will quote Scripture and appear as one who is an authority of God's truth and way. He will tell us that he is going to provide us with some deep truths, or he has an easy way for us to obtain the truth.

However, Paul, John, and the author of the letter to the Hebrews realized it was important to progress step by step. Paul says, *I have fed you with milk, and not with meat* (solid food): *for hitherto ye were not able to bear it, neither yet now are ye able* [1 Cor. 3:2]. Hebrews says, *Ye have need that one teach you again which be the first principles of the oracles* (sayings) *of God; and are become such as have need of milk, and not of strong meat* (solid food) [Heb. 5:12].

Another ploy of the devil is to say that there is no opposition to the Lord Jesus Christ and His Gospel, but have you considered such-and-such or what so-and-so has to say? The devil will try to hide himself and say that he does not exist. There was a time when people wanted to amend a church catechism and eliminate all mention of Satan or the devil. The devil loves to conceal himself. What does a deer hunter do when he goes hunting? He conceals himself.

After considering the false teachings and the methods employed by the devil, there is a question to consider: How can we stand against *the wiles* (schemes) *of the devil*? William Gurnall states it concisely and forthrightly, "Take heed of him as a seducer." We are to be aware of the tools he uses and the methods he employs. We are to be ever alert and on guard because he is a relentless foe. We are to obey the basic truths contained in Scripture as revealed through the Master's teachings, as well as the apostles, regarding the devil.

Do not be led down a primrose path that is laced with nice questions diverting one's attention or leading one to stray off-course, or Scripture taken out of context, or dark providences misleading us. When encountering *the wiles* (schemes) *of the devil* be sure to call upon God for help. We are to use the example of the Lord Jesus, who when tempted by the devil said, *Get thee behind me, Satan* [Luke 4:10]. Say in the name of God, *The Lord rebuke thee* [Jude 9]. Recall that the promises of the Gospel state that God gives us a new heart, a clean heart, and fulfills His promises. He will not forsake us in our hour of need.

In closing, it is well to consider the abiding strength and power of the Lord Jesus Christ.

> *And he that keepeth his commandments dwelleth in him, and he in him. And hereby we know that he abideth in us, by the Spirit which he hath given us* [1 John 3:24].

> *Ye are of God, little children, and have overcome them: because greater is he that is in you, than he that is in the world* [1 John 4:4].

Yes, the devil is a formidable, subtle, deceitful foe. Yes, there are false teachings, and devious methods are employed.

But, we are to turn to the Lord, obey His commandments and become knowledgeable. We are to grasp the strength available from the

Lord Jesus, fight against this subtle foe, and defeat him by God's grace, power, and might. This requires obtaining the proper knowledge about God and His teachings, exerting the necessary effort in learning how to use God's armor, and becoming proficient in using it to repel Satan's attacks, as we serve the Lord Jesus day in and day out.

Amen!

16

Those Damnable Heresies

> *Put on the whole armor of God, that ye may be able to stand against the wiles* (schemes) *of the devil.*
> *For we wrestle not against flesh and blood, but against principalities, against the rulers of the darkness of this world* (age), *against spiritual* (hosts of) *wickedness in high places* [Eph. 6:11–12].

"God is love." What a beautiful statement! It conjures up all sorts of ideas and feelings. It is a truthful statement, yet a very emotional one when made by a number of people.

Jesus says, *If ye love me, keep my commandments* [John 14:15]. A condition is laid down. Yes, God is love, but now I must do something if I really love Him. I must keep His commandments. First, I must learn them, then I must keep them. If God is love, will He really make me do things? Will He really place demands upon me? Jesus says, *If ye keep my commandments, ye shall abide in my love: even as I have kept my Father's commandments, and abide in his love* [John 15:10]. Now the cheese gets a little more binding. There is a way in which we are to conduct ourselves. There is a standard. We are to learn about it and practice it.

This is followed by another commandment of the Master's, *This is my commandment, That ye love one another, as I have loved you* [John 15:12]. How is that possible? How can we do these things? We thought, "God is love," and that nothing else matters. When we fall short or fail to follow His teachings, is it okay since God is love.

There are two sides to a coin. How are those thoughts reconciled with our Lord's comments at the close of the Sermon on the Mount?

> *Not every one that saith unto me, Lord, Lord, shall enter into the kingdom of heaven; but he that doeth the will of my Father which is in heaven.*
>
> *Many will say to me in that day, Lord, Lord, have we not prophesied in thy name? and in thy name have cast out devils? and in thy name done many wonderful (miracles) works?*
>
> *And then will I profess unto them, I never knew you: depart from me, ye that work iniquity* (lawlessness) [Matt. 7:21–23].

Pretty strong words! To whom are they directed? What about the warnings contained in the Lord Jesus' teachings? What about John the Baptist and the letters of the apostles? They all contain warnings and exhortations. They are all explicit. They tell us what we are to do and how we are to conduct ourselves as members of Christ's body.

We are to know the love of God as it comes to us through His Son, our Lord and Saviour. Yes, we are to know it, but we are to know much, much more. We are to know those things which can keep us from the love of Christ and from obeying His commandments. Therefore, it is important to know about *those damnable heresies*, as Peter identifies them, and *the wiles of the devil*.

Those damnable heresies are the false teachings that lead to destruction. Peter and Paul both talk about prophets. Peter is not talking about those who are outside the church. *He is talking about those who are within the church* about those who mislead the people and lead them down the path to destruction and ruin. They are false teachers; they twist the scriptures when addressing the saints and faithful in subtle ways and in not so subtle ways.

> *And God hath set* (appointed) *some in the church, first apostles, secondarily prophets, thirdly teachers, after that miracles, then gifts of healings, helps, governments, diversities* (varieties) *of tongues.*
>
> *Are all apostles? are all prophets? are all teachers? are all workers of miracles?*
>
> *Have all the gifts of healing? do all speak with tongues? do all interpret?*
>
> *But covet earnestly the best gifts: and yet show I unto you a more excellent way* [1 Cor. 12:28–31].

Paul is talking about prophets and teachers. However, an explanation is needed. The prophets of whom he is speaking are not the ones who had been endowed with the gift of foretelling.

The prophets to whom he is referring are those who are "Blessed with the unique gift of dealing with scripture, not only by interpreting it, but also by the wisdom they show in making it meet the needs of the hour," as properly explained by John Calvin. Why does Calvin say this? Because Paul is stressing the importance of prophecy as it relates to edifying Scripture and to enlightening the hearers. It is more important in this context, than predicting future events.

These prophets were to console, encourage, and teach. They were first century people endowed with a remarkable ability to interpret Scripture properly, an unusual capacity for grasping the needs of the church, wisdom in meeting and satisfying the requirements of that day, delivering God's message in an unadulterated way, not as the people may want to hear it.

On the other hand, teachers have the slightly different tasks of preserving and propagating the teachings of God and the Lord Jesus Christ, presenting the truth as it is found in Christ, and preserving the purity of the faith as expressed by the saints and followers.

Prophets and teachers have a formidable task. They are to acquire skill, experience, and knowledge in order "to make known the will of God, by applying prophecies, threats, promises, and all the teachings of scripture to the current needs of the called out," as clarified and described by John Calvin.

The Apostle is concerned about the performance and practice of the prophets and teachers so that the people will be enlightened and properly understand Scripture. There is to be an upbuilding of the members. This can be accomplished only through presenting the truth and having the Holy Spirit interpret it in the minds and hearts of the hearers. The members are to devote themselves to their own upbuilding and to the upbuilding of their fellow members.

When this happens, *those damnable heresies* become evident, and the hearers know that biblical teachings are being distorted, twisted, misinterpreted, or misrepresented. Heresy is always a danger when the Word is presented. Most people want to soften it. Unfortunately, it happens "wherever the church in its proclamation makes a given or inherited human, self-understanding into the criterion of the Word," as Otto Weber warns us with his direct, incisive statement.

How does this happen? "Invariably, with the best of intentions: to mitigate the strangeness of the proclaimed Word; to make it easier for the listener to find access to the Word; and to make it possible for the believer to exist in his 'world,'" as further defined by Otto Weber. And to make the Word more palatable, more in conformity to the world, and far less demanding.

The Word may be presented in such a way as to confirm worldviews and to reflect them. The teachings become focused on man, his existence, his importance, his creatureliness, his capabilities, his ideas, and his beliefs. The focus is not upon God, the giver of life, nor upon the Lord Jesus Christ as man's Redeemer and strength.

The Word may be presented in such a way that it does not appear to contradict Scripture. As a matter of fact, it may even use Scripture and appear to be pious, moral, or rational, when in reality it is distorting the truth as it is in Christ. This is one of *the wiles of the devil*. He wants us to fall, not to stand. One thing needs to be clarified and realized: the devil is not a principle, he is a person.

On what authority, you may ask? None other than the Lord Jesus Himself. He said to the spirit, *Come out of him, and enter no more into him* [Mark 9:25]. You do not say that to a principle, you say that to a person. If you deny that the devil is a person then you are denying that the Lord dealt with him in that manner. You are establishing yourself in a position of knowledge and understanding that is above and beyond the Lord Jesus. As Lloyd-Jones said, when you do that "you are involved in the whole question of revelation and authority."

Why pursue this point? Why probe the scriptures? Why seek the truth? First and foremost, so that we come to know the Lord Jesus Christ, His teachings, and His concerns. The apostles and the other writers of the New Testament knew Him, loved Him, respected Him, and wanted to share all that and more with the saints and faithful. They wanted to inform others regarding the real truths about Him.

That is why Paul is instructing the Ephesians. He wanted them to know not only the wiles, but the devil himself. He wanted them to be aware of the real thing. He did not want them to substitute an evil principle for a personal devil that attacks individuals.

This is an important point. Do we believe in a spiritual realm or not? Do we believe what Scripture says or not? Where do people get their information and place their confidence? Scripture speaks of the Holy Spirit as well as the devil and his forces. Do we believe all the scriptures or just the parts that agree with our background and experience?

Where are the people coming from? Remember the apostles were with the Lord, they knew Him and they proclaimed His Gospel. They knew full well the impact He had had on their lives. Therefore, they wanted to share it.

One admirable feature of the New Testament writers was that they presented the whole Gospel, not just the part about love, or miracles, or joyful teachings. Therefore, they talked about and discussed *those damnable heresies* that originate with the devil. They wanted the people to know that heresies occur within the body of Christ. They happen with people who accept the basic teachings of the Christian faith, but go wrong in interpreting and presenting them. The devil takes an interest in these things. Why? So he can disturb the life of the saints and faithful, so he can shake the confidence of people and spoil the work of Christ.

Where did *those damnable heresies* come from in the first century, and since then? From the experience and mindsets of people accepting Christ and joining the church, from people trained in philosophy, from people who were new in the faith, from those who had followed the scribes and Pharisees, and from other educated and respectable sources.

What has been their impact? They threatened the vitality of the members and in some cases the very existence of the called-out congregations. They threatened the proclamation of the Gospel of the Lord Jesus Christ in its full glory and power.

What has been the answer to these conditions and threats through the ages? The truth of the Gospel has been proclaimed and the Word has been revealed. First we had the Letters of the Apostles, then the Gospels. We had apostles, prophets, evangelists, pastors, and teachers. And people who wanted to hear and to know the full truth. Then we had the great councils of the organized church, which resulted in the Nicene and Apostles' creeds.

After the Reformation Period began Confessions of Faith were developed. They include the Belgic Confession (1561 and 1619), the French Confession (1559), and the Second Helvetic Confession (1566). These three Confessions begin by declaring that Scripture is the sole authority on both the matters of faith and God revealing Himself in the Lord Jesus Christ. Then, there were the Augsburg Confession, the Westminster Confession, the Heidelberg Catechism, and the Thirty-Nine Articles of the Church of England.

Why did these developments occur? To state in writing what is true and not true according to the teachings of Christ. These writings were developed to guide the teaching and preaching of prophets, pastors, and teachers, and for the edification of the people of God who are not called to one of these offices. It always amazes me when some ministers and teachers say words to the effect, "Oh, well, that can only be understood by those who have received special training."

Yet if the Holy Spirit interprets the true meaning in our hearts and minds then all the members of Christ's body should be able to understand Christ's teachings, the Creeds, and the Confessions. One of the great preachers and pastors of the twentieth century was Martyn Lloyd-Jones. Yet he never went to seminary. The Holy Spirit wants us to know the truth as it is revealed in the Lord Jesus and to have a meaningful knowledge of Him.

What factors keep one from having a knowledge of the truth and a right relationship with God? First, there are evil and false statements or communications.

> *Be not deceived: evil communications* (company) *corrupt good manners* (habits).
> *Awake to righteousness, and sin not; for some have not the knowledge of God* [1 Cor. 15:33–34].

"When Satan cannot make a direct attack upon us, he deceives us by pretending that there is nothing wrong in our starting all sorts of speculations for the sake of finding out what the truth is," as John Calvin warns us. Therefore, Paul wants us to be on guard against either imparting or receiving the wrong information. Why? Because it corrupts a person and causes him or her to depart from a pure faith, or it causes him or her not to attain a pure faith as he or she begins walking with Jesus or continues to do so.

Consequently, the Apostle wants the saints and faithful awake to righteousness. He wants them to turn to those things that are good and holy. Yet he realized that some of them had little or no knowledge of God. They were ignorant of Him. Therefore, the Apostle warns them and wants them to become knowledgeable.

A second consideration is that if your doctrine is wrong, there will be errors in your daily living. There is an old saying that applies to athletes and to performers. It goes like this, "the way you play or perform is according to how you practiced or rehearsed." There are people who act and conduct themselves as wonderful Christians when everything is going well, or according to their desires. Then trouble strikes, and what happens? They do not know what to do or which way to turn. They may even begin to doubt God.

They say, "Look, we have been going to church, we have committed our lives to God, and now look what is happening to us. How could this happen? What are we going to do? What can be said about such a situation and many like it?"

The problem is that these people do not have a clear understanding of the Christian faith. "They have an utterly inadequate notion of what Christianity means. Their idea of Christianity was or is: Believe in Christ and you will never have another trouble or problem; God will bless you, nothing will ever go wrong with you," as Martyn Lloyd-Jones observed after many years in the ministry and searching Scripture.

What does Scripture say to this? Luke tells how they *preached the gospel* and *taught many* and then says, *Confirming* (strengthening) *the souls of the disciples, and exhorting them to continue in the faith, and that we must through much tribulation enter into the kingdom of God* [Acts 14:21–22].

Paul says, *And in nothing* (be) *terrified by your adversaries: which is to them an evident token* (proof) *of perdition* (destruction) *but to you of salvation, and that of God. For unto you it is given in the behalf of Christ, not only to believe on him, but also to suffer for his sake* [Phil. 1:28–29].

Our Lord says these wonderful words of wisdom and encouragement, *In the world ye shall have tribulation: but be of good cheer; I have overcome the world* [John 16:33]. Pray God that you can see the importance of presenting the Gospel through sound preaching and teaching; and understanding the truths revealed in and through the Lord Jesus Christ.

There are going to be afflictions, trials, tribulations, and difficulties in our lives, and there is eventually going to be death. The question is: how are we going to handle them? Is our strength going to come from the Lord Jesus Christ, or will we allow *the wiles* (schemes) *of the devil* to create doubts, and to make us question our relationship with the Master?

We are to be aware of the fact that there are heresies within the modern church. There are teachings, events, and programs that lead from Christ, not to Him. Therefore, it is extremely urgent to know the true teachings of Scripture and to study the Word. It is important to know what Jesus said and taught in order to realize that the Holy Spirit is active, working, and exercising amazing power when we let him and when we call upon Him. But a word of caution: the Holy Spirit does not "honor anything except His own Word," as positively stated by Martyn Lloyd-Jones.

Remember, the New Testament writers received the Word that they wrote by revelation. They were not expressing their own thoughts. They were true to the Lord Jesus Christ. We are to be the same. We are to hear and to understand according to Scripture. The Holy Spirit will honor His Word, but nothing more, nothing less, nothing else.

The fourth area keeping us from a knowledge of the truth and a right relationship with God is the emphasis on numbers. Yes, it would be nice to have more people professing faith in the Lord Jesus Christ. But the main thing is to present the truth as it is found in Christ and revealed in Him. God said, and, oh how often we forget, *Ye shall be holy: for I the Lord your God am holy* [Lev. 19:2]. This is what needs to be preached and taught: the holiness of God, not the demands or rationalizations of man.

William Lloyd Garrison said, "One with God is a majority." It is the power of God that matters. Certainly, there are things that distract, annoy, and divert us, but they are not to separate us from the love of God or keep the Holy Spirit from working within us, or keep us from learning the truths of Scripture, and from walking with the Lord Jesus Christ.

What really matters is the spiritual truths as given by the Holy Spirit. Think of Jeremiah: the majority in his time had gone wrong. They had left the teachings of God. But Jeremiah knew the truth and spoke the truth as it was revealed to him. He did not say the popular things. He did not like his role of being unpopular, being disliked, being laughed at, or being ridiculed, but he continued proclaiming the Word of God. In continuing to proclaim God's Word, Jeremiah continued suffering from the abuses and taunts of men."

There is a fifth point prevalent today. It involves primarily several secular things: we must all get together and put aside our differences; we must have programs, activities, events; and we must attract the young people, the masses.

Think of the apostles. How much easier it would have been on them individually if they had accepted the differences, if they had toned down the Gospel and if they had not proclaimed the full Gospel, but only part of it? The world would have absorbed them, and there would have been darkness, not light. Praise God that they turned the world upside down instead.

Is it not interesting? The New Testament writers were not concerned with the size of the church, but they were concerned with the purity of Christ's body. How did they do it? They were true to Paul's statement to Timothy admonishing him,

> *If thou put the brethren in remembrance of these things, thou shalt be a good minister of Jesus Christ, nourished up in the words of faith and of good doctrine, whereunto thou hast attained* (carefully followed).
> *But refuse profane and old wives' fables, and exercise thyself rather unto godliness* [1 Tim. 4:6–7].

They emphasized the teachings of Christ, the love of God, the wrath of God, the displeasure of God, the Cross, the shed blood, the sinful nature of man, man's disobedience to God, the need to repent, and the need to practice daily the teachings of the Master.

And the early church grew. The Reformed Church grew in the sixteenth, seventeenth and eighteenth centuries. The whole Gospel needs to be expounded. If not, *the wiles of the devil* will cause it to fall.

In closing, just think where we would be if God had not worked with one man almost five hundred years ago. God worked in Martin Luther, He struggled with him, and finally Luther could stand and say, "Here I stand, I can do no other, so help me God."

We cannot start the great Reformation as Luther did. But we can stand on the truth as it is revealed in the Lord Jesus Christ. It *does* matter what you believe, and it *does* matter where you stand.

Pray God that He will keep us from *those damnable heresies* and that we *may be able to stand against the wiles of the devil.*

When considering the teachings of the apostles and our Redeemer may we ponder the meaningful words of Charles Wesley in his beautiful hymn "O for a Thousand Tongues to Sing."

> *O for a thousand tongues to sing*
> *My dear redeemer's praise,*
> *The glories of my God and King,*
> *The triumph of His grace!*
>
> *Jesus, the name that charms our fears,*
> *That bids our sorrows cease;*
> *'Tis music to the sinners ears,*

'Tis life, and health, and peace.

He breaks the power of reigning sin,
He sets the prisoner free;
His blood can make the sinful clean,
His blood a-vailed for me.

My gracious Master and my God,
Assist me to proclaim,
To spread through all the earth abroad,
The honors of thy name.

Amen!

17

Road Blocks and Detours

> *Finally, my brethren, be strong in the Lord, and in the power of his might.*
> *Put on the whole armor of God, that ye may be able to stand against the wiles (schemes) of the devil.*
> *For we wrestle not against flesh and blood, but against principalities, against powers, against the rulers of the darkness of this world* (age), *against spiritual* (hosts of) *wickedness in high places* [Eph. 6:10–12].

Often we become so immersed in what we are doing that we ignore or forget what the Master did. Though we are concerned with a number of things, we allow our minds to wander or to become restricted by putting on blinders. When driving an automobile, you need to be cognizant of the traffic on the road you are traveling, and you also need to be aware of the side streets, the countryside, and the existing conditions; all of it needs to be tied together.

The reality of the devil and his wiles should be a real concern to everyone. Our primary concern is the Lord Jesus Christ and our relationship with Him, but we must recognize those things threatening to disturb our focus and relationship. Certain roads lead to Christ, but impediments and distractions try to get us off the right road and keep us from traveling along it.

When considering the manifest and obscure *wiles* (schemes) *of the devil* it is well to bear in mind the words of our Lord, who prays to His Father,

> *I have given them thy word; and the world hath hated them, because they are not of the world, even as I am not of the world.*
>
> *I pray not that thou shouldest take them out of the world, but that Thou shouldest keep them from (the) evil (one).*
>
> *They are not of the world, even as I am not of the world.*
>
> *Sanctify (set apart) them through thy truth; thy word is truth.*
>
> *As thou hast sent me into the world, so have I also sent them into the world.*
>
> *And for their sakes I sanctify myself, that they also might be sanctified through the truth* [John 17:14–19].

Note the Lord's words and thoughts as He prays: *Given them thy word.* Calvin states that Jesus prays to God saying, "It is for thee to protect those who are hated by the world because of the word."

Christ does not pray that the Father take them out of the world or that he set them up in some protected area. No, He does not do that! What does He do? He prays that God will keep the disciples (you and me) from that which is evil and from the evil one.

We should learn that Christ does not ask the Father to put a protective shield around each of us, but prays for each of us be "in-filled" with God's power and truth. He prays for the inner person to be strengthened and to withstand external pressures with its vexations and enticements to pleasure, ease, and safety.

We are to realize from studying these verses that Christ neither prays for nor promises freedom from anxiety, cares, and toil. But He does pray that we should receive the power and strength to keep us from being conquered, overwhelmed, or deceived by external forces and that which is evil. Calvin says clearly and concisely, "If we want to be kept according to the rule which Christ laid down, we must not desire immunity from evils or pray to God to convey us straightway into blessed rest, but must remain content with the certain assurance of victory, and meanwhile resist bravely all the evils from which Christ prayed to His Father that we might have a happy issue."

Oh, how at times we would like to take the easy way. But God wants us to be witnesses in the world and to the world, yet not to be of the world. Can you think of one person in either the Old Testament or the New Testament called of God who had an easy time, who was fully protected from the world and *the wiles of the devil*? I cannot. There is not one. They all had problems.

However, there is not one who was overwhelmed or who did not receive strength from God. How does Christ pray that we be sanctified? That it be done automatically or instantaneously? No, no, no! He prays that the Father sanctify them through what? Through the Father's truth, and what is that? Thy Word is truth.

People write about sanctification and wanting to be sanctified, and what do they do for the most part? Ignore God's Word. Yet the Lord prays for us to be sanctified and at the same time tells us how to be sanctified. It is by the revealed Word of God.

What does the process of sanctification include? God's righteousness and His kingdom. God's renewing power and strength, which He makes available to us. Christ "asks that the Father would first sanctify the disciples; that He would consecrate them entirely to Himself and defend them as His sacred property," as John Calvin noted and assures us.

Think about that! God the Father, creator, omnipotent, omniscient, omnipresent; God who was, is, and will be; God the Alpha and Omega has consecrated the believers in the past and will consecrate each of us to Himself, and He will defend us today as He has done for each one in the past. This is mind-boggling!

How is this accomplished? Through His Word. His Word is truth! Christ is explicit. The way God sanctifies His people is through the truth which is in the Word. Jesus said, *I am the way, the truth, and the life* [John 14:6]. John begins his Gospel: *IN the beginning was the Word, and the Word was with God, and the Word was God* [John 1:1].

What is meant by *sanctify them through the truth; thy word is truth* [John 17:17]? It means teaching the Gospel that Christ proclaimed. It cannot be done outside the Word and the truth as it is found in Christ. It can only be done through it. Christ concludes these few verses praying *. . . and for their sakes I sanctify myself, that they also might be sanctified through the truth* [John 17:19]. Christ is to be our example. He consecrated Himself to the Father. It is through Him that we are consecrated. He does it for us.

However, we are to recognize that *the wiles of the devil* do not want us to proceed through the process of sanctification. Therefore, there are additional factors to consider. The devil wants to keep us from God and Christ. He will erect barricades along the path, he will create detours, he will change the road signs, he will point us in the wrong direction, and he will give us false directions. These are some of the things that he will do to those who profess faith in Christ and are members of His body. What are some of the ways by which Satan tries to mislead the saints and the faithful?

One way is through what are commonly referred to as the cults. A cult is identified according to the Shorter Oxford dictionary as "devotion to a particular person or thing as paid by a body of professed adherents." You will note that it may be devotion to a certain person. There are many cults, such as Christian Science, Jehovah's Witnesses, Mormonism, and others. They will use Christian names and terminology, but they do not have much, if anything, in common with the truth as contained in the scriptures and expounded by our Lord and His apostles.

They also have the ability to present themselves in an attractive manner to people who are experiencing difficulties, such as illness, sorrow, the loss of a loved one, bitter disappointment, business worries, anxieties, rejection, and ill feelings.

What are the characteristics of the cults? First, they manage to sound like they are discussing Christianity. They want to imply something that they are not. They use terms and statements that appear to be in the Christian context, but they remove or ignore the basic truths of the New Testament found in the Lord Jesus Christ.

They talk about Christ and the blessings available through Him, but they compromise His deity, His authority, His Sonship. They give emphasis to the teachings or writings of people other than what is contained in Scripture, or based upon the Word.

They offer blessings in a quantity and proportion beyond what the Christian denominations seem to provide or make available. They attractively package their offerings.

In the last chapter we discussed *those damnable heresies*, whereas now we are considering the cults. You may well ask, what is the difference? A heresy is when a professing Christian goes wrong on a particular doctrine or truth. The cults are different; they are counterfeits. They are not part of the body of Christ. That is the essential difference. They do not accept the basic truths revealed in Scripture about the Lord Jesus Christ. However, some traits of the cults are their sincerity and enthusiasm. They are usually known or regarded as zealous, active workers.

What differentiates the cults from faith in the Lord Jesus Christ? Primarily, the cults began during the nineteenth century and were founded by one person. The founder is usually someone who had a revelation that appeared only to him or her.

The cults may recognize the Bible, but they are governed by an authority or writings in addition to or in place of Scripture. They claim that since the revelation was given to a particular person, that individual's writings or teachings are authoritative, not Scripture.

Some cults claim to believe in the Bible, and some do not. Some ignore it, some do not. But they all claim to have additional insight or knowledge that is above and beyond what is contained in the Bible. Therefore, if you want to understand what the Bible says, you must interpret it in light of this special revelation given to the founder.

The cults betray their fallacies on certain basic doctrines contained in Scripture, such as God Himself and His deity, the incarnation, the person of the Holy Spirit, the Holy Trinity, creation, sin and redemption, salvation, prayer, and the presence of God. The cults may appear to be harmless or innocuous, but they can lead people down the wrong road and keep them from walking *worthy of the vocation* (calling) *wherewith ye have been called.*

What are we called to be and to do? The Old Testament reveals, *Ye shall be holy: for I the Lord your God am holy* [Lev. 19:2]. The New Testament reveals that we are to practice the teachings of the Master and be in a right relationship to God. This is made possible only by Christ's shed blood on Calvary's Hill.

What does the Bible stress? It stresses our relationship to God through the Lord Jesus Christ and being sanctified through the Word, God's truth, but it does not stress how you or I feel. How we feel is not the important thing.

You will recall the parable of the Pharisee and publican. To whom did Jesus tell it? He told it to those *which trusted in themselves that they were righteous, and despised others* [Luke 18:9].

> *Two men went* (up) *into the temple to pray.*
> *Note the words the Master uses: The Pharisee stood and prayed thus with himself, God, I thank thee, that I am not as other men are, extortioners, unjust, adulterers, or even as this publican (tax collector).*
> *I fast twice a week, I give tithes of all that I possess* [Luke 18:10–12].

The Pharisee felt good about himself, what he was doing, and what he had done. He was self-satisfied and proud. What about the publican? He beat his breast, he bowed down, he did not pray with himself. He turned to God and beseeched Him, saying, *God be merciful to me a sinner* [Luke 18:13].

What happened when they left the temple? The publican went to his house justified, but not the Pharisee. Our relationship to God is of primary importance.

How do the cults say you will receive the blessings that will or should come your way? Usually by learning a certain formula or by practicing a prescribed method. But the formulas or methods are not based upon Scripture. Why?

Because they did not receive them from Scripture. They may quote excerpts from the Bible, but their formulas or methods are not based upon the Word. This is in direct contrast to the great teachings of the Christian faith, which are based upon an exposition of Scripture and expounding the truths of the Holy Trinity.

The cults want to start with some practical teaching. This is in direct contrast to the New Testament, which always starts with doctrine and the basic truths of God. The New Testament does not start by saying you need practical help. It starts with God and His truths. Just think, it is not until Ephesians 4:1 that the Apostle says *I . . . beseech you that ye walk worthy of the vocation* (calling) *wherewith ye are called.* Paul does not present the practical until he presents the truths of God.

The cults do not have much to say about the Holy Spirit. Yet the New Testament places significant emphasis upon the Holy Spirit working within the members of Christ's body. The Holy Spirit teaches, strengthens, stimulates, enables, and comforts us.

In addition, the cults want their followers to believe their formula is easy, simple, and a great cure-all. Further, it is the salve for all your troubles and problems. That approach is in direct contrast to Paul's statement,

> *But we have this treasure in earthen vessels, that the excellency of the power may be of God, and not of us.*
> *We are troubled (hard pressed) on every side, yet not distressed (crushed); we are perplexed, but not in despair;*
> *Persecuted, but not forsaken; cast (struck) down, but not destroyed;*
> *Always bearing about in the body the dying of the Lord Jesus, that the life also of Jesus might be made manifest in our body* [2 Cor. 4:7–10].

Paul emphasizes God's power and what He can do. He points out that no matter how capable or great a person may be by reason of birth, intellect, wealth, or accomplishment, he is an unworthy vessel for the inestimable treasure that God through Christ may bestow upon him.

When we are cornered or troubled, the Lord opens a way. When we are oppressed or perplexed, He comes to our aid. When we are surrounded, He strengthens and supports us. When we are in deep trouble, He will support us and stay with us. He will not allow us to be destroyed or overwhelmed. Remember: *We wrestle not against flesh and blood, but against principalities, against powers, against the rulers of the darkness of this world* (age), *against spiritual* (hosts of) *wickedness in high places.*

There is another point peculiar to the cults. They promise instant success that is foolproof. Just like Jell-O or pudding, pour the ingredients in a bowl, add water, and stir. Then you will receive your blessing or cure instantly. That is not what the Bible teaches. Scripture says, thank God you have accepted Christ. You are to obey His commandments. *If ye love me, keep my commandments* [John 14:15]. But it never says that your whole life will be one of ease and that trouble will never stop at your door. It is not a case of "they lived happily ever after."

What does the New Testament say? It says you are in the world, but you are not of the world. What else does it say? Lloyd-Jones succinctly states, "You are in a very difficult world, a sinful world, a world that is dominated by the devil and his cohorts. These principalities and powers! It tells you that you will often find it difficult just to stand on your feet at all. Indeed you will need the whole armor of God; you will need to be 'strengthened' with might by his Spirit in the inner man; you will need to be 'strong in the Lord, and in the power of his might.' Then you will be able to stand, but only then. 'Quit you like men; be strong!'" That is what the New Testament says. That is laying it on the line and telling it like it is!

How do people react to that? Some say, I want instant relief as in Rolaids. Some say, I do not want to struggle, or sweat, or fight. Some say, I want my problems solved, no messing around. However, the New Testament talks about growing in grace, growing in the knowledge of the Lord, working out your salvation with fear and trembling, obeying the commandments of the Lord, and denying yourself. That type of talk does not sound like a shortcut to some utopian village.

How does the New Testament work? It starts with the basic truths of Christ, with the Word. It presents the Gospel of the Lord Jesus Christ in all its glory and power. It describes the Holy Spirit working within the members of Christ's body. It reveals the need for mortifying the deeds of the flesh and the body.

There is another interesting aspect to the cults. They always start with you. Your needs, wants, desires, troubles, worries, burdens, and anything else that bothers you, or you want to do, or you want to achieve. Further, the cults say they can address and take care of each and every one.

What is different about the Gospel? The Gospel always starts with God. Why did Christ come into the world?

> *For Christ also hath once suffered for sins, the just for the unjust, that he might bring us to God, being put to death in the flesh, but quickened* (made alive) *by the Spirit* [1 Pet. 3:18].

> *For God, who commanded the light to shine out of darkness, hath shined it in our hearts, to give the light of the knowledge of the glory of God in the face of Jesus Christ* [2 Cor. 4:6].

The Gospel starts with knowing God, not with you or me. If we are right with God, really right with Him in Spirit and in truth, then our particular situations will be resolved or handled in the light of the Gospel.

The good news of the New Testament is the proclamation of Christ's coming in the flesh to give us a true knowledge of God as God and the Lord Jesus Christ as His Son. *And this is life eternal, that they might know thee the only true God, and Jesus Christ, whom thou hast sent* [John 17:3].

Calvin stressed two things concerning our relationship to God: worshipping God; and acquiring knowledge of God, His plans, and His purposes. Yes, we are to worship God and reverence Him day in and day out. We are to search the scriptures and to learn the Word, *for thy word is truth*. It is through these disciplines and God's grace, power, and might that we are sanctified.

What does this mean? Abiding by a certain moral code or refraining from doing things? No, a thousand times no! It means becoming like the Lord Jesus Christ. It means putting into thought and practice the teachings, the attitude, and the actions of the Master. Jesus prays,

> *Neither pray I for these alone, but for them also which shall believe on me through their word;*

> *That they all may be one; as thou, Father, art in me, and I in thee, that they also may be one in us: that the world may believe that thou hast sent me* [John 17:20–21].

In closing, what does Scripture stress above everything else? The person and work of the Lord Jesus Christ. His life and His death on the Cross are central to the teachings of Scripture, to the Word, and to the truth. Any teaching that detracts from or minimizes the Lord Jesus Christ as the Son of God and our Lord and Saviour is not of the Word, but is of *the wiles of the devil*. The only way we come to the Father is by the Son. You cannot deny the Son and go to the Father.

> *And lo a voice from heaven, saying, This is my beloved Son, in whom I am well pleased* [Matt. 3:17].

> *I am the way, the truth, and the life; no man cometh to the Father, but by me* [John 14:6].

How do we have access to God? How do we have knowledge of Him? Through the Son. How are we sanctified? How do we come to the Father? Through the Word.

> *Thy word is truth* [John 17:17].

> *IN the beginning was the Word, and the Word was with God, and the Word was God* [John 1:1].

Please bear in mind two thoughts from Paul's letter to the Colossians:

> *As ye have therefore received Christ Jesus the Lord, so walk ye in Him:*
> *Rooted and built up in him, and stablished in the faith, as ye have been taught, abounding therein with thanksgiving.*
> *Beware lest any man spoil* (plunder) *you through philosophy and vain* (empty) *deceit, after the tradition of men, after the rudiments of the world, and not after Christ* [Col. 2:6–8].

May you understand the reality of the devil and his wiles, as you continue on your life's journey, but may you be guided by God's Word as you walk with the Lord Jesus as His disciple.

Life in the world is fraught with dangers. The committed followers of the Lord Jesus will encounter an inordinate number of temptations, tests, and tribulations as they endeavor to obey His commands and teachings. It is not a life of ease, nor is it for the faint hearted. That is why

Christ and His apostles encourage us to acquire knowledge and grow in our relationship with Him. This will enable us to become strong in the faith, to withstand the attacks of Satan, and to emerge victorious.

Therefore, it is prudent to remember the meaningful words of "What a Friend We Have in Jesus" by Joseph Scriven that apply to our daily living and the challenges that we face:

> *What a Friend we have in Jesus, All our sins and griefs to bear!*
> *What a privilege to carry Everything to God in prayer!*
> *O what peace we often forfeit, O what needless pain we bear,*
> *All because we do not carry Everything to God in prayer!*
>
> *Have we trials and temptations? Is there trouble anywhere?*
> *We should never be discouraged: Take it to the Lord in prayer!*
> *Can we find a friend so faithful, Who will all our sorrows share?*
> *Jesus knows our every weakness—Take it to the Lord in prayer!*
>
> *Are we weak and heavy laden, Cumbered with a load of care?*
> *Precious Savior, still our refuge—Take it to the Lord in prayer!*
> *Do thy friends, despise, forsake Thee?*
> *Take it to the Lord in prayer!*
> *In His arms He'll take and shield Thee,*
> *Thou wilt find a solace there.*

These words are worth reading again and again. How blessed we are to have the Lord Jesus as our friend!

Amen!

18

Watch and Pray

> *Finally, my brethren, be strong in the Lord, and in the power of his might.*
> *Put on the whole armor of God, that ye may be able to stand against the wiles* (schemes) *of the devil.*
> *For we wrestle not against flesh and blood, but against principalities, against powers, against the rulers of the darkness of this world, against spiritual* (hosts of) *wickedness in high places* [Eph. 6:10–12].

Each of us realizes changes have occurred during our lifetimes reflecting the attitude of society in general. These developments have had an impact upon individuals as well as large groups and especially upon church organizations and literature. Just think of the printed material, movies, and television programs. One wonders what is going to happen next.

What then is the relationship between freedom and accountability? Where is the line between ignorance and the responsibility to learn? How do we distinguish between our self-centeredness and the will of God as made known through the Lord Jesus Christ? How do we mature to the point where we can deny self and become obedient to Christ's commandments?

Why does the Master challenge the teachings and proclamations of the Pharisees and scribes and tell the people, *But seek ye first the kingdom of God, and his righteousness* [Matt. 6:33] and tell Peter, *feed my lambs . . . feed my sheep* and *follow me*? Why is there conflict within the church as we know it? Why do some people want to supplement the teachings of the Master and how they are to be applied to daily living? Why do some stress the importance of works in contrast to the need to know and to obey?

These questions are asked in order to look not only at Scripture, but to focus upon the Lord Jesus Christ. Everything else is secondary, tertiary, or even more remote.

Too often we forget that God is almighty. We limit Him because of our spiritual impoverishment or our finite view of His majesty. We want Him to love us, to do our will, to comfort us, and to sympathize with us, but we want to limit His almighty power.

Oswald Chambers states it concisely saying, "Suppose there is a well of fathomless trouble inside your heart, and Jesus comes and says, 'Let not your heart be troubled:' and you shrug your shoulders and say, 'But, Lord the well is deep; you cannot draw up quietness and comfort out of it.' No, He won't. He will bring them down from above. Jesus does not bring anything up from the well of human nature or from earthen vessels." Think of that when you ponder these questions or when you think about yourself.

There is another significant point that Chambers makes in this context, which is that while "We have Christian attributes and experience, we do not abandon ourselves to Christ; we do not commit fully and completely to Him. 'When we get into difficult circumstances, we impoverish His ministry by saying, 'of course He cannot do anything,' and we struggle down into the deeps and try to get the water for ourselves. Beware of the satisfaction of sinking back and saying, 'It cannot be done.' You know it can be done if you look to Jesus. Too often the wiles of Satan defeat or discourage us. Where do we focus? Where do we concentrate? Where do we seek help?"

The Lord Jesus spoke to His disciples in a forthright manner from the beginning to the end of His public ministry. He told them what to do and what not to do. He held nothing back from them, and they did not dispute His sayings and teachings, nor did they ignore them, or select only the portions they liked, or reject what they did not like.

Before considering these verses in more detail, consider how Luke describes what Jesus said after they left the upper room but before the Master was apprehended: *And the Lord said, Simon, Simon, behold, Satan hath desired to have you, that he may sift you as wheat: But I have prayed for thee, that thy faith fail not* [Luke 22:31–32]. Matthew and Mark extend what is said in this account to all the disciples, but Luke singles out Peter. That is not the crux of the matter.

What really matters is what Jesus said and did, and to whom He was speaking. Right after participating in the Lord's Supper, the Lord Jesus warns the disciples about *the wiles of the devil*. He tells us to beware, that we will have to struggle, but "At the same time He promises them victory," as John Calvin joyfully tells us.

What else does the Master say to His disciples? First, He tells them *. . . the sheep of the flock shall be scattered abroad. But . . . I will go before you into Galilee* [Matt. 26:31–32]. Is this not true of us? Cannot you see it? We have communion with Him. We are in His presence; we are together as members of His body. Then we scatter to different places, but He goes before us.

If my wife and I drive separate cars to class and church, then she tells me that she is going home and will meet me there, naturally she will be there before me. Doesn't it stand to reason that Christ will also be there, regardless of our decision to greet Him or not?

Second, He said unto them, *Sit ye here, while I go and pray yonder* [Matt. 26:36]. The Master did not want to unduly burden them. However, He wanted to prepare them for the tests that would come, for the conflicts they would experience, and for the fact that He would not be present with them in the flesh.

The disciples were to grow in strength, faith, and obedience. So are we! The Lord Jesus will be gentle and loving with us and even protective, so that we will not be exposed to certain hardships, conflicts, and strife before our condition has received ample strength and enlightenment. "Christ particularly has in mind what He did with twelve apostles, yet He also teaches us, that while we are still novices and weak in faith He will for the time, be gentle, until we grow up into men: so they are wrong who use His times of quiet for self-indulgence which softens the strength of faith," as John Calvin enlightens us.

Do not think for a moment that Christ is not aware of you and your requirements. The question is, "Are we aware of His almighty power and the living waters with which He can fill us?" Remember: He prepares the members of His body.

Jesus came to His disciples after praying and found them asleep. It is enlightening to know the Greek word used for sleep in this verse [Matt. 26:40]. It is *katheudō* and has three meanings: "natural sleep," "carnal indifference to spiritual things on the part of (get this) believers," and "a condition of insensibility to divine things, involving conformity to the world."

Do these things apply to us after we have had communion with the Lord? We go to sleep when He tells us to wait. We exhibit carnal indifference to spiritual things, and we are insensible to divine things. We are earthen vessels and cannot draw from the bottom up. We need to be filled from above.

What does Jesus say when He has the disciples attention, when He has our attention? He says, *Watch and pray, that ye enter not unto temptation: the spirit indeed is willing, but the flesh is weak* [Matt. 26:41]. What beautiful words and thoughts! What an appropriate exhortation! No wonder Paul says to the Ephesians, *Finally, my brethren, be strong in the Lord, and in the power of his might. Put on the whole armor of God, that ye may be able to stand against the wiles* (schemes) *of the devil* [Eph. 6:10–11].

Christ urges us to do two things: *Watch and pray*. Why? He does not want us to succumb to *the wiles of the devil*. He wants us to stand. Please note how we stand: by watching and praying; by focusing, concentrating, and converging on Christ; and by turning upward and outward, not inward and downward.

Recall the situation. They have left the upper room; Jesus has cared for them in the flesh for more than three years; Jesus knew what was going to happen. What about the disciples and ourselves? We have had a joyful experience. Now, we are sad and grieving because of our impending loss. We are turning inward. We are beset by the things of the world. We are fair game for *the wiles of the devil*.

How do we handle these situations? Certainly not by relying upon our own power and strength. We need to depend upon the power and strength of God to infill us. Calvin notes sanguinely, "Our watchfulness will do no good without prayers." Jesus said after telling us to *Watch and pray, . . . the spirit indeed is willing, but the flesh is weak* [Matt. 26:41]. These words should make us realize that the flesh struggles, and needs the Holy Spirit to strengthen it through prayer. Every saint and faithful person needs the abiding presence of the Holy Spirit to sustain him or her, and to keep him or her from temptation.

Pray God we can understand what He is telling us. There is not one of us that has the strength in our earthly vessels to keep from succumbing to temptation. We are not to be dismayed or frightened by this truth, but we need to recognize *from whence cometh my help* [Ps. 121:1].

What does this account of our Lord ministering to His disciples have to say to those thinking they go to church every Sunday and all is well in their relationship to God in Christ? He tells them within a few hours of the Last Supper to *Watch and pray* [Matt. 26:41].

What does the word *watch* mean as used by Jesus? It comes from the Greek word *Grēgoreō*, which means "keeping awake," "being spiritually alert," and "being vigilant." This definition more accurately describes the Lord's command to His disciples.

Why does Jesus tell His disciples to *Watch and pray*? Because the devil is a very subtle and dangerous foe. Further, the Master does not want us to assume anything. He wants us to take the necessary precautions. Just because a person has accepted Christ does not mean that he or she can go to sleep and forget to be vigilant. The devil is a cunning, crafty predator who seeks to attack those people who let their guard down or rest upon their experiences.

In addition to watching and praying, Scripture tells us two other things.

> *And that from a child thou hast known the holy scriptures, which are able to make thee wise unto salvation through faith which is in Christ Jesus.*
> *All scripture is given by inspiration of God, and is profitable for doctrine, for reproof, for correction, for instruction in righteousness:*
> *That the man of God may be perfect, thoroughly furnished* (equipped) *unto all good works* [2 Tim. 3:15–17].

One of the best ways to *watch and pray* is to become knowledgeable regarding Scripture. That requires reading and studying it!

The scriptures are the inspired word of God and are provided for our edification and obedience. They contribute substantially to realizing a profitable and joyful life. They enable us to know *the wiles of the devil* and the commands of our Lord.

Another way to watch is by self-examination, which is extremely difficult. It is hard to maintain a balance between being too harsh or too lenient in examining ourselves. Scripture says, *Examine yourselves, whether ye be in the faith; prove your own selves. Know ye not your own selves, how that Jesus Christ is in you, except* (unless you don't stand the test) *ye be reprobates* [2 Cor. 13:5]. When examining ourselves, we are acknowledging what we have received from Christ. True faith in Christ depends upon the grace God bestows upon us.

When we have been blessed with faith in Christ *we are to claim it and grasp it with a firm, unyielding assurance that He is able to keep that which He has promised. The wiles (schemes) of the devil do not want us to come to that realization.*

However, we are to examine ourselves and ask certain questions. Are we watching and praying? Diligently reading Scripture? Fearful of entering into temptation? Being superficial? Paying lip service? Giving five minutes here or there to watching and praying? Too busy to give more than a few minutes to the Master?

The New Testament explicitly says we are to:

- *Watch and pray;*
- *Obey my commandments;*
- *Follow me;*
- *The spirit indeed is willing, but the flesh is weak;*
- *Feed my sheep;*
- *Examine yourselves;*
- *Be strong in the Lord, and in the power of his might;*
- *Put on the whole armour of God, that ye may be able to stand against the wiles* (schemes) *of the devil.*

These things require a commitment. They require heeding our Lord's exhortation to *Watch and pray, that ye enter not into temptation* [Matt. 26:41].

There should be a balance between the mind, experience, and practice if one is to stand, not fall. As individuals we are to give the proper attention to each of the three. Of course, the devil would like to create an imbalance between the mind, experiences, and practice. Each needs to receive attention, each needs to be fed, and each needs to be disciplined.

If you spend too much time on your mind, then your experience or your practice will suffer. If you spend an inordinate amount of time practicing or doing, then your mind and understanding will be penalized.

It is important to have the right ingredients in the proper proportions. A balance is to be sought and maintained. Some people want to give too much attention or place too much emphasis on their mindsets, or experiences, or habits instead of maintaining the proper balance. This is evident not only in individuals but also in a class or in a church.

Second, are our experiences. By that I mean our exposure to events and developments, and our reaction to them. "A goodly portion of our lives is lived in the realm of experiences, feelings, sensations, sensibilities, desires, moods, and states. This is more elemental than the mind, and we should always be struggling to attain a mastery over it by using the mind and the understanding," as an enlightened Martyn Lloyd-Jones expressed it.

Third, our behavior is what we do and what we do not do. It is influenced by our minds and our experiences. We are blessed with a mind, feelings, and emotions and with the ability to do something regarding these three. Therefore, it is important to maintain a balance and not allow one of the three to become predominant and block out the other two.

Why should we seek and maintain a balance between the mind, experiences, and behavior? What do the New Testament Epistles reveal? They express affection, love, concern, and feelings. They contain doctrine and the truths of Christ, which are to feed the mind and impart understanding. The Epistles tell us what we are to do and how we are to live and conduct ourselves.

Paul after his conversion became a balanced individual. His whole being was committed to Christ. This was evident in his mind, his affections, and his experiences, plus his behavior and performance.

God's way is to have the whole person, not just bits and pieces or a part-time relationship. "We have no right to pick and choose. God's way of salvation takes up the intellect, the heart (emotions), the will, the understanding, the sensibilities, the experience, the practice, everything, the whole man . . . ," according to Martyn Lloyd-Jones. Anything less is not acceptable. *The spirit indeed is willing, but the flesh is weak* [Matt. 26:41b]. Thank God for His mercy, love, and forgiveness. There is to be a balance. We are to *Watch and pray, that ye enter not into temptation* [Matt. 26:41a].

Radio personality Paul Harvey said, "That is not all of the story." After Jesus came the first time and found them asleep, he exhorted them to *Watch and pray*. Then he went away a second time and prayed. What did He find when He returned? The disciples were asleep. They were not awake, they were not spiritually alert, and they were not being vigilant. They were not obeying Christ's command.

So what did Jesus do? He left them the third time and went away to pray. How many times do we go to sleep after we have been with Jesus?

How many times have we struggled to stay awake? How many times has He come back to us? Thank God He keeps coming back to fill us from above. May we continually keep in the forefront of our minds to *Watch and pray, that ye enter not into temptation* [Matt. 26:41a].

May we realize and give thanks continuously for "*Love so amazing, so divine, Demands my soul, my life, my all*," that was penned in the beautiful, wonderful hymn "When I Survey the Wondrous Cross" by Isaac Watts.

Amen!

19

False and True Teachings

Finally, my brethren, be strong in the Lord, and in the power of his might.

Put on the whole armor of God, that ye may be able to stand against the wiles (schemes) of the devil.

For we wrestle not against flesh and blood, but against principalities, against powers, against the rulers of the darkness of this world (age), *against spiritual* (hosts of) *wickedness in high places* [Eph. 6:10–12].

The Gospel of the Lord Jesus Christ is an amazing dichotomy. It is both simple and complex. It can reach and satisfy the child, the unlearned, and the scholar. Men and women, boys and girls, with varying gifts, aptitudes, talents, and resources have come to know Christ, to accept Him, and to follow Him. Basically, there is only one thing that keeps a person from grasping the Gospel, and that is self.

Genesis states it very aptly, *And the serpent said unto the woman, Ye shall not surely die: For God doth know that in the day ye eat thereof, then your eyes shall be opened, and ye shall be as gods* (God), *knowing good and evil* [Gen. 3:4–5]. Note the serpent said, *For God doth know*. This was the argument used to get Adam and Eve to succumb. It has been used ever since. How often have similar arguments been used, saying God will not know or God will forgive you?

Compare this with the words of John the Baptist when a confrontation developed between some of his disciples and the Jews regarding purification:

> *John answered and said, A man can receive nothing except it be given him from heaven.*
> *Ye . . . bear me witness, that I said, I am not the Christ, but that I am sent before him* [John 3:27–28].
>
> *He must increase, but I must decrease.*
> *He that cometh from above is above all . . . he that cometh from heaven is above all* [John 3:30–31].
>
> *For he whom God hath sent speaketh the words of God: for God giveth not the Spirit by measure unto him.*
> *The Father loveth the Son, and hath given all things into his hand.*
> *He that believeth on the Son hath everlasting life: and he that believeth not the Son shall not see life; but the wrath of God abideth (remains) on him* [John 3:34–36].

John states several truths in this revealing encounter. He acknowledges that a person receives nothing except what comes from above. John looked to God, not to himself. Then he said, *He must increase, but I must decrease* [John 3:30]. John had disciples. He had people committed to him. Yet he did not seek to usurp that which had been given to him. He realized his position was temporary. He was satisfied to do the will of God and to obey His commands. Further, John asserts a significant truth: Jesus comes from above, and He is above all. He is not of the earth or earthly. He came from heaven. In these verses, John sets a definite standard for preachers and teachers when proclaiming the Gospel by acknowledging who Christ is and stating it unequivocally.

John was bearing witness to Christ, to what he had learned, to what had been revealed to him, and to the truth that he had seen and heard. He was bearing witness to the truth as found in Christ Jesus. He was not adding other thoughts or topics to the Gospel. John did not subscribe to idle rumors, or teachings diluted by the Pharisees and the scribes, or the teachings of men. John knew that Christ had been sent by our heavenly Father, that He had been taught by the Father and was obedient unto Him. Therefore, John stated that God gave the Spirit to Christ in unlimited measure.

There is no bottom to the well from which it cometh or to the container which will hold it. However, recall these words of the Apostle, *But unto every one of us is given grace according to the measure of the gift of Christ* [Eph. 4:7]. None of us receives a measure or an amount whereby we can be satisfied with ourselves and with what we have. We need to draw from the other members of Christ's body and from the Head, which is Christ. We need one another. We need to receive strength from others. We need to give strength. We need the nourishment made available to the members of His body.

The fourth chapter of Ephesians describes how Christ imparts his unity to the body of believers, how we are to walk, how Christ bestows gifts upon different people, how we are to increase in knowledge, how we are to learn Christ, what the new man is to do, and how he or she is to live.

Adam and Eve were interested in themselves, in something specific, something finite. John the Baptist was interested in: what God wanted; in Christ Jesus, the Son of God; in Christ's ministry; and in proclaiming the Gospel. It did not bother him one iota that he was to decrease and Christ was to increase. Pray God that preachers and teachers increase in Christ and decrease in themselves.

There is an enlightening point to consider in these two accounts in Genesis and John's Gospel. In Genesis, Eve says, *We may eat of the fruit of the trees of the garden: . . .* (but) *God hath said, Ye shall not eat of it, neither shall ye touch it, lest ye die* [Gen. 3:2–3]. Note John says, *He that believeth on the Son hath everlasting life: and he that believeth not the Son shall not see life; but the wrath of God abideth* (remains) *on him* [John 3:36]. Certainly there is a contrast. These events relate to us, they impact the mind, the heart, the experiences, and abiding in them. Adam and Eve did not maintain the proper balance. John the Baptist did.

What are we to do? We are to maintain a balance! We are to use our minds, control our experiences, and conduct ourselves according to the Master's teachings. When doing these things it is profitable to open our hearts and minds to the truths proclaimed by Him. First, consider certain points in general, then examine Scripture and what our Lord has to say.

For the most part, people desire to know and to do. That does not mean that they will always do the right thing, even when they want to. Some people like to know and to do merely for self-satisfaction or because of covetousness. Adam and Eve wanted to know and to do in order to gratify themselves to serve their own desires.

What about John the Baptist? His mind increased, his experiences and his heart increased, and his conduct was for the benefit of others. He knew that Christ was to increase and he was to decrease. He supported that. He knew that true knowledge came from God, and that was all the knowledge he needed concerning life and the things of God. Further, he knew that all he needed to know about God was revealed through His Son. He did not seek for more or look for other sources or other people.

Oh, what a testimony we have in the witness of John the Baptist. It would be enlightening if we knew more about the Lord's cousin, but we do not. However, that leads to the next point. What do we know about God? What does Scripture say about acquiring more knowledge regarding God, the Father?

So often people wish to start with themselves, their limited knowledge, and their own experiences when it comes to knowing God. A person desiring to become an aeronautical engineer or a physicist cannot hope to practice in those areas without acquiring knowledge, experience, and practice in that field. How we can be Christ's disciples without exercising similar disciplines is beyond understanding.

The great minds of Scripture, the Reformation, and other periods had one thing in common. They started with God as revealed by and through the Lord Jesus Christ. The most dramatic illustration is the Apostle Paul. Immediately after his conversion, he discarded his previous mindset, experiences, and practices. Look at Calvin, Luther, Knox, Wesley, Whitefield and others.

While proceeding with this study, there are certain thoughts to consider concerning the mind, learning, and knowledge: "How foolish it is to wish to measure God's immensity by our measure," as John Calvin wondered. He also said, "that even the greatest geniuses are like a traveler passing through a field at night who in a momentary lightning flash sees far and wide, but the sight vanishes so swiftly that he is plunged again into the darkness of the night before he can take even a step, let alone be directed on his way by its help," as Calvin expressed in amazement regarding God's power and wisdom. He further states our concern should not be with "What is God" but rather "What God is like to us."

The key point expressed by John Calvin is that "[i]n understanding faith it is not merely a question of knowing that God exists, but . . . of knowing his will toward us." That is a significant difference.

Consider what certain learned individuals have to say about God. Calvin states in his Institutes, "For it is not so much our concern to know who he is in himself, as what he wills to be toward us." Ford Lewis Battles summarized it beautifully, stating, "patiently God, through our history, accommodates his ways of revelation to our condition. Thus, par excellence, the Word made flesh and the written Word from which he speaks is God accommodating Himself to us." Roland Frye said, "What we most need to know about God can come only from God, and it does come through God's self-disclosure in the incarnate Word and the written Word; . . . furthermore, that self-disclosure is typically couched in terms accommodated to the limits of human capacity."

Calvin expresses God's accommodation in the following way: "the Father, himself infinite, becomes finite in the Son, for he has accommodated himself to our little measure lest our minds be overwhelmed by the immensity of his glory." How simple and remarkable are these words about God the Father. God reveals Himself to us so that we can understand Him, so that we can grasp the truth as it is revealed to us.

Some things we are to grasp and not let go. However, we need to recognize that we like to reason and generate our own explanations. Therefore, when so doing remember the brilliant Blaise Pascal said, "It is the supreme achievement of reason to show that there is a limit to reason."

Unfortunately, people do not want to accept the fact that there is a limit to their ability to reason. There comes a time when, if we are honest, we realize that our capabilities are finite, and when we reach our capacity to reason we must accept the fact that we must look elsewhere. Lloyd-Jones stated it in an enlightening and humble way, "I confess that I do not know, that I cannot understand. I become 'as a little child,' and I look up into the face of Him who is the Way, the Truth, and the Life! But from the moment you enter it in that way you begin to use your understanding, and it grows and develops, and there is literally no end to it." That is what certain learned people have to say about God and the Lord Jesus Christ.

What does Scripture have to say about the mind, knowledge, experience, and practice?

> *Beware lest any man spoil* (plunder) *you through philosophy and vain* (empty) *deceit, after the tradition of men, after the rudiments of the world, and not after Christ. For in him dwelleth all of the Godhead bodily* [Col. 2:8–9].

> *Except ye be converted, and become as little children, ye shall not enter into the kingdom of heaven* [Matt. 18:3].

> *Let no man deceive himself. If any man among you seemeth to be wise in this world* (age), *let him become a fool, that he may be wise* [1 Cor. 3:18].
>
> *But the natural man receiveth not the things of the Spirit of God: for they are foolishness unto him: neither can he know them, because they are spiritually discerned* [1 Cor. 2:14].

These verses are appropriate when considering man's mind and how he is going to act. The Colossians were a very intelligent people. They were knowledgeable and intent upon acquiring more learning. However, the Apostle Paul warned them to be careful. He did not want them to be led astray. He did not want them to follow false teachings. He wanted to protect them. He did not want them to fall prey to false wisdom. He did not want anything added to God's Word, or taken away from it. Paul was concerned that philosophy and vain deceit would either compromise or dilute the teachings of Christ.

The Colossians were to focus directly on Christ Himself and so are we. We are to be aware of false teachings when it comes to knowing God, to learning about Him, and to doing His will. The scriptures reveal, not only from the beginning of Christ's ministry but from the time of Adam and Eve that people have tried to distort, disguise, change, alter, and subvert God's word. His truths are revealed so that we may come into a right relationship with Him through Christ and remain there forever and ever." *I am come that they might have life, and that they might have it more abundantly* [John 10:10]. These truths are provided so that we may strengthen one another and be strengthened in turn.

Throughout the Bible one point is clear. God reveals Himself through the written Word and the Word incarnate. Conversely, through Scripture and Christ man is revealed in his natural condition and need. If only man will look and see what he is like, what he really needs, and what is available for him. Pray God that our minds and hearts may be open to the knowledge of the truth contained in Scripture. Pray God that we may not only have our needs revealed to us, but that we may live as God through Christ would have us to live.

"There is no ultimate knowledge of God apart from the Lord Jesus Christ and the full and the perfect revelation that is in Him," as Martyn Lloyd-Jones proclaimed. However, there is a critical point to consider with respect to that statement. We are to guard against becoming more interested in learning the intellectual aspects of God's truths and teachings than in knowing the Lord Jesus Christ Himself.

What is the purpose of acquiring the knowledge in Scripture? It is to know the Lord Jesus. To know Him as He is, the Son of God, and to remember what John the Baptist said.

Members of Christ's body are to worship God and to acquire knowledge. This means learning the truths contained in Scripture so that we will know them, and rejecting false teachings when they appear or are proclaimed.

When studying Scripture we are not to focus on things, we are to focus on the person, the Lord Jesus Christ. Why say that? Because it is through Him that we know God. Because it is on Him that God poured the Spirit in an immeasurable abundance. It is from Him that we receive the living waters and that we receive knowledge and strength.

The wiles of the devil do not want us to know the Lord as we should. They want us to get sidetracked, to look for meanings hidden in numbers, to consider or emphasize differences in the different translations of the Bible, and to create doubt in our hearts and minds. What should we do?

We have considered Genesis, Adam and Eve, John the Baptist, Calvin, New Testament statements, and expository comments by Christian scholars. What else is there? What about the teachings of our Lord?

In the tenth chapter of John, Jesus reveals a great deal about His life, His purpose, and His conduct. He says,

> *. . . I am the door of the sheep.*
> *I am the good shepherd: the good shepherd giveth his life for the sheep.*
> *The hireling fleeth, because he is a hireling, and careth not for the sheep.*
> *I am the good shepherd, and know my sheep, and am known of mine.*
> *. . . and I lay down my life for the sheep.*
> *Therefore, doth my Father love me, because I lay down my life, that I might take it again.*
> *No man taketh it from me, but I lay it down of myself. I have power to lay it down, and I have power to take it again. This commandment have I received of my Father* [Selections from John 10:7–18].

In these verses, Jesus is dealing with the scribes and priests who were considered the shepherds of the people. Therefore, He was both amplifying upon something the people could understand and fulfilling the teachings of God.

At that time there was a door to the sheepfold, but only one door. There was a porter, or doorkeeper, who would open the door. However, he was to open it only when he recognized the voice of the shepherd. Then the shepherd would lead the sheep into the sheepfold. Since the sheep knew the voice of the shepherd they would follow him.

During that time there were people who would not enter the sheepfold by the door. Why? Because they were thieves and robbers. They wanted to steal the sheep or lead them away. Jesus says, *I am the door of the sheep* [John 10:7]. What does this mean? He is affirming, as Calvin puts it, that He is "the head of all spiritual teaching." Therefore, it is through Him that we are fed and enlightened.

This teaching comes immediately after Jesus had healed the blind man and was confronted by the Pharisees. Jesus answered the Pharisees, *For judgment I am come into this world, that they which see not might see; and that they which see might be made blind* [John 9:39]. Jesus tells us that He is the door by which the sheep are saved and that it is the only way: into the sheepfold; into a right relationship with God; to acquire proper knowledge; and to lead the sheep through the door. The false teachers and preachers do not want to use that door. They want to find other ways into the sheepfold, or they want to lead the sheep in other directions.

Jesus says several things in these verses. First, the sheep are to hear the Shepherd. They must remain in hearing distance. They are not to wander off so that they cannot hear the Shepherd, or allow other noises to drown out His voice.

Second, they are to know the voice of the Shepherd. They are to know what He means, what He is telling them. The sheep are to know when they go into the fold by the door that they will find care and protection, and when they go out to pasture they will find food and nourishment. Jesus says, *By me if any man enter in, he shall be saved, and shall go in and out, and find pasture* [John 10:9].

Next, the good Shepherd wants the sheep to have life and to have it more abundantly. Why? Because they will obey His commands and live an abundant, joyful life.

Further, the good Shepherd gives His life for His sheep. Need we say more?

Also, the door is the gateway to the Father. The Voice calls us to the door. May we hear and know that voice, those words, and that truth.

May we learn to turn away from the false teachings and the false prophets, whether they are outside the sheepfold, or have gained entrance falsely.

Last, the good Shepherd knows His sheep. And, thank God He says that He is known by His sheep.

May we learn from Adam and Eve, John the Baptist, scholars, Scripture, and the teachings of the Master. More importantly, may He reveal Himself to us and may we hear His voice.

But even more importantly, may we respond to Him and know Him as the way, the truth, and the life. May we have life more abundantly by going in and out through the door and finding pasture in the fertile fields God has prepared and made available for increasing our faith, knowledge, strength, and wisdom.

Amen!

20

Truth and Experience

> *So when they continued asking him, he lifted (raised) up himself, and said unto them, He that is without sin among you, let him first cast a stone at her.*
>
> *When Jesus had lifted (raised) up himself, and saw none but the woman, he said unto her, Woman, where are those thine accusers? hath no man condemned thee?*
>
> *She said, No man, Lord. And Jesus said unto her, Neither do I condemn thee: go, and sin no more.*
>
> *The Pharisees therefore said unto him, Thou bearest record (witness) of thyself; thy record (witness) is not true (not valid as testimony).*
>
> *Jesus answered and said unto them, Though I bear record (witness) of myself, yet my record is true: for I know whence I came, and whither I go; but ye cannot tell whence I come, and whither I go* [Selections from John 8:7–14].

Questions are asked. Why, in the final verses of Ephesians, are we examining portions of other books in the New Testament and Genesis? Why are we still considering *the wiles of the devil*? What is Scripture saying in the early years of the twenty-first century? How can the New Testament teachings be applied to our daily living? These and other questions are appropriate.

Consider two additional questions. What did the eleven who became apostles and Paul bring to Christ when they were called? Their minds, hearts, experiences, personalities, and practices. What did the eleven plus Paul have after their encounter with the Lord Jesus? Certainly, they had their minds, hearts, experiences, personalities, and practices. But they had more. They had knowledge, obedience, faith, confidence, and an intense desire to serve the Lord. However, they did not have a life of ease nor a life free from tests, temptations, opposition, taunts, revilings, hardships, sufferings, and persecutions.

What are we looking for? A life that is "comfy and cozy" or the strength to proceed under difficult circumstances and to persevere when conditions are less than favorable?

Much emphasis has been placed throughout the twentieth century and into the twenty-first century upon beautiful and truthful teachings that meet important needs and comfort us: that God is love, that Jesus loves me, and that we can "let go and let God." These thoughts impact us and color our thinking. However, Christ realizes we have burdens and cares as we proceed through life and that we need help to overcome them, not that we are to abandon them or allow them to overcome us. It is Christ who strengthens us in our time of need and provides us with His wisdom.

Therefore, Christ says, *Come unto me all ye that labor and are heavy laden* [Matt. 11:28] and I will help you through your trials, tests, and temptations. In addition, Paul provides us with these comforting and encouraging words, *And now abideth faith, hope, charity* (love), *these three; but the greatest of these is charity* (love) [1 Cor. 13:13]. Yes, we may have faith, hope, and charity as we encounter the challenges, obstacles, and pitfalls of life, but we are to persevere boldly and confidently, knowing that the Lord Jesus is with us and will enlighten us. These are beautiful, truthful teachings that meet some of our basic needs. Thank God for them!

But there is more, much more. One of the basic deficiencies of the church at large during the last century and into this one has been *not* presenting the full Gospel. There has been picking and choosing. The demands, challenges, persecutions, rejections, and requirements have been neglected and soft-pedaled. Selected teachings of Scripture may have been presented, but the agonies and ordeals that our Master experienced during His earthly ministry have been ignored.

Previously, we considered certain aspects of our minds, experiences, and practices regarding our faith in the Lord Jesus Christ and *the wiles of the devil*. The truths revealed in Scripture should help us better understand Jesus Christ and His teachings provided for our instruction and benefit.

However, a word of caution when considering the broad realm of people's experiences: it is difficult to identify *the wiles* (schemes) *of the devil*. We are trying to deal with what we have done or experienced which is something that is inside us. For the most part it is subjective and incorporates our feelings, emotions, moods, and opinions.

It is much easier to analyze something involving other people or an objective truth. When self is involved, that is a different question. Sometimes the issues get cloudy or hazy, or the mind gets muddled, or we cannot see the trees for the forest. Individuals accepting Christ and putting on the new man are still confronted by temptations that they would just as soon not experience.

Two factors impact upon us: truth as it is revealed; and experiences impacting our thinking and conduct. Sometimes people place their entire emphasis upon experiences, what has happened or should have happened. These people are not particularly interested in what caused the experiences or in the truths that brought them about. Other people are interested in acquiring the truth or knowledge about the truth, but they are not particularly interested in experiences.

There needs to be a balance between obtaining a knowledge of the truth and understanding it, and having experiences that strengthen our faith and enhance our relationship with the Lord Jesus Christ and His Father. There may have been a time when we had a meaningful experience or when God revealed Himself in a special way, enabling us to have understanding. However, that does not mean we will have meaningful experiences or that our minds will be illuminated easily without continuous effort.

There are things to do. We are to search and seek for God's guideposts, read and study Scripture, pray for enlightenment, and obey the will of the Father.

These tasks require effort, concentration, and self-control. We are not called to remain in grade school or high school or to have a diet of milk only. We are called to progress to the limits of our capabilities, to persevere in the face of obstacles, to pursue knowledge and understanding as it relates to the will of the Father, and to eat meat, even tough meat. These objectives are not for those who place themselves first, but for those who follow in the footsteps of John the Baptist.

What can we say about John the Baptist? He knew the truth as it had been revealed to him. He pursued the truth. He proclaimed the truth, and he applied it to his daily living. He had experiences, but he did not dwell upon them. He proceeded to do the will of God. John the Baptist maintained a balance between objectivity and subjectivity. We are to strive to do the same.

There are questions to address. What do we know about the truth as it has been revealed in the Lord Jesus Christ? Where do we get our knowledge? What have been our experiences with the Lord Jesus Christ? What is our relationship to Him? "Make no mistake about this, the truth of God is something that is to be experienced. It is not a philosophical system, it is not a mere ethical teaching. The whole object and end of the Christian (faith) is to bring us to a knowledge of God; and God is not some kind of philosophic 'X.' He is not an abstraction, a mere postulate in philosophy. God is! He is a personal deity. And He is to be known," as appropriately described by Martyn Lloyd-Jones. This bears repeating, remembering, and applying.

The Apostle John says,

> *THAT which was from the beginning, which we have heard, which we have seen with our eyes, which we have looked upon, and our hands have handled, of the Word of life* [1 John 1:1].
>
> *That which we have seen and heard declare we unto you, that ye also may have fellowship with us: and truly our fellowship is with the Father, and with His Son Jesus Christ* [1 John 1:3].

John knew the truth and experienced it. Then he proclaimed it, saying, *Our fellowship is with the Father, and with his Son Jesus Christ.* Our fellowship is with them. It is to be a fellowship that is not only experienced, but the truth of it known and realized. As members of Christ's body, we are to know the truth and to experience it.

The eighth chapter of John's Gospel contains truths expressed by the Lord Jesus during an encounter He had with the Pharisees and scribes as they sought to discredit Him. This experience contains beneficial and valuable teachings of our Lord Jesus for today and tomorrow.

Jesus was in the temple teaching when suddenly the scribes and Pharisees physically brought a woman into his presence who had been caught in the act of adultery. Why did they do this? To punish or make an example of the woman? No. They did it in order to ensnare Christ by His answer. They had an ulterior motive.

The scribes and Pharisees were opposed to the Master. Therefore, they wanted to trap Him and cause Him to fall in disrepute or to offend either the Roman or Jewish authorities. The Lord Jesus had enemies. Do we? They were opposed to Him and did not want Him teaching the people. The Master's response was two-fold. His initial response exhibited that it was not worth listening to them when He stooped down and wrote in the sand. Next, He spoke those immortal words, *He that is without sin among you, let him first cast a stone at her* [John 8:7]. He hit them right between the eyes, smack, bam! They could not continue to face Him in the light of that statement.

However, it did not mean that any of the scribes and Pharisees were converted or that their opposition lessened. Jesus did not condemn the woman. He *said unto her, Neither do I condemn thee; go, and sin no more* [John 8:11]. Why did Jesus say those words? Because when a sinner (that is, you or me) is reconciled to God, he or she should show their gratitude by endeavoring to live a holy and godly life. When we are forgiven, we should express our appreciation by striving to obey His commandments. As Calvin so appropriately notes, "The same Word of God that offers us pardon, calls us at the same time to repentance."

After the encounter with the scribes and Pharisees, Jesus returned to teaching the people assembled. He said unto them, *I am the light of the world: he that followeth me shall not walk in darkness, but shall have the light of life* [John 8:12]. Guess what? The Pharisees had come back and were listening to Jesus. They did not want to learn from Him. They were not interested in the truth or in a meaningful experience. They were opposed to Him and wanted to get Him. Therefore, the Pharisees said to Jesus, *Thy record* (witness) *is not true* [John 8:13]. Then after Jesus answered and left no doubt that His record was true, the Pharisees said unto Him, *Where is thy Father* [John 8:19]? The Pharisees undoubtedly asked this question in order to mock Him. They made fun of Him because of the way He spoke about His Father.

Note how Jesus responded to the Pharisees. He came right back at them, saying, *Ye neither know me, nor my Father: if ye had known me, ye should have known my Father also* [John 8:19]. Jesus, even though He is being attacked and maligned, is true to His Father. His first allegiance is to the Father. We are to have the same allegiance. We are to be true to our heavenly Father.

After this encounter in the temple the situation calmed down a little bit. Then they said to Jesus, *Who art thou* [John 8:25]? Jesus answered their question and explained who he was. The scribes and Pharisees did not understand, but as Scripture says *many believed on him* [John 8:30]. When this happened Jesus said to the Jews who believed, *If ye continue* (abide) *in my word, then are ye my disciples indeed: And ye shall know the truth, and the truth shall make you free* [John 8:31–32]. The word *continue* means *to abide in the Word*.

Jesus tells the believers that they are to learn the truth and they are to practice it according to His instructions. Here we have two sides of the same coin—knowledge and experience. Then things began to heat up. Some of the Jews and Pharisees saw that many believed and that Christ was instructing them in what they should do. Therefore, they said to Jesus, *We be Abraham's seed* (descendants), *and were never in bondage* (enslaved) *to any man: how sayest thou, Ye shall be made free* [John 8:33]?

Jesus responded wanting them to focus on His teaching. Therefore, he says,

> *Whosoever committeth sin is the servant of sin* [John 8:34].
>
> *I know that ye are Abraham's seed* (descendants); *but ye seek to kill me, because my word hath no place in you.*
> *I speak that which I have seen with my Father: and ye do that which ye have seen with your father* [John 8:37–38].

Note how Jesus goes back to the truth of His Father, who is God, and to His experiences with the Father.

Then Jesus' opponents became testy and obnoxious. They *said unto him, Abraham is our father* [John 8:39]. What did they mean by this? Not just that they were of the lineage of Abraham, but that "they were a holy race, the heritage of God and the children of God," according to John Calvin. They did not say they were doing the will of God or that they were obedient to the teachings of Scripture. No. They were depending upon their ancestry, on what someone else had done. Jesus responds directly to their shallow statements, saying,

> *If ye were Abraham's children, ye would do the works of Abraham. But now ye seek to kill me, a man that hath told you the truth, which I have heard of God: this did not Abraham. Ye do the deeds of your father* [John 8:39–41].

Abraham's foremost quality was his obedience to the will of God. Christ differentiates between those who know the will of the Father and those who seek to obey their own ideas and interpretations. He is not interested in their lineage but in their relationship to God and their knowledge of Him.

He contrasts that by acknowledging what they intended to do to Him, that is, to kill Him. Then He points out that He had been telling the truth about God, which also Abraham had done, but the people had not sought to kill Abraham.

Then what happens? The Jews get nastier. They said to him, *We be not born of fornication: we have one Father, even God* [John 8:41]. Why did they say this? Once again, to state that they were of Abraham's lineage. Therefore, they were of God. Further, they want to depend upon the fact that they could trace their ancestry back to the patriarch. The devil uses his wiles so that people will consider things that are irrelevant. The devil does not want them to stress faith, truth, knowledge, and obedience.

The Jews were stressing their ancestry. Jesus responds to them by saying they are so obstinate that they not only do not understand His speech but will not even listen to His words. Jesus tells these so-called holy people that they are of their father, the devil, that the devil is a liar and the father of lies. He tells them straightforwardly that they are not the children of Abraham and God. Then Jesus adds these telling words. *He that is of God heareth God's words: ye therefore hear them not, because ye are not of God* [John 8:47]. Remember to whom Jesus directs those words, the scribes and Pharisees, even though there were other people present listening to this exchange.

So what did the Jews say next? They were not faring very well. They were losing face, losing support, and becoming emotional. Therefore, they said something intended to incite the people and to defame Him. They let their acrimony show when they said to Jesus, *Say we not well that thou art a Samaritan, and hast a devil* [John 8:48]? The antipathy keeps building. Jesus responded, *I honor my Father, and ye do dishonor me* [John 8:49]. He adds to this, *I say unto you, If a man keep my saying* (word), *he shall never see death* [John 8:51].

This was too much for the Jews. They said unto Jesus, *Now we know that thou hast a devil. Abraham is dead, and the prophets; . . . Art thou greater than our father Abraham, which is dead? And the prophets are dead: whom makest thou thyself* [John 8:52–53]? The Jews were putting more emphasis on Abraham and the prophets than the Word of God and the truth being revealed to them.

> *Jesus answered, If I honor myself, my honor is nothing: it is my Father that honoreth me; of whom ye say, that he is your God:*
> *Yet ye have not known him; but I know him: and if I should say, I know him not, I shall be a liar like unto you: but I know him, and keep his saying* (word) [John 8:54–55].

Jesus was not interested in a popularity contest. He knew that it was the Father who was honoring Him, the same God that the Pharisees claimed was theirs. Jesus points out that they knew neither God nor His teachings. Then Jesus adds the clincher that culminates His encounter with the Pharisees. He says, *Your father Abraham rejoiced to see my day: and he saw it, and was glad* [John 8:56]. Abraham's object was to see Christ's kingdom flourish, and he ardently longed for it. *Then said the Jews unto him, Thou are not yet fifty years old, and hast thou seen Abraham* [John 8:57]? The Jews were thinking of the flesh. Then Jesus said, *Verily, verily, I say unto you. Before Abraham was, I am* [John 8:58].

With these words Christ, "claims for himself a heavenly and divine power, the perception of which was diffused from the beginning of the world throughout all ages," as beautifully described by John Calvin.

This was too much for the Jews. Their words, their accusations had come to naught. Therefore, they took up stones to cast at Him. Jesus did not have an easy time. He was attacked, persecuted, and vilified. Yet He was obedient to the will of His Father. He maintained a balance between knowledge and experience. His mind and His heart were devoted to the Father and to serving Him. He did not waver from the truth as He received it from His Father, and in turn He revealed it to us.

May we have the capacity as we face challenges, tests, and temptations to know what Christ would do and what He would have us to do. When we experience opposition, rejection, acrimony, the evils of the world, suffering, hurts, and injuries may we also realize that our Lord and our God, when He was in the flesh, suffered much more than we, and He was without sin. He deserved nothing less than honor, glory, adoration, adulation, praise, worship, and obedience.

Yes, it is important to know the teachings of Scripture, but it is much more important to know the Lord Jesus Christ and what He experienced during His earthly ministry.

Amen!

Outline Questions

Chapter 1

CHILDREN, OBEY YOUR PARENTS

> CHILDREN, obey your parents in the Lord: for this is right.
> HONOUR THY FATHER AND MOTHER; which is the first commandment with promise;
> THAT IT MAY BE WELL WITH THEE, AND THOU MAYEST LIVE LONG ON THE EARTH.
> And, ye fathers, provoke not your children to wrath: but bring them up in the nurture (training) and admonition of the Lord [Eph. 6:1–4].

What is the qualification and the admonition in the command *Children, obey your parents in the Lord: for this is right*?

How are parents to raise their children?

Why does Paul use the word *obey*?

What reasons does Paul cite for the lack of harmony in the home?

Why did Paul direct his teaching to both the children and parents?

What is the difference between morality and righteousness?

What divine obligation do parents have to their children and the children to their parents?

How did Jesus exhibit obedience to His earthly parents?

What duties are children to discharge to their parents?

What did Jesus say to the Pharisees and scribes?

Who can distort the teachings of God?

Why are children to *obey* their parents?

What does the fifth commandment mean in its full context?

Chapter 2

DISCIPLINE

> CHILDREN, obey your parents in the Lord: for this is right.
> HONOUR THY FATHER AND MOTHER; which is the first commandment with promise;
> THAT IT MAY BE WELL WITH THEE, AND THOU MAYEST LIVE LONG ON THE EARTH.
> And, ye fathers, provoke not your children to wrath: but bring them up in the nurture (training) and admonition of the Lord [Eph. 6:1–4].

What did Jesus do during His earthly ministry that has had an impact on people for two thousand years?

What is a person to do when he or she accepts Christ as Lord and Saviour?

Why is it important to be knowledgeable regarding divine teachings and biblical truths?

Why are people to learn to live in the most intimate and complex relationships?

How are family relationships to be conducted?

How are we to walk in family relationships?

What does Paul say to the different types of people at the close of the fifth chapter and the beginning of the sixth?

What should our prayer be regarding infirmities?

What teachings does Paul provide for our instruction, growth in faith, and right relationship with Christ?

How important is discipline in our life with Christ?

What factors or teachings have become evident in the last one hundred years regarding discipline?

What does the Bible reveal with respect to discipline and the nature of people?

How is God revealed in Scripture?

Where and how does God punish sin?

Why was the Atonement necessary?

Chapter 3

MAN'S RELATIONSHIP TO GOD

> *Servants, be obedient to them that are your masters according to the flesh, with fear and trembling, in singleness* (sincerity) *of your heart, as unto Christ;*
>
> *Not with eyeservice, as menpleasers; but as the servants of Christ, doing the will of God from the heart;*
>
> *With good will doing service, as to the Lord, and not to men:*
>
> *Knowing that whatsoever good thing any man doeth, the same shall he receive of the Lord, whether he be bond* (slave) *or free.*
>
> *And, ye masters, do the same things unto them, forbearing* (giving up) *threatening: knowing that your Master also is in heaven; neither is there respect of persons with him* [Eph. 6:5–9].

To what kind of a living faith are we called?

What specific truths did Paul address to the Ephesians?

What spiritual blessings did he bring to their attention?

Why was God's grace given to the Ephesians?

How are we to walk through life?

What does Paul say we are to do?

Where is the emphasis to be placed?

What is peculiar or significant about the Apostle's message?

What must we do to apply a doctrine or teaching?

What is the Apostle Paul doing as he addresses the servants and slaves?

Why does Paul tell the servants to *be obedient . . . as unto Christ*?

What do the apostles stress regarding man's various relationships?

What is the primary teaching of the Bible?

What relationships come first in the Bible?

What is the chief function of the church?

What is to be the guiding light for a Christian's conduct?

Chapter 4

PRIORITIES

> *Servants, be obedient to them that are your masters according to the flesh, with fear and trembling, in singleness (sincerity) of your heart, as unto Christ;*
> *Not with eyeservice, as menpleasers; but as the servants of Christ, doing the will of God from the heart;*
> *With good will doing service, as to the Lord, and not to men* [Eph. 6:5–7].

What are your priorities?

How does God make us clean and whole?

What are our responsibilities with respect to our salvation and sanctification?

What are we to do when facing difficulties, obstacles, and our daily tasks?

What is the primary task of the church?

What is required of church members today?

What does the Bible stress?

What principles emerge from this portion of Ephesians?

What does the Apostle say regarding our conduct in all aspects of life, even when the situations or circumstances are not ideal?

How is a member of Christ's body to react to life's challenges?

Where and how does Paul say we are to serve God?

What does Scripture teach regarding our primary relationships?

What is the primary concern of the person who accepts Christ?

How can individuals and social conditions be improved?

What did John Wesley preach about when he went into the poorest of poor districts in London?

What happened as a result of Wesley's preaching?

What happens when the church produces Christians?

Chapter 5

CHRIST'S SLAVES

> *Knowing that whatsoever good thing any man doeth, the same shall he receive of the Lord, whether he be bond (slave) or free.*
> *And, ye masters, do the same things unto them, forbearing (giving up) threatening: knowing that your Master also is in heaven; neither is there respect of persons with him* [Eph. 6:8–9].

To whom are the masters or employers to give obedience?

Who are Christ's slaves?

What are the servants and masters to learn?

When is a member of Christ's body required to take a stand?

What type of conduct are masters and servants to exhibit?

What do the words *fear and trembling* mean?

How are we as adults in Christ to be like children?

What does *in singleness of your heart* mean?

What characteristics or traits are we to exhibit?

What does the Apostle mean when he says, *as to the Lord, and not to men*?

What is Paul telling the Ephesians and us to do?

What does Paul mean when he tells the servants not to obey their masters *with eyeservice, as menpleasers*?

How does this teaching impact upon those who are members of Christ's body?

Who and what is the saint or faithful person in Christ Jesus?

What is to be the first consideration of the saint, or the faithful, in Christ Jesus?

How does Paul, under the influence of Christ, tell us to conduct ourselves?

Chapter 6

KNOWING YOUR MASTER IN HEAVEN

> *And, ye masters, do the same things unto them, forbearing (giving up) threatening: knowing that your Master also is in heaven; neither is there respect of persons with him* [Eph. 6:9]

How are masters to treat their servants?

To whom are the masters accountable?

What does Paul tell the earthly masters they are to do?

Where do most troubles, disagreements, clashes, and discords occur?

What principles does the Apostle Paul lay down to guide an earthly master's conduct?

What does Scripture say about being accountable to *your Master . . . in heaven*?

What does Scripture say about the judgment seat of Christ?

What does Calvin say about evil deeds and God's grace?

What are the masters and servants to know?

Why does Paul add the phrase *knowing that your Master also is in heaven*?

What does the phrase *neither is there respect of persons with him* (God) mean?

What is God's concern for each of us?

What really matters in this world?

What does the parable of Lazarus and the rich man say to us?

Why are we to search the scriptures?

What are we to do with these teachings?

Chapter 7

FINALLY MY BRETHREN, BE STRONG . . .

> *Finally, my brethren, be strong in the Lord, and in the power of his might.*
> *Put on the whole armor of God, that ye may be able to stand against the wiles* (schemes) *of the devil* [Eph. 6:10–11].

What does Paul present to the brethren before telling them to *be strong in the Lord*?

How are the saints and faithful to live?

To whom is Paul addressing the culmination of his letter?

What confronts the saints as they journey through life?

Why does Paul say, *Finally, my brethren, be strong in the Lord*?

What does Ruth Paxson say about the "arch enemy" and "spiritual pacifist(s)"?

What sustained, strengthened, and enabled Paul?

How did Paul show his complete dependence upon God?

Why does Paul shift his emphasis from Christlike conduct and marriage to the outside enemy?

What general observations are we to grasp and retain as we continue to go through life with Christ?

How does Paul issue his call to battle?

How are we to conduct ourselves?

Chapter 8

SEPARATING OURSELVES

> *Finally, my brethren, be strong in the Lord, and in the power of his might.*
> *Put on the whole armor of God, that ye may be able to stand against the wiles* (schemes) *of the devil* [Eph. 6:10–11].

What should Paul's command to *be strong in the Lord, and in the power of His might* stimulate us to do?

Why are we to continue to focus our minds on the Lord Jesus Christ?

With what do we have to contend?

What does William Gurnall say about preaching and hearing God's word?

What is the Apostle defining in these final verses of Ephesians?

To whom is Paul directing his exhortation?

What does Scripture say about dealing with life's problems?

Why does Paul expound upon Christ's words in Ephesians?

Why is more needed than moral schemes and teachings?

What is it that Paul does not say?

How is the Christian to act as a member of Christ's body?

Why did Christ come?

What does Scripture stress about the flesh?

What do we wrestle against?

What did Martin Luther discover?

Who provides a witness to the Gospel of Christ?

What method does Scripture propose that Christ's followers are to exemplify?

Chapter 9

STRENGTH, POWER, AND MIGHT

> *Finally, my brethren, be strong in the Lord, and in the power of his might* [Eph. 6:10].

What do the words *strong, power*, and *might* mean as used by Paul?

Why does the Apostle want us to become strengthened inwardly?

What steps are the saints and faithful to take in applying this teaching?

What is the saint to do when exhibiting courage and resolution?

How are the four commands of Paul summarized?

What produces strength for the saint and faithful follower?

How is this strength acquired from the Lord?

What happens through prayer and as a result of it?

Why should we receive strength from God?

What type of strength, *power*, or *might* is received from God?

What does Paul want us to do?

Why are we to depend on the power of the Lord?

Who is it that God loves?

Chapter 10

TO FALL OR TO STAND

> *Put on the whole armor of God, that ye may be able to stand against the wiles* (schemes) *of the devil* [Eph. 6:11].

What enables us to fall or stand?

What do we encounter as we travel along life's road?

On whom did David depend?

How do we obtain a firm conviction that God will not forsake us?

What does receiving this firm conviction require?

What relevant factors should be considered regarding God's strength?

What does God do regarding these relevant factors?

What does Paul mean by *light* and *darkness*?

What are we to do regarding these relevant factors?

Why are we to put on the *whole armor of God*?

What is a person like who does not have the *whole armor of God*?

What are the characteristics of *the whole armor of God*?

What happens when the saints and faithful do not use God's armor?

What are the saints and faithful to do when they put on *the whole armor of God*?

Chapter 11

PREPARE TO WRESTLE

> *Finally, my brethren, be strong in the Lord, and in the power of his might.*
> *Put on the whole armor of God, that ye may be able to stand against the wiles (schemes) of the devil.*
> *For we wrestle not against flesh and blood, but against principalities, against powers, against the rulers of the darkness of this world* (age), *against spiritual* (hosts of) *wickedness in high places* [Eph. 6:10–12].

Who is the enemy?

What is the greatest need in the world today?

Why does Paul, under the influence of the Holy Spirit, want us *to stand against the wiles* (schemes) *of the devil?*

Who are the saints and the faithful?

What do the words *stand, wrestle, devil,* and *wiles* mean?

How does Paul use the pronoun *we* to describe our relationship with Christ?

How can a person wrestle with God?

How are we to wrestle?

Why does Satan initiate combat with us?

Why do we have struggles and temptations?

Why do *we wrestle* continuously?

Why are the saints and the faithful to be trained?

What enables us to triumph when *we wrestle*?

Chapter 12

SATAN

> *Put on the whole armor of God, that ye may be able to stand against the wiles* (schemes) *of the devil.*
> *For we wrestle not against flesh and blood, but against principalities, against powers, against the rulers of the darkness of this world* (age), *against spiritual* (hosts of) *wickedness in high places* [Eph. 6:11–12].

What is the problem with man?

What changes man?

What do man's problems have to do with the devil?

Why is it that people do not believe there is a spiritual realm?

How do people question the authority of Scripture?

What is the way to God the Father?

Outline Questions

What is of primary importance if we are to *walk worthy of the vocation* (calling) *wherewith ye have been called*?

What does Christ do on the Cross?

What does Scripture say about Satan?

What are the names and characteristics of Satan?

What does Ephesians say about the power of Satan?

What else can we say about Satan?

What does Jesus say about Satan?

What is Satan's plan?

What is the result of Satan's revolt plus his activities?

What did Paul know regarding the devil and the Lord Jesus Christ?

Chapter 13

THE COMBATANTS

> *For we wrestle not against flesh and blood, but against principalities, against powers, against the rulers of the darkness of this world* (age), *against spiritual* (hosts of) *wickedness in high places* [Eph. 6:12].

What is meant by the *wiles of the devil*?

What does the Apostle Paul exhort us to do?

Who is involved in *the wiles of the devil*?

What are we to bear in mind as we study *the wiles of the devil*?

What are we to do regarding our battles with Satan?

Why is Satan at enmity with God?

Why were the devil and other angels cast out of heaven?

How has history been influenced by Satan and Adam?

What impact does God's action against Satan and Adam have on us?

Why are the saints and faithful to be strengthened by the power of God's might?

Who is Satan's adversary with the ability to defeat him?

What limitations are placed upon Satan?

Chapter 14

THE DEVIL AND HIS FORCES

> *Put on the whole armor of God, that ye may be able to stand against the wiles* (schemes) *of the devil* [Eph. 6:11].

What is our relationship to be with the Lord Jesus Christ?

What three basic relationships concerned Paul?

To what did Paul know that we would be exposed?

What does Paul say to the Corinthians that is so meaningful?

What does the devil do to people?

What does Scripture say about forgiveness and Satan?

What does Scripture say about sin?

What must we do *to stand against the wiles of the devil*?

What are various *wiles of the devil*?

How are we to respond to the wiles?

Where are we to take refuge?

Why does Satan continue to taunt us?

Chapter 15

THE DEVIL'S DISGUISES

> *Put on the whole armor of God, that ye may be able to stand against the wiles* (schemes) *of the devil* [Eph. 6:11].

Why are we to be concerned about the devil?

What is meant by being *subtle*?

Why did Paul warn the Christians in Ephesus?

What did Paul realize after his encounter on the road to Damascus?

Why did the New Testament authors write as they did about Satan?

How does the devil attack us?

Why does Calvin stress the importance of worshipping God and acquiring knowledge?

About what are we to pray to God?

How does the devil work in the organized church?

Why does Scripture remind us of false teachers and prophets?

What other ways does Satan use to assault the members of Christ's body?

What does the Bible state unequivocally?

What methods does Satan use to deceive Christ's followers?

What does the devil love to do?

What is Gurnall's assessment of Satan?

What are we to do when encountering *the wiles of the devil*?

Chapter 16

THOSE DAMNABLE HERESIES

> *Put on the whole armor of God, that ye may be able to stand against the wiles* (schemes) *of the devil.*
> *For we wrestle not against flesh and blood, but against principalities, against powers, against the rulers of the darkness of this world* (age), *against spiritual* (hosts of) *wickedness in high places* [Eph. 6:11–12].

What commandments does Jesus give regarding love and God's love?

What are we to know about God's love?

To whom does Jesus direct His commands and statements?

What are we to know about *those damnable heresies*?

What did the first century prophets do regarding Scripture and Christ's followers?

What tasks were performed by the first century teachers?

What is a constant threat to the Word of God?

What happens when the Word is proclaimed but the focus is not upon God and Christ?

Why are we to probe the scriptures and seek the truth?

How did the New Testament writers present the Gospel?

What is the source of *those damnable heresies*?

What has been their impact?

What has been the answer to *those damnable heresies*?

Why were the different confessions of faith developed?

What can keep a person from a knowledge of the truth and having a right relationship with God?

What does Scripture say about proclaiming the Gospel and its truths?

What interested the New Testament writers regarding the church and its members?

Chapter 17

ROAD BLOCKS AND DETOURS

> *Finally, my brethren, be strong in the Lord, and in the power of his might.*
> *Put on the whole armor of God, that ye may be able to stand against the wiles (schemes) of the devil.*
> *For we wrestle not against flesh and blood, but against principalities, against powers, against the rulers of the darkness of this world* (age), *against spiritual* (hosts of) *wickedness in high places* [Eph. 6:10–12].

How does the Lord Jesus pray regarding that which is evil?

For what does Christ pray regarding those who have been given to Him by God?

Can you think of one Old Testament or New Testament person who was protected from the world and *wiles of the devil*?

What does the process of sanctification include?

What does *sanctify them through thy truth* mean?

What does the devil want to do?

What are the characteristics of cults?

What differentiates the followers of the cults from those who have faith in Christ Jesus?

What are we called to be and to do?

What do the cults say about the Holy Spirit?

What does Paul emphasize regarding our heavenly Father?

What does the New Testament say?

What does Lloyd-Jones say?

What are the differences between the message of the cults and the Gospel?

What does Calvin stress concerning our relationship to God?

What does Scripture stress above everything else?

Chapter 18

WATCH AND PRAY

> *Finally, my brethren, be strong in the Lord, and in the power of his might.*
> *Put on the whole armor of God, that ye may be able to stand against the wiles* (schemes) *of the devil.*
> *For we wrestle not against flesh and blood, but against principalities, against powers, against the rulers of the darkness of this world* (age), *against spiritual* (hosts of) *wickedness in high places* [Eph. 6:10–12].

How can we mature to the point where we can deny self and obey Christ's commands?

How do we limit Christ's power and strength?

Why don't we abandon ourselves to Christ?

What should we affirm when partaking of the Lord's Supper?

What did Christ say and do after the first Lord's Supper?

What were His disciples to do after the first Lord's Supper?

What are we to do after the Lord's Supper?

What happened after Jesus *went a little farther . . . and prayed*?

What does the Greek word for "sleep" mean?

Why does Jesus tell us to *watch and pray*?

What does the flesh need as it struggles?

What does the word "*watch*" mean as used by Jesus?

Why does Jesus tell His disciples to *watch and pray*?

How should we learn to *watch and pray*?

What are we to realize when we have been blessed with faith in Christ?

Why should each individual *watch and pray*?

Why are we to maintain a balance between the mind, experience, and practice?

What does God's way of salvation include?

Chapter 19

FALSE AND TRUE TEACHINGS

> *Finally, my brethren, be strong in the Lord, and in the power of his might.*
> *Put on the whole armor of God, that ye may be able to stand against the wiles* (schemes) *of the devil.*
> *For we wrestle not against flesh and blood, but against principalities, against powers, against the rulers of the darkness of this world* (age), *against spiritual* (hosts of) *wickedness in high places* [Eph. 6:10–12].

What keeps a person from God and Christ?

What does John the Baptist say about Jesus?

To whom did John the Baptist bear witness?

What does the fourth chapter of Ephesians decribe?

What are the differences between Adam and Eve and John the Baptist?

What did John the Baptist know?

What does Scripture say about acquiring a knowledge of God?

Where have the great minds of Scripture begun their spiritual journeys?

What is God like to us?

From whom do we learn what we need to know about God?

What does Scripture say about the mind, experience, knowledge, and practice?

Why did Paul warn the Colossians?

Upon whom are we to focus regarding true and false teachings?

What is the purpose for acquiring knowledge of the scriptures?

Who are we to focus upon when studying Scripture?

What is meant by Jesus saying, *I am the door of the sheep*?

Chapter 20

TRUTH AND EXPERIENCE

> *Finally, my brethren, be strong in the Lord, and in the power of his might.*
> *Put on the whole armor of God, that ye may be able to stand against the wiles (schemes) of the devil.*
> *For we wrestle not against flesh and blood, but against principalities, against powers, against the rulers of the darkness of this world* (age)*, against spiritual* (hosts of) *wickedness in high places* [Eph. 6:10–12].

What did the apostles bring to Christ when they were called?

What did they have after their initial encounter with Christ?

What type of life did they experience after accepting and following Christ?

What type of life do you expect after accepting Christ?

What two factors should impact upon us?

What can we say about John the Baptist?

What do we know regarding the truth as revealed in the Lord Jesus Christ?

What does Lloyd-Jones say regarding the truth of God?

Why did the scribes and Pharisees seek to discredit Jesus?

Why did Jesus have enemies?

Why did Jesus say to the woman *neither do I condemn thee; go, and sin no more*?

Why did the Pharisees come back to hear Jesus?

What did Jesus say to the Pharisees?

What did the Jews mean when they said, *Abraham is our Father*?

What was the one significant quality of Abraham?

What does Satan want people to do?

What happened when the Pharisees said to Jesus, *Who art thou*?

What truths were presented during that encounter?

What did Jesus do when He was attacked, persecuted, and vilified?

Bibliography

Volume Seven

Barth, Markus. *Ephesians 1-3*. Garden City, NY: Doubleday & Company, Inc., 1974.
———. *Ephesians 4-6*. Garden City, NY: Doubleday & Company, Inc., 1974.
Calvin, John. *Calvin's New Testament Commentaries*. Grand Rapids, MI: William. B. Eerdmans Publishing Company, 1959, 1960, 1961, 1963, 1965, 1972, 1973.
———. *Calvin's Sermons on The Epistle to the Ephesians*. Carlisle, PA: The Banner of Truth Trust, 1973.
———. *Institutes of the Christian Religion*. Philadelphia, PA: The Westminster Press.
Chambers, Oswald. *My Utmost for His Highest*. New York, NY: Dodd, Mead & Company.
Holy Bible. *The King James Study Bible*. Nashville, TN: Thomas Nelson, Inc., 1988.
Gurnall, William. The Christian in Complete Armour. Reprinted in 1987. The Banner of Truth Trust. 3 Murrayfield Road, Edinburgh EH12 6EL. P.O. Box 621, Carlisle, Pennsylvania 17013, USA
Lloyd-Jones, Martyn. The Christian Warfare. Baker Book House, 1981 Grand Rapids, MI.
———. Life in the Spirit. Baker Book House, Grand Rapids, MI 1974, 1981
Paxson, Ruth. *The Wealth, Walk and Warfare of the Christian*. London and Edinburgh: Oliphants, Ltd., 1941.
Presbyterian Hymnal. Louisville, KY: Westminster/John Knox Press, 1990.
Vine, W. E. *Vine's Expository Dictionary of New Testament Words*. McLean, VA: MacDonald Publishing Company.
Weber, Otto. *Foundations of Dogmatics. Volumes 1 & 2*. Grand Rapids, MI: William B. Eerdmans Publishing Company, 1981, 1983

Scripture Index

GENESIS

1:31	113
2:17	112
3:1	122
3:2–3	165
3:4–5	163
6:3	94
6:5	18
17:1	82

LEVITICUS

19:2	142, 149

JOSHUA

1:5	74
1:7–8	75

JUDGES

6:13	96
6:14	82

1 SAMUEL

15:29	77

1 CHRONICLES

21:1	125

JOB

1:6	111
1:7	111
40:2	95

PSALMS

19:7–10	123
56:3	81
119:97–104	88
121:1	158
138:3	78

ECCLESIASTES

8:8	91

ISAIAH

9:6–7	115
14:12–14	105
26:4	79
45:9	94
45:24	82
53:5	35

EZEKIEL

28:6	111

HOSEA

14:2	78

ZECHARIAH

1:1–4	95
1:6	95

MATTHEW

3:17	153
4:6	132
4:9	116
6:33	155
7:21–23	136
7:23	18
11:28	173
12:26	103
15:4–6	7
18:3	167
22:17–21	25
22:21	26
22:36–40	27
23:23	27
24:11	131
24:24	131
25:41	103, 107
26:31–32	157
26:36	157
26:40	157
26:41	158, 159, 160
26:41a	161, 162
26:41b	161
28:18	116

MARK

4:14–20	103–104
9:25	138
12:30	42

LUKE

1:13	80
1:18	80
2:46–50	6
2:51	6
2:51–52	6
4:10	133
11:18–19	106
12:30	79
12:35	87–88
12:44	49
12:46–48	49
16:19–20	53
16:22–23	53
16:24–25	53
16:29	53, 94
16:30	53
16:31	53
18:9	149
18:10–12	149
18:13	150
22:31–32	116, 156
24:49	85

JOHN

1:1	147, 153
1:29	43
3:27–28	164
3:30	164
3:30–31	164
3:34–36	164
3:36	165
8:7	176
8:7–14	172
8:11	176
8:12	176
8:13	176
8:19	176
8:25	177
8:30	177
8:31–32	177
8:33	177
8:34	177
8:37–38	177
8:39	177
8:39–41	177
8:41	178
8:44	106
8:47	178

Scripture Index 227

8:48	178	**ROMANS**	
8:49	178		
8:51	178	1:18	4
8:52–53	178–179	1:22	66
8:54–55	179	1:28	3, 4
8:56	179	1:30–32	3
8:57	179	4:20–21	80
8:58	179	5:1	54
9:39	170	5:8–9	54
10:7	170	6:14	113
10:7–18	169	6:14–15	17
10:9	170	6:16	17
10:10	168	7:15	77
10:30	76	7:23	69
12:21	84, 92	7:24	69
12:31	103	7:25	69
14:6	18, 63, 101, 107, 147, 153	8:37–39	71
		11:16	31
14:7	120	12:2	76
14:15	8, 135, 151	13:1	116
14:30	103	13:8–10	86
15:5	60, 77	13:12–14	86
15:10	135		
15:12	135	**1 CORINTHIANS**	
16:11	103		
16:33	141	2:3	40
17:3	152	2:14	168
17:11	77	3:2	132
17:14–19	146	3:13	49
17:17	147, 153	3:18	168
17:19	63, 147	5:19	50
17:20–21	152–153	6:2	98
		6:3	98
ACTS		7:14	31
		7:20	32
4:12	65	7:22	32
7:51	94	7:22–24	32
8:1	97	8:5	120
9:1	97	12:28–31	136
9:5	97	13:13	173
14:21–22	141	15:24	107
24:16	87	15:33–34	140
26:17–18	105		
26:18	113		

2 CORINTHIANS

2:10–11	121
3:5	77
3:5–6	60
4:2	120
4:4	103, 120
4:6	119, 152
4:7–10	150
5:10	49, 52
5:17	43
5:21	18
7:15	40
11:14–15	132
12:9	14
13:5	159

GALATIANS

2:20	56
3:24	17

EPHESIANS

1:1	21, 43, 50, 93
1:3	21
1:3–4	47
1:4	54
1:7	93
1:10	98
1:17–19	47–48, 78
1:18	21
1:18–19	55
1:19	68, 72
1:21	68
2:2	103, 113
2:5	93
2:6	93
2:8	21
2:10	93
2:12	87
2:18	93
2:18–19	21
3:3–6	65
3:16–17	21
3:17	97
3:19	21, 54
4:1	1, 55, 56, 59, 88, 98
4:7	164
4:14	131
4:15	97
4:17	59
4:24	86
4:25	93
5:8	87
5:15	55
5:18	1, 9, 50, 85, 97
5:18–20	30
5:21	1, 50
5:30	93
6:1	1, 2, 5, 8
6:1–4	1, 10, 182, 184
6:4	2, 5, 9, 11
6:5	40, 41, 42
6:5–6	38, 39
6:5–7	20, 29, 43, 44, 188
6:5–9	186
6:7	42
6:8	50
6:8–9	38, 190
6:9	38, 46, 48, 50, 51, 59, 192
6:10	56, 72, 125, 198
6:10–11	54, 60, 63, 102, 107, 108, 117, 158, 194, 196
6:10–12	89, 145, 155, 163, 202, 214, 216, 218, 220
6:11	81, 89, 118, 200, 208, 210
6:11–12	64, 99, 127, 135, 204, 212
6:12	66, 70, 91, 106, 108, 206
6:12–13	57

PHILIPPIANS

1:28–29	141
2:12	40, 41
2:13	61, 77

COLOSSIANS

1:13	113
2:6–8	153
2:8–9	167
2:13–15	101
2:15	116

2 THESSALONIANS

2:3–4	107
2:9–10	105
2:9–12	131–132

1 TIMOTHY

1:14–15	44
3:6	111
3:7	111
4:1	122
4:6–7	143

2 TIMOTHY

3:1–5	4
3:5	4
3:15–17	159

HEBREWS

2:14–15	115
5:12	132–133
7:25	116
13:5–6	82

1 PETER

2:15	26
2:18	26, 34, 41
2:24	18
3:18	152
5:8	102, 110

2 PETER

2:1–3	129
2:3	131
2:4	112

1 JOHN

1:1	175
1:3	175
1:9	124
2:14	98
3:8	115–116
3:24	133
4:4	133
5:4	98
5:19	113

JUDE

6	112
8–10	111
9	133

REVELATION

3:21	98
5:10	98
12:17	106
20:2–3	116